Social Science and the Idea of Process

Social Science
and the Idea of Process

The Ambiguous Legacy
of Arthur F. Bentley

by Paul F. Kress

45129

UNIVERSITY OF ILLINOIS PRESS

Urbana   Chicago   London

To my parents

Contents

Preface

THERE IS CURRENTLY in American political science a considerable amount of dispute about the nature of theory and its relationship to empirical research. In part this involves familiar questions which have disturbed economists, psychologists, and sociologists for some time—the legacy of the empirical revolution—but the state of political science is more complex, perhaps because the revolution has achieved so much success in this field. We now know much more about the possibilities and the limitations of empirical techniques, enough, certainly, to be dissatisfied with arguments that might have appeared decisive twenty-five years or even a decade ago. This means that exploration of fundamentals in contemporary political science requires much greater sophistication and much more knowledge than does inquiry into the sociology of the 1930s. We have, to this extent, benefited from our legacy.

American social theory in general, and certainly American political science, has often been indicted for its lack of profundity. It is not always clear what this means, but I think it must be conceded that we have not produced the social theorist who is also a systematic philosopher. Where, for example, is our Hegel, our Marx, Locke, or Hobbes? Beside these men our Madisons and Calhouns look like political tacticians. Whatever the causes and the broader implications of this situation, it is indisputable that the study of politics and society in America has been conducted at a theoretical level different from that of European study. I do not suggest that this empirical inclination has been without its positive aspects. It has enabled us to get on with the business of learning about politics and society and largely to ignore the task of creating a systematic philosophy of man and the universe such as those which have entrapped many continental philosophers. It is possible to spend one's life laying foundations which are, as Georg Simmel astutely remarked, often less secure than the structure built upon them. But the converging currents of natural science and philosophy that compose the empirical revolution, and the accompanying interest in the rigor and reliability of knowledge, demand greater theoretical depth than American social theory has thus far possessed.

In America we have drawn a line between "philosophy," or speculation, and "scientific" methodology, often narrowly conceived as what Paul Lazarsfeld has called "research techniques." An imperfectly understood positivism has encouraged us to consign theoretical endeavor to one category or the other, thereby denying the existence of that broad and difficult area that combines truly speculative thought and the methods of scientific procedure. The result is often a lack of coherence and unity, as expressed in C. Wright Mills's description of the hiatus between grand theory and abstracted empiricism. This tendency of American social and political science colors the kind of original work that is done and provides a framework within which the contributions of the past are evaluated. An example of this second result is the reception accorded the work of Arthur F. Bentley. Interpretations of his work vary, but the context in which he is placed does not. He is viewed as the father of American "group theory," a school whose contemporary members include, most prominently, David Truman and Earl Latham. Both of these men have acknowledged their indebtedness to Bentley, and the aim of their writing has been the refinement and extension of Bentley's vision—a group interpretation of politics.

Group theory is a subcategory of the broader perspective we call pluralism, which is so much a part of American political thought and practice that we often seem unable to think outside it. For example, it is not at all uncommon to find the group approach to politics described as a steady development from Madison to Bentley to Truman, and the presentation is superficially plausible. My own dissatisfaction with this interpretation began with a reading of Bentley's *The Process of Government* and Truman's *The Governmental Process*. I had anticipated discovering a relationship of prophecy and fulfillment, but that was not the result. Part One of *The Process of Government*, "To Prepare the Way," is devoted to a discussion of methods of investigation and of explanation in the social sciences generally. Here Bentley introduces the concept of "process" and juxtaposes it to other, antagonistic methods of investigation. In Part Two, where he gives examples of how the "tool" he has fashioned might be put to use, the "group" becomes a central concept. *The Governmental Process* summarizes and reformulates our knowledge of uniformities in group activity, but there is little interest in the kind of inquiry Bentley thought necessary to prepare the way. My reading of other group theorists has convinced me that Truman was not alone in selecting the second, more empirical, section of *The Process of Government* as his focus. Those political scientists who have accepted Bentley's teaching seem to have made the "group" their central concept and to have allowed "process" to become the general milieu in which the group "functions." As a consequence, the *level* of theoretical focus has been shifted from the philosophical to the empirical plane.

One result of shifting the level of inquiry has been a concentration on the validity and utility of the group concept in empirical research. No fault can be found with this, but it must not be concluded that Bentley's contribution stands or falls with the fate of the group concept, nor that the direction taken by other group theorists is necessarily consistent with his teaching. Bentley was absorbed in problems of epistemology, theory of signs, and the logic of scientific method—all fundamental philosophical concerns.

xi

Part One of *The Process of Government* is, and was intended to be, revolutionary. Contemporary political science, Bentley was saying, is barren and formalistic, and he continued to characterize it as animistic, sterile, ghost-ridden, and static, but the indictment was documented less from political science itself than by examples drawn from various sciences of man. It is perhaps this revolutionary critical character that induces us to "explain" the concept of process negatively—that is, in terms of what Bentley rejected.

It is characteristic of American social science that the empirical Bentley, the Bentley of groups and the demand for scrutiny of fact, should be remembered; but if we reorient ourselves toward Bentley's work by placing process at the center of inquiry, we will see different questions and different lines of development. "Process" is a word that has found its way unobtrusively into the accepted vocabulary of political science, so that we now speak easily and confidently of the legislative and judicial processes, of the decision-making process, and even of the entire political process. We believe that process is a meaningful term, that when we say "the political process" or "the process of administration" we are saying something different from, perhaps something more than, "the political" or "administration." We are encouraged to accept it as an advance in conceptualization or at least as a liberation from previous strictures, but as soon as one attempts to state the precise nature of the advance, or the kind of liberation, it becomes very difficult to do more than speak negatively or metaphorically. This book is an attempt to explore the meaning of the idea of process, especially as it was developed by Arthur Bentley. Process can be considered on several levels, and, though my primary concern is with its application in social science, I shall suggest and on occasion explore its wider implications. I hope to present both an account of the historical evolution of an idea and an analysis and evaluation of a concept. As far as this attempt is successful, it constitutes an inquiry into that shadowy area which lies between the philosophical and the methodological realms. I have tried to make each chapter a development both in historical time and in conceptual refinement, but the persistence of certain central concerns has made some repetition essential. Since the concept of process has almost infinite dimensionality and an inexhaustible literature, the central problem of this book is to achieve a focus relevant to theoretical social science and at the same time to suggest connections with the larger matrix of metaphor, ontology, and value.

An effort of this kind is necessarily informed by so many and such diverse sources that specific indebtedness is impossible to acknowledge adequately. Three books, however, merit special mention. David Easton's *The Political System* is a valuable summary statement of the current state and prospects of systematic political theory, and, while I have disagreed with it at many points, it has lent a very useful orientation to my thought. Thomas Kuhn's *The Structure of Scientific Revolutions* has helped me understand some of the crucial features of change in basic scientific beliefs and is a notable contribution to the history and sociology of science. C. A. O. van Nieuwenhuijze's careful analysis in *Society as Process* suggests an intriguing and challenging future course for social science and represents the kind of theoretical inquiry that has been regrettably absent from the American scene.

I am indebted to my Berkeley teachers Seymour M. Lipset, John Schaar, and the late Peter Odegard for the generous contribution of their interest and advice. Conversations with my former associates John Gunnell, Matthew Stoltz, and Richard C. Snyder have given me helpful suggestions on a number of difficult problems, and the critical acumen of my Northwestern colleagues Scott Greer, Harold Guetzkow, and James J. Sheehan has often forced me to a clarity of statement I should not have achieved alone. David Braybrooke's careful reading and insightful knowledge of Bentley have saved me from many missteps. I have benefited most from my association with Norman Jacobson, who enthusiastically shared, sustained, and informed my interest in a difficult and frequently discouraging effort. This book would be better had I learned more from all of them.

My wife Charlotte has lived with this book as long as I have, and

xiii

her many contributions far exceed a tolerance of its demands and duration. Those errors and inadequacies which remain are entirely my own responsibility.

Finally, I wish to thank the Committee for Political Theory and Legal Philosophy of the Social Science Research Council for a grant which made possible much of the research for this book.

Paul F. Kress
Chicago, Illinois
December, 1969

Social Science and the Idea of Process

Introduction

> *Socrates*: But now, since not even white continues to flow white, and whiteness itself is a flux or change which is passing into another colour, and is never to be caught standing still, can the name of any colour be rightly used at all?
>
> *Theodorus*: How is that possible, Socrates, either in the case of this or any other quality—if while we are using the word the subject is escaping in the flux?
>
> —*Theaetetus*

THE SIMULTANEOUS EXISTENCE of endurance and change has perplexed the Western mind from its earliest ventures into the mystery of reality. The question formulated by Socrates and Theodorus in Plato's *Theaetetus* was not new to the Athens of the fourth century B.C. Early in that dialogue Theodorus says that the problem is at least as old as Homer, but it is Heraclitus, the mysterious Eleatic who wrote around the turn of the fifth century B.C., whom historians have credited with the discovery of process and its expression in the succinct aphorism, "all things flow." His importance consists not simply in the discovery that change is a problem, but in the challenge it posed for his successors. "Heraclitus' discovery influenced the development of Greek philosophy for a long time. The philosophies of Parmenides, Democritus, Plato, and Aristotle can all be appropriately described as attempts to solve the problems of that changing world which Heraclitus had discovered."[1]

We should not wonder that the effect of Heraclitus' teaching, when fully understood, was terrifying. "He visualized the world not as an edifice, but rather as the totality of all events, or changes,

[1] Karl Popper, *The Open Society and Its Enemies* (Princeton: Princeton University Press, 1950), 15.

3

or facts."[2] This belief constituted a formidable challenge to the infant natural philosophy. What if the fact of physical change forced the conclusion that the cosmos was unstructured, that there was no endurance, hence no substance, and finally no edifice? If it is true that nature yields no ordered structure, then our bold attempt to achieve immanent comprehension is halted before it is under way. Western man may count himself fortunate that Heraclitus was not a solitary genius in a constellation of mediocrity. Parmenides, Plato, and Aristotle rose to his challenge, and in doing so they gave permanent shape to the scientific and philosophical dialogue of twenty-odd centuries.[3]

But the idea of process threatened at least as much destruction to social as to natural speculation. Heraclitus was perhaps the first philosopher to treat at length "ethico-political problems," and Karl Popper has suggested that the turbulent political conditions of Ephesus decisively conditioned the philosopher of change to the idea of impermanence. Heraclitus is thought to have been a member of the Ephesian aristocracy, and though he did not participate in public life he supported his class in its vain struggle against the democratic revolution. His remark that the cosmos was a "rubbish heap scattered at random" suggests an awareness of the moral and political implications of his natural philosophy. History, however, rewarded the Greeks with successors to Heraclitus who were capable of formulating alternative natural and ethico-political systems. Parmenides of Elea (540–470) replied directly to Heraclitus; he denied the reality of change and postulated the permanence of being. These polar philosophies were to find their union in the great Aristotelian synthesis of being and becoming, and in Aristotle's effort to link the ontological principle of being to a logic built upon the principle of identity.[4]

[2] *Ibid.*

[3] For a comparison of Aristotelian and Galilean conceptions of change, see Clifford Pierson Osborne, *The Problem of Change in Greek Science* (Chicago: Private Edition, distributed by University of Chicago Libraries, 1934).

[4] For a useful classification of Greek systems of natural philosophy, see F. S. C. Northrop, *Science and First Principles* (New York: Macmillan, 1931).

Behind these secular articulations lay more shadowy antecedents, rooted in the depths of culture, myth, and the structure of human experience, which the light of the rational mind illuminates occasionally and uncertainly.

> Philosophy, when she puts aside the finished products of religion and returns to the "nature of things," really goes back to that original representation out of which mythology itself had gathered shape. If we now call it "metaphysical," instead of "supernatural," the thing itself has not essentially changed its character. What has changed is, rather, man's attitude towards it, which, from being active and emotional, has become intellectual and speculative.[5]

F. M. Cornford has written that the religious concepts of *Moira*, which included the ideas of "allotted portion," spatial boundedness, and fixed destiny, and *Dike* or "way through life," an idea suggesting passage and transcendence of barriers, foreshadow early scientific theories of permanence and flux, discreteness and continuity.[6] While some sort of view of the cosmos as process seems fundamental to the Western mind, it has also played an interesting intermediary role as the transition between polarities. Wilmon Sheldon has explained process as the motion of walking, which is itself the imbalance created by the alternate movement of "polar" feet; in this view process is the mediator between stabilities. "In sum, we have equilibrium plus advance; which again is the polar couple, stability and process. Polarity itself has its own polar opposite, which is process."[7] Whether conceived as mediator or as polarity, the idea of process has been a basic category of Western experience for at least twenty-five centuries. Alfred North Whitehead found the coincidence of permanence and change illustrated in the hymn,

---

5 F. M. Cornford, *From Religion to Philosophy* (New York: Harper, 1957), ix.

6 For a discussion of the relation of myth and theory, see John Gunnell, *Political Philosophy and Time* (Middleton, Conn.: Wesleyan University Press, 1968).

7 Wilmon Henry Sheldon, *Process and Polarity* (New York: Columbia University Press, 1944), 12.

"Abide with me/ Fast falls the eventide"—here, he says, "we find formulated the complete problem of metaphysics."[8]

If process was a basic metaphor of ancient natural philosophy, its historical development has owed as much to speculation about social phenomena. Social scientists who habitually look to natural science for models and metaphors might ponder the words of Stephen Toulmin and June Goodfield, who begin their study of time with the cautionary statement that "physical cosmologists today may have more to learn than they yet recognize from the theoretical quandaries facing their predecessors in geology, and even in political theory."[9] This point is especially important to the people and ideas with which this study is concerned, for, however ancient its origins, the idea of process emerges with new force and direction in the nineteenth century. A recent collection devoted to "philosophers of process" seems to consider them phenomena of the last 150 years. This may be a bit parochial, but it accurately reflects the impact of the historical philosophies of Comte, Hegel, and Marx, the evolutionary excitement of Darwinism, the vitalism of Nietzsche or Bergson, and the pragmatism of James and Dewey.[10]

Encompassing and diverse as these currents undeniably are, the modern idea of process must be seen against an even broader background of human experience. Insofar as process has been found congenial by Romanticism, it has appeared as an alternative aesthetic to the assertedly "static" forms of classicism, and its promise of freedom was at least as attractive to the artists who made the revolution in twentieth-century painting.[11] "An artist of our own day, Georges Braque, has recently spoken of the thrill and awe with which he discovered the fluidity of our categories, the ease

---

[8] Alfred North Whitehead, *Process and Reality* (New York: Harper, 1960), 318.

[9] Stephen Toulmin and June Goodfield, *The Discovery of Time* (New York: Harper and Row, 1966), 15.

[10] Douglas Browning (ed.), *Philosophers of Process* (New York: Random House, 1965). See especially the introductory essay by Charles Hartshorne.

[11] See Geoffrey Clive, *The Romantic Enlightenment* (New York: Meridian, 1960). The nature of Clive's analysis is indicated by his chapter headings; each section describes a "breakdown" in the organization of particular aspects of the human experience.

with which a file can become a shoehorn, a bucket a brazier."[12] Again, we might consider the revolt against established modes of creation and expression in the music and literature of the same period. Within the narrower context of social science, the idea of process preserves the dual promise of liberation from suffocating formalism and of hope for a genuinely new vision of society.

The advantages of the broad perspective, in which modes of creation and reporting in art and social science are seen as norms, governed by similar images and values, should be apparent, but that scope and splendor can obscure certain important ambiguities. This is, perhaps, the point at which several serious theoretical difficulties should be faced. The analysis of a concept so basic as process frequently requires treatment at the level of symbolism or imagery. At this level we encounter those metaphors which shape and express our fundamental categories of thought and perhaps also our perceptions. The struggle to understand and articulate these images is arduous and frustrating, but, as Reinhard Bendix and Bennett Berger point out, much disagreement among social theorists "stems from the failure of many discussants to reflect on the sense of the 'real' which lies behind their conflicting definitions of 'social fact.' "[13] As we advance to a more explicit elaboration of basic categories of analysis, the influence of these images is readily apparent.

Our image of society determines how we think about society. If we use mechanical models for thinking about society, we say nothing very rigorous about communication as a symbolic interaction or roleplaying unless we reduce communication to "signaling," "feed-back," "built-in purposes," and so on. The same holds true, of course, for models derived from aesthetic or religious experience. When we say society is a "configuration," like that of a

[12] E. H. Gombrich, *Art and Illusion* (Washington: Bollingen Foundation, 1961), 313. I have elsewhere undertaken to suggest some thematic convergences among literature, art, and social science. See my "Self, System and Significance: Reflections on Professor Easton's Political Science," *Ethics*, LXXVII (October, 1966).

[13] See Reinhard Bendix and Bennett Berger, "Images of Society and Problems of Concept Formation in Sociology," *Symposium on Sociological Theory*, ed. Llewellyn Gross (Evanston, Ill., and White Plains, N.Y.: Row, Peterson, 1959), 93.

great painting, there is little we can say about verbal communication because paintings do not talk.[14]

Study of the concept of process must undertake analysis at the metaphorical as well as at the explicitly conceptual level; it must seek further to understand the intricate transactions between these realms. The latter obligation is particularly difficult to discharge since our theorists often move very freely across the boundary. This freedom of movement illustrates a further difficulty of this enterprise, namely, that explicit norms of scientific procedure, of proper methodology, of the nature of explanation and theory, are inextricably intertwined with images and metaphoric elements; and it is often not possible to find clear logical interdependencies among them. This means that an analytic account must sometimes meander with the course of the theory. These observations apply to many efforts at conceptual analysis, and most practitioners in this field learn by painful experience the twin but frequently jealous commandments of clarity and fidelity. The concept of process, however, presents two especially perplexing problems.

First, it is unclear whether process has been predominantly a "basic" polarity or whether it has served as a second-order mediator between polarities. For example, if the principle of substance or being is taken as one pole, its negation has sometimes been said to be change or becoming. The question then arises, does process itself constitute a polarity synonymous with change, or does it refer to some unspecified, but less fundamental, transitional state? The issue is not simply a verbal one, for it raises the question of whether there can be a fundamental category, posture, or vision rooted in the idea of process. Insofar as process has implied transition, flux, and impermanence, it has had to endure the Platonic scorn reserved for the ephemeral and for mere appearance. Within the realm of social scientific discourse, process philosophy has often seemed to support certain polar positions on such issues as

---

[14] Hugh D. Duncan, "Simmel's Image of Society," *Georg Simmel, 1858–1918*, ed. Kurt Wolff (Columbus: Ohio State University Press, 1959), 100.

the nature of society, the nature of explanation, reduction, and emergence, and the units appropriate to social analysis. It is this we see in an Henri Bergson and an Arthur Bentley—the attempt to criticize the established scientific paradigm and to supplant it with a new universe of observation and discourse informed by the image of process.[15]

Although it has assumed this polar position in the sociological sense of providing an alternative belief system for the scientific community, the idea of process, like other master conceptions in science, has been imperialistic in its refusal to be contained within existing categories. Thus, despite its role as polarity, it has consistently sought to transcend dualistic categories and abolish their claims to legitimacy. In this sense, the image of process has striven to assert its continuity against all forms of polarity and discreteness.[16] This situation requires that analysis be conducted within the process universe itself and also within the wider belief system of which it is a competing member.

As succeeding discussion will indicate, it is probably impossible to construct a single, self-consistent "process position," even within comparatively recent social science. Were this a feasible undertaking, it would still fall far short of the task of elaborating a full process vision embracing nature and man. This is not, however, to say that there are not definite inclinations and proclivities among those who embrace a process philosophy. Certain predispositions favor the overarching metaphysic of their larger vision. It is the existence of these inclinations and intimations that makes the narrower task of this book at all possible of accomplishment.

The analysis offered here seeks to explore the contours of a paradigm case of process theory, specifically, the theoretical tradition of special importance to sociology and political science which emerged from Arthur Bentley's now classic study *The Process of*

---

[15] On the idea of scientific paradigms, see Thomas S. Kuhn, *The Structure of Scientific Revolutions* (Chicago: University of Chicago Press, 1962).

[16] See W. T. Jones, *The Romantic Syndrome* (The Hague: Martinus Nijhoff, 1961), for an exposition of the use of polarities in theoretical analysis.

9

Government. The word "paradigm" is used here in the rather special sense it receives in the history and philosophy of science by Thomas Kuhn.[17] A primary requisite of the paradigm is that it perform the function of illustrating the proper mode of scientific research and reporting, that is, that it articulate and embody the norms which are to govern the science. These norms include not only the formal imperatives of scientific methodology but also the basic conceptions of the subject matter and the kinds of questions or problems which require attention. The latter point is especially important; students of social and political thought have catalogued exhaustively the answers given by their tradition, but they have been less energetic in understanding how and why certain questions were perceived as problems. The history of science can be written as the continued redefinition of problems, rather than as the progressive accumulation of knowledge.

In order for a particular work to attain the status of a paradigm, it must not only *be* a piece of actual research, it must also be perceived by a community of investigators as a source of imperatives for their own research energies. Insofar as the efforts of the scientific community remain faithful to the norms of problem selection, resolution, and reporting, they are said to be "elaborating the paradigm," or conducting "normal science." To speak of scientific progress in this way is to describe the success of the community in solving problems defined by the paradigm according to methods it holds legitimate. Knowledge, in this view, would be said to be cumulative only within the context of a particular paradigm.

While it is useful to approach *The Process of Government* in these terms, it is necessary to adopt certain reservations about the practice of some historians of political science who have sought to

[17] This account is based upon Thomas Khun's analysis, especially his Chaps. 1–3. Two recent attempts to apply this interpretive framework to political science are David B. Truman's presidential address to the American Political Science Association, "Disillusion and Regeneration: The Quest for a Discipline," *American Political Science Review*, LIX (December, 1965), and Sheldon S. Wolin, "Paradigms and Political Theories," *Politics and Experience: Essays Presented to Michael Oakshott*, ed. Preston King and B. C. Parekh (Cambridge: Cambridge University Press, 1968).

convince us that Bentley's effort stimulated a cohesive and self-conscious response, sufficient to be considered a constituency if not a community.[18] This interpretation appears more than a little parochial in that the actual convergence of themes far transcends disciplinary boundaries; but, even though a healthy measure of skepticism about the continuity of this tradition is salutary, Bentley was the direct inspiration of certain landmark studies which have been viewed as the normal science of *The Process of Government*.[19] If we should suspect the continuity and self-consciousness of this account, we must also wonder whether it is accurate in other respects. A major thesis of the present study, and one which requires some modification of Kuhn's terminology, is that though American observers of the social structure have announced their membership in the paradigmatic community of process, they have misunderstood the nature of Bentley's message. This misunderstanding has been in part the result of ambiguities in Bentley's first book, but the thrust of his later work demonstrates a force and clarity of purpose which are unmistakable.[20]

The task, however, is not simply one of reinterpreting Bentley's work, for the idea of process was not exclusively his. Max Lerner's essay in the first edition of *The Encyclopaedia of the Social Sciences* lists Ward, Giddings, Small, Ross, Bentley, Ellwood, Dewey, Mead, Thomas, and Cooley as Americans for whom that concept was central.[21] Many of these names appear three decades later in Ber-

[18] Heinz Eulau, Samuel Eldersveld, and Morris Janowitz (eds.), *Political Behavior: A Reader in Research and Theory* (Glencoe, Ill.: Free Press, 1956), 7. This parochialism is reinforced by the willingness of behaviorism's critics to acquiesce to the historical accuracy of this account. See, for example, Bernard Crick, *The American Science of Politics* (Berkeley and Los Angeles: University of California Press, 1959).

[19] Peter H. Odegard, personal communication in reference to the origins of his *Pressure Politics: The Story of the Anti-Saloon League* (New York: Columbia University Press, 1928).

[20] In the context of the discussion of paradigm functions, it is instructive to note that the opening section of *The Process of Government* is much less concerned with providing answers than with instructing us in the kinds of questions we ought to be asking about man and society.

[21] Max Lerner, "Social Process," *Encyclopaedia of the Social Sciences*, ed. Edwin Seligman and Alwin Johnson (New York: Macmillan, 1935), XIV, 148–51.

tram Gross's account of the political process.[22] My attempt to explore the idea of process takes Bentley's work as its focus, but it seeks also to illuminate a wider context of meaning.

[22] Bertram Gross, "The Political Process," *The International Encyclopaedia of the Social Sciences,* ed. David L. Sills (New York: Macmillan and Free Press, 1968).

I

History as Process

Surely, at every point in history when an orientation
has been radically brought into question, we may look
for a nudist sect—and we may look for a parallel cult
of nudism in the remoter areas of thought. Nudism
represents an attempt to return to essentials, to get at
the irreducible minimum of human certainty, to re-
emphasize the *humanistic* as the sound basis above
which any scheme of values must be constructed.

—Kenneth Burke

Philosophy can exclude nothing. Thus it should
never start from systematization. Its primary stage
should be termed "assemblage."

—Alfred North Whitehead

We now raise the question whether there is a concept which can reveal the common structure of philosophy and politics. We believe this concept to be the idea
of *Prozess*.

—Hans Barth

BENTLEY AND THE AMERICAN TRADITION

IN 1893 two young men, recent graduates of Harvard and Johns
Hopkins, were crossing the Atlantic en route to Germany for the
enjoyment of that birthright of the well-to-do American student—
his *Wanderjahre*. Such at least was the intention of Hutchins Hapgood, for, though he had an interest in philosophy, the trip appeared to him as a romantic quest; but Hapgood's shipboard
acquaintance, "a strangely vivid young man," had a more serious
purpose. Arthur F. Bentley was even then "passionately determined
to solve the mystery of society."[1] Bentley, in 1893, was as Victorian
and inexperienced as his new friend. He had entered Johns Hopkins University three years earlier, after an education in the public
schools of Freeport, Illinois, and Grand Island, Nebraska, and a

[1] Hutchins Hapgood, *A Victorian in the Modern World* (New York: Harcourt,
Brace, 1939), 84.

13

little more than a year of study at York College, Nebraska, and the University of Denver. He graduated from Johns Hopkins in June, 1892, having produced a rather conventional thesis entitled "The Condition of the Western Farmer as Illustrated by the Economic History of a Nebraska Township,"[2] and had remained in Baltimore for a year of graduate work in economics and sociology.

Bentley had been attracted to Hopkins by the reputation of the economist Richard T. Ely, but Ely left for the University of Wisconsin a year after Bentley's arrival, and no one else among the faculty made much of an impression on the young man. Many years later Bentley recalled this period.

> My situation had its amusing features. I went to Johns Hopkins University because Richard T. Ely was there, my goal being economics, and indeed I have still fancied myself, until the last decade or two, an economist in the making. Ely left the University, I stayed, I don't know why. During my years of graduate study there was no faculty in economics, only a bright young instructor or two and a few lecture courses from the outer world. Political economy hung from the ankles of political science, and political science from the ankles of history. In other words I was on the loose.[3]

This description of academic life at Hopkins tells us two important things. First, it indicates something about the state of the social science that Bentley was shortly to attack so vigorously, and second, it suggests the circumstances in which he could develop his particular vision. Intellectually, he was indeed on the loose, but it is possible to discern the beginnings of his life-long preoccupations and something of the unusual personal character that was to sustain them.

Bentley's early experiences in his father's bank may account for his interest in economics, especially labor relations, but from the

---

[2] Bentley's thesis was published in the *Johns Hopkins University Studies in Historical and Political Science*, Series 11, Nos. VII–VIII (Baltimore: Johns Hopkins University, July–August, 1893).

[3] Arthur F. Bentley, "Epilogue," in *Life, Language, Law: Essays in Honor of Arthur F. Bentley*, ed. Richard W. Taylor (Yellow Springs, Ohio: Antioch University Press, 1957), 210–11.

beginning of his career he displayed considerable intellectual independence and a desire to "operate freely outside of the conventional controls."[4] In Ely's absence Bentley took courses from John Bates Clark and Simon Patten (visiting faculty from Columbia and the University of Pennsylvania, respectively). E. A. Ross, just returned from Germany and completing his doctorate in Baltimore in 1891–92, was "vivid and interesting in conversation," but Bentley found in him no continuing source of inspiration. His independent reading of the classical British economists and of Karl Menger seems to have been more influential than any individual teacher or colleague. Of the academic interests that sent him abroad, Bentley recalled, "at a guess my aim in the background was to find how to fit the marginal utility theories of Karl Menger into a fully behavioral sociology."[5] Menger's *Grundsatze der Volkswirtschaftslehre* appeared in 1871, and Bentley was probably most familiar with it, but a second work published twelve years later may also have claimed his attention—the *Untersuchungen über die Methode der Socialwissenschaften und der politischen Oekonomie insbesondere.*[6] Louis Schneider indicates in his introduction to the English edition that the *Untersuchungen* received very little attention from Anglo-American scholars. This is hardly surprising, for it is a highly theoretical and methodological tract and a polemic against the so-called "historical school" of economics (notably Gustav Schmoller). As such, it bore the ponderous trappings of German scholarly dispute and was difficult to fit neatly or comfortably into American categories of social science. It did, however, undertake the *kind* of inquiry into science and society that was to occupy Bentley throughout his long and vigorous intellectual life.

---

[4] *Ibid.*, 211. For biographical details of Bentley's early life, see Sidney Ratner, "A. F. Bentley's Inquiries into the Behavioral Sciences and the Theory of Scientific Inquiry," in *ibid.*

[5] Bentley, "Epilogue," 211.

[6] The *Grundsatze* is now available in an English edition, James Dingwall and Bert Hoselitz (trans.), *Principles of Economics* (Glencoe, Ill.: Free Press, 1950). An abridged version of the *Untersuchungen* has also been published, Louis Schneider (ed.) and Francis J. Nock (trans.), *Problems of Economics and Sociology* (Urbana: University of Illinois Press, 1963).

The young Bentley's preoccupation with the mystery of human society, with collective life as a puzzle, had roots deeper than intellectual curiosity, however intense that might have been. During the year Bentley and Hapgood shared a room in Berlin, Hapgood noted that "Bentley's passionate desire to discover the sociological ultimate revealed an infinite mental turmoil. He was an unhappy soul, bitterly critical of himself and his inability to reach the heights."[7] Despite his diligence and his obedience to the demands of German scholarship, Bentley's European experience produced neither happiness nor satisfaction. Hapgood recorded this rather somber memory.

> Bentley made those demands on himself with great intensity, and worked very hard, but on the whole unhappily. Sometime later, when he was in London, I got an eloquent letter from him about his passionate disappointment in not being able to solve the mystery of sociology. He had been wandering through the slums of London, and had seen such a mass of suffering human beings, he said, so unhappy that they didn't know they were unhappy; an objective impersonal misery that put him into a state almost of insanity. Ever since that time Bentley has been working, and still is working, on that effort to solve the problem of human beings in organized society.[8]

Hapgood's observation was perceptive, though the suggestion that Bentley sought a more powerful social science for the alleviation of human suffering may be exaggerated. This memory does reveal the unhappiness and the passionate nature of the young Bentley; he was a man capable of sustaining profound intellectual and emotional commitments.

While in Berlin Bentley studied with Adolph Wagner, Hermann Grimm, Gustav Schmoller, Wilhelm Dilthey, and Georg Simmel. Simmel made the greatest impression, and Bentley was later to call him "perhaps the keenest and most searching investigator so-

7 Hapgood, 9. It is of historical interest to note that another resident of the Berlin house in which Bentley and Hapgood lived was Celestin Bouglé, later to attain prominence as the author of *Les idées égalitaires* and professor of sociology at the Sorbonne.

8 *Ibid.*, 112.

ciety has yet had, undoubtedly the one with the greatest yield of permanently applicable knowledge."[9] It is characteristic of Bentley that he praised Simmel's "working attitudes" and attached most importance to his general orientation rather than remembering any particular substantive contribution. Another important influence was the work of the Austrian conflict theorist Ludwig Gumplowicz. Bentley's eclecticism is revealed by the inscription he penned on the first outline of *The Process of Government*, drafted in 1905–6: "To John Dewey, Georg Simmel, Ludwig Gumplowicz, Walt Whitman, and the many other makers of this book."[10] Eclecticism remained a primary characteristic of Bentley's work, matched only perhaps by his intellectual solitude. When his European education was terminated by the depression of 1893, he resumed graduate studies at Johns Hopkins, reading economics and sociology widely and independently in English, French, and German. He received his doctorate in 1895, presenting a dissertation entitled "The Units of Investigation in the Social Sciences."[11] Bentley was soon to repudiate the mental and psychical categories on which that paper was based, but his interest in the epistemological and methodological aspects of the subject remained intense.

Bentley's first and only regular academic position was at the University of Chicago in 1896, but he had little success as a teacher. He later remarked that the result of his graduate study in Germany and at Hopkins "was to unfit myself for academic status." He tried to discuss French and German systems of sociology with a few students, but early sessions produced universal agreement to discontinue efforts to study such arduous material. (His brief academic experience at Columbia in 1941, presumably arranged through John Dewey, does not seem to have been much more successful.) Chicago's social science faculty was most impressive at that time—it included Dewey, George Herbert Mead, J. R. Angell, Wesley Mitchell, Thorstein Veblen, Franz Boas, and Jacques Loeb—but Bent-

[9] Arthur F. Bentley, *Relativity in Man and Society* (New York: G. P. Putnam's Sons, 1926), 163.
[10] Sidney Ratner, "Bentley's Inquiries into the Behavioral Sciences," 32.
[11] *Annals of the American Academy*, V (May, 1895).

ley had little contact with any of them. He did attend Dewey's seminar for a time (an association which was to develop to intimacy much later), and he knew W. I. Thomas personally, but for the most part he preserved his solitary habits. This lack of success and probable lack of interest in the academy soon terminated Bentley's association with the university, and in 1897 he became a reporter for the Chicago *Times-Herald* and the *Record-Herald*. By 1903 he had advanced to an editorial position, which he held until 1911, when his health forced him to retire to a farm near Paoli, Indiana. He was then forty-one years old.

Part of the damage to his health was occasioned by the task of writing his classic book, *The Process of Government*, in about three years. The achievement was remarkable even though his position allowed him blocks of free time to visit the nearby Crerar Library. The attraction of an editorial position was its relative flexibility and the absence of conventional restrictions. The newspaper provided him with a salary without making many demands on his time and energy, but it contributed something else of equal importance —a torrent of facts, "raw data." "All the politics of the country, so to speak, was drifting across my desk."[12] This sense of tremendous social activity taking place daily and hourly, of men doing things, was as significant an experience as any book or teacher Bentley might have known. From his editorial desk in the heart of Chicago, Bentley could know the misery of the London slums and much, much more besides. If we try to imagine what the social world must have looked like from that chair, we gain a better understanding of how Bentley used words like "activity" and "brute fact" in his scientific writings. It may also help us to understand why his vision of social reality seems contradictory. On the one hand he insists on the "hardness" of concrete factuality, but on the other he has a curious detachment from the activity described; it is the journalist's perspective of a greatly expanded horizontal vision that often seems to lack a "depth" dimension.

With his health restored, Bentley resumed his studies and pub-

12 Bentley, "Epilogue," 211.

lished a steady stream of articles and four more books; the last, written in collaboration with John Dewey, appeared in 1949, when Bentley was seventy-nine. Bentley's only active political involvement occurred in 1924, when he chaired Robert LaFollette's Indiana campaign committee and served as a national committeeman of the Progressive party.[13] Sidney Ratner suggests that Bentley preferred the programs of reformers like LaFollette and Louis Brandeis to the more radical social analysis of Thorstein Veblen, though he did profess admiration for the latter. Apparently he thought that small businessmen, farmers, and laborers could best improve their situation by operating within the pluralistic framework of American politics. His thoughts on this subject were advanced in a manuscript of some 100,000 words, a study of American business entitled "Makers, Users and Masters in America." It was rejected by two or three publishers, and Bentley apparently was not sufficiently interested in its publication to press further.[14]

Apart from sustained intellectual effort Bentley's life must be viewed as rather uneventful, without the shattering interruptions that bent and broke so many twentieth-century intellectuals. He did not follow Hapgood and any number of academic, literary, and journalistic figures into bohemia or radical and reform politics. In contrast to the wide range of involvement in political and social problems of his friend Dewey, Bentley seems like a recluse. The contrast is strikingly illustrated by the two decades of correspondence between them. From the brief and formal note, dated November 15, 1932, which Bentley sent with a copy of his *Linguistic Analysis of Mathematics* (Dewey did not acknowledge it for six months), the correspondence developed to a regular and intimate exchange. It was a remarkable chapter in the history of American social thought, not only because the best-known philosopher of his

[13] Sidney Ratner, "Bentley's Inquiries into the Behavioral Sciences," 36.

[14] See the comments of Sidney Ratner, "Arthur F. Bentley's Voyage of Social Discovery," paper prepared for the Arthur F. Bentley Seminar on the Great Society, National Planning Program, Maxwell Graduate School of Citizenship and Public Affairs, Syracuse University, May 27, 1966. Ratner has recently edited that manuscript; see Arthur F. Bentley, *Makers, Users and Masters* (Syracuse, N.Y.: Syracuse University Press, 1969).

day carried on such an exchange with the obscure orchard owner of Paoli, and not even because that association ripened into a joint publication when both men were in their twilight years; it was remarkable also because the obscure Midwesterner dominates the exchange—identifying problems, proposing and rejecting solutions, tirelessly criticizing, evaluating, and urging. It is the Columbia professor who expresses gratitude and admiration for his friend's insights, and a willingness to entertain challenges to positions held over a lifetime. In terms of modesty, generosity, and energetic dedication, the correspondence does credit to both.[15]

The life of the scholar (Bentley would have said "scientist") seems appropriate, as does his decision to forsake the city for the halcyon charm of Paoli.[16] These considerations suggest a possible parallel between his personal life and the conduct of his scholarship. In both he avoided the conventional in favor of a highly individual and personal style. It is true that illness shortened his journalistic career, but it is difficult to imagine his prolonged association with that profession—indeed, it is more revealing that Bentley abandoned the academy in the first place for the scarcely intellectual or prestigious world of the metropolitan reporter. Certainly the realization that he had unfitted himself for the teaching profession must have come quite early, and his renunciation seems not to have been accompanied by much regret. It is not pure conjecture to suggest an intimate relationship between Bentley's rejection of his contemporary social science and his desertion of the university. If Bentley found himself unsuited to the conventional occupations of intellectual and scholar, his thought and work defy the usual categories of social scientific labor. Bentley was a singular man professionally and intellectually. He has been considered a political scientist for *The Process of Government*, a sociologist for

15 These letters are now available in a collection, Sidney Ratner, Jules Altman, and James E. Wheeler (eds.), *John Dewey and Arthur F. Bentley: A Philosophical Correspondence 1932–1951* (New Brunswick, N.J.: Rutgers University Press, 1964).

16 Bentley was here, perhaps, true to the American mistrust of urbanism. See Morton and Lucia White, *The Intellectual Versus the City: From Thomas Jefferson to Frank Lloyd Wright* (Cambridge, Mass.: Harvard University Press and M.I.T. Press, 1962).

Relativity in Man and Society, a mathematician for *Linguistic Analysis of Mathematics,* a psychologist or social psychologist for *Behavior Knowledge Fact,* and an epistemologist and logician for *Knowing and the Known;* and Bentley considered himself an "economist in the making" for many years. Beyond these areas, Bentley had a considerable interest in theoretical physics, from which he frequently drew analogies. His writing displays technical erudition, though it is employed in an off-hand, almost casual manner. Seldom does his approach seem that of a professional in "his" field; rather, we gain the impression that he has focused on a problem and is willing to reach anywhere for clues to its solution.

I have stressed the qualities of independence and individuality in Bentley's personal and intellectual life as a preliminary to presenting him as a true revolutionary. He saw himself as a pathfinder, a scientific radical who would sweep away the intolerable tangle of fact, theory, and speculation which was the social science of his day and rebuild it on tested, secure foundations.[17] Bentley was to struggle with the vocations of critic and theory-builder for most of his life, but in 1908 the critical function seemed more imperative. The underdeveloped state of social science appeared less a result of the intractability of its subject matter, of innate limitations of the human mind, than it was a legacy of misconceptions, a history of malpractice. Without an appreciation of the intensity of this conviction, one is likely to be puzzled by the genuine rage and caustic scorn that boil within *The Process of Government.* We must not mistake the withdrawal to Paoli as a sign of a lack of concern with the future of social science. Bentley continued to read widely in professional journals, and, despite his isolation and the obscurity of his work, he retained a firm conviction that his investigations would one day serve as the basis of a new social science. It is remarkable that Bentley could sustain these difficult labors in self-imposed exile, believing most of his contemporaries to be fundamentally mistaken, and remain convinced that his work would

[17] I take it that this is analogous to what Peter Winch has called the "underlaborer" conception of philosophy's role in social science, *The Idea of a Social Science* (London: Routledge and Kegan Paul, 1958).

ultimately be vindicated. The confidence, the ego strength, that this suggests is reminiscent of a Veblen or a Peirce.[18] The tranquillity of Bentley's personal life may have prepared him to live in sustained intellectual turbulence. Few men have been given the opportunity to remake both the categories and rules by which their worlds have ordered social relations and those which govern the acquisition of knowledge of such relations. Bentley chose to conclude a truce with the former and to raze and rebuild the latter.[19]

I have stressed the revolutionary aspects of Bentley's vision because his work has often been absorbed into larger movements within American social science and society.[20] One such movement has been characterized by Morton White as "the revolt against formalism." White's study of American social thought extends to history, law, philosophy, and economics and includes such individual scholars as Charles Beard, James Robinson, Oliver Wendell Holmes, John Dewey, and Thorstein Veblen. Although White does not discuss Bentley, his conception of what these insurgents were trying to do has undeniable parallels with the program of *The Process of Government.* "All of them insist upon coming to grips with life, experience, process, growth, context, function. They are all products of the historical and cultural emphases of the nineteenth century, following, being influenced by, reacting from its great philosophers of change and process."[21] "Abstraction," broadly

18 Bentley's letters to Dewey illustrate the eagerness with which he greeted the opportunity of sharing his accomplishments and ambitions with an intelligent and sympathetic mind, but even with Dewey communication was sometimes a problem. An instructive account of Peirce's difficulties with the academy is C. Wright Mills, *Sociology and Pragmatism* (New York: Oxford University Press, 1966), Part II.

19 Bentley may not have been without some regrets about this decision. In February, 1941, he wrote to Dewey: "I occasionally wish I had let myself run free instead of compressing myself so severely in an academic world." See Ratner et al., 85. "Academic" here refers to intellectual pursuits, not to situation of employment.

20 For an interesting discussion of the interplay between the science and practice of politics, see Norman Jacobson, "Political Science and Political Education," *American Political Science Review,* LVII (September, 1963).

21 Morton White, *Social Thought in America: The Revolt against Formalism* (Boston: Beacon Press, 1957), 13. It should also be noted that Bentley could be included in this group by chronological as well as intellectual proximity. He was born

construed so as to include deductive logic, was the enemy; the rebels' objection struck primarily at what might be called the hollowness of abstraction. White's phrase "coming to grips with life" may be taken quite literally as indicating an almost physical effort. "Life" meant "the way things are"; it tendered all the respect for brute existence contained in Peirce's famous remark that "facts are hard things which do not consist in my thinking so and so, but stand unmoved by whatever you or I or any man or generations of men may opine about them." The vitalism of Henri Bergson and the organicism of Charles Darwin and Herbert Spencer lent the associations implicit in words like "growth," "context," and "function." The demand that the continuity, the "connectedness," of the social universe be recognized fostered a respect for historical antecedents that White calls "historicism" and defines as "the attempt to explain facts by reference to earlier facts."[22] The search for connection and relatedness among social phenomena extended "vertically" through history's temporality, while "cultural organicism" expanded inquiry "horizontally" across various disciplines. Dewey's political thought illustrates this theme very clearly. "The fundamental element on which Dewey's political system was built is the fact of human association. As it applies to politics, this postulate is simply a representation of the belief in interconnectedness of all aspects of the world. . . . Thus he began with a kind of organicism in which, in the final analysis, everything takes its meaning from its relationship to the totality."[23]

thirteen years after Veblen, eleven years after Dewey, and four years before Beard; C. S. Peirce, William James, and Holmes were in their thirties.

[22] *Ibid.*, 12. This is not a satisfactory definition of a word in such wide and often polemical use. For examples of its use, see Frederick von Hayek, *The Counter-Revolution of Science* (Glencoe, Ill.: Free Press, 1952); Karl Mannheim, *Ideology and Utopia* (New York: Harcourt, Brace, 1936); Ludwig von Mises, *Theory and History* (New Haven: Yale University Press, 1957); Karl Popper, *The Poverty of Historicism* (Boston: Beacon Press, 1957); Leo Strauss, *Natural Right and History* (Chicago: University of Chicago Press, 1953); and Glenn Tinder, "The Necessity of Historicism," *American Political Science Review*, LV, No. 3 (September, 1961).

[23] David W. Minar, *Ideas and Politics: The American Experience* (Homewood, Ill.: Dorsey, 1964), 366.

The Americans were empiricists in the sense that they sought to ground their inquiries in experience rather than in *a priori* principle, but there is a much more important sense in which neither they nor Bentley was sympathetic to a major stream of empiricist thought. Dewey and Veblen criticized such prominent British empiricists as Jeremy Bentham and John Stuart Mill for their adherence to associationist psychology and epistemological dualism. Dewey rejected the notion of discrete states of consciousness implied by Hume's analysis, and Veblen objected to the very basis of Mill's economics.[24] Mill's essay "On the Definition of Political Economy and the Method of Investigation Proper to It" had sought to distinguish economic science from more inclusive studies of social man by limiting its scope to the consequences of the pursuit of wealth. "Political economy considers mankind as occupied solely in acquiring and consuming wealth, and aims at showing what is the course of action into which mankind, living in a state of society, would be impelled, if that motive . . . were absolute ruler of all their actions."[25] Mill used the phrase "would be . . . if" as an heuristic device, explicitly stating that, in fact, men were not so simply motivated, but this did not save him from Veblen's censure. Veblen could not accept the "counter-factual conditional" as a methodological device even though it greatly simplified certain problems. In this refusal is perhaps reflected his objection to an empiricism that did not describe things as they were. Empiricism, at least the classical British variety, simply was not empirical enough.[26]

24 For an historical commentary on British utilitarianism, see Elie Halévy, *The Growth of Philosophic Radicalism* (Boston: Beacon Press, 1955), especially Part I, Chap. 1, and Part III, Chap. 3. Dewey's position is set forth in many places; see his famous essay "The Reflex Arc Concept in Psychology," reprinted in *Philosophy, Psychology and Social Practice*, ed. Joseph Ratner (New York: G. P. Putnam's Sons, 1963). The papers published by Dewey and Bentley as *Knowing and the Known* (Boston: Beacon Press, 1960) are an attack on the dualism of empiricist epistemology.

25 Quoted in Morton White, 22–23. Mill's position is more generally presented in *A System of Logic* (London: Longmans, Green, 1961), especially Book III concerning induction. See Winch, Chap. III, for a recent critical commentary. Veblen's extended remarks may be found in the essay "Why Is Economics Not an Evolutionary Science," *The Portable Veblen*, ed. Max Lerner (New York: Viking Press, 1950).

26 For a more general discussion of these themes, see Charles W. Morris, *Logical Positivism, Pragmatism and Scientific Empiricism* (Paris: Hermann et Cie, 1937).

The American revolt against formalism sought the destruction of "artificial" boundaries between the social sciences. Charles Beard forcefully expressed this attitude.

> We are coming to realize that a science dealing with man has no special field of data all to itself, but is rather merely a way of looking at the same things—a view of a certain aspect of human action. The human being is not essentially different when he is depositing his ballot from what he is in the counting house or at the work bench. In the place of a "natural" man, an "economic" man, a "religious" man or a "political" man, we now observe the whole man participating in the work of government.[27]

These words appeared in 1908, the year in which *The Process of Government* was published. Historically, and on the political level, sentiments such as Beard's have been associated with pragmatism, pluralism, and the Progressive movement, and Bentley's now famous book could easily be read as echoing the same themes. Beard himself perceived the community of interest between group theory and the kind of inquiry he had launched in his economic interpretation of the framing of the American Constitution, and he assigned Bentley's book to the students in his Columbia seminar.[28] The desire for a social science that could "get behind" form and appearance had a genuine parallel in the technique of the Muckrakers' exposé.[29] When Bentley wrote of activity and interest as the raw materials of political science, he echoed the "harsh reality" tone of his age. Richard Hofstadter has described the Progressive's vision of the political universe this way: "At bottom, I think, it had three characteristics: it was rough and sordid; it was hidden, neglected, and, so to speak, off-stage; and it was essentially a stream of external and material events, of which psychic factors were a kind of pale reflex. Reality was the bribe, the rebate, the bought franchise, the sale of adulterated food."[30]

[27] Quoted in Richard Hofstadter, "Charles Beard and the Constitution," *Charles A. Beard*, ed. Howard K. Beale (Lexington: University of Kentucky Press, 1954), 79.
[28] Charles A. Beard, *An Economic Interpretation of the Constitution of the United States* (New York: Macmillan, 1961), 12.
[29] See Minar, Chaps. X and XI.
[30] Hofstadter, 87.

25

Arthur Bentley's place in this intellectual and political current must be conceded, but to leave the matter there is to domesticate him, to sublimate the revolutionary in the reformer. On the level of political action he may indeed have remained a Progressive, but his vision of social science was less a revolt against formalism than a lifelong commitment to its utter elimination and its replacement by genuinely new categories and methods. Some political scientists sought to expand the scope of their discipline beyond the confines of an institutional description of "government," and Beard would have dispensed with political man altogether, but Bentley extended the revolt until it became something else—the vision of a process universe. In this respect at least he was the paradigm scientific radical.

But Bentley's place in such indigenous American movements is only half the story. His early thought in particular was framed by his European studies, notably of French and German sociology. This experience was not at all exceptional; Bentley and Hapgood were only two of an estimated 9,000 Americans who studied in German universities during the century following 1820.[31] What was unusual in Bentley's case was the unique way in which he sought to extend and transcend that legacy. Bentley's early attempts to formulate the concept of process reflected a dualism which emerged in the late nineteenth century; the full dimensions of this dualism cannot be examined here, but some mention must be made of the two traditions which nourished the process idea. In Arthur Bentley's experience, these two strains were represented by the sociologies of Georg Simmel and Ludwig Gumplowicz. Gumplowicz will be discussed only briefly here, since his position and that of Albion Small will be developed later.

THE EUROPEAN BACKGROUND

Behind both sociologies lies a varied and complex history of ideas which was eventually to culminate in the divorce of the social

31 Jurgen Herbst, *The German Historical School in American Scholarship* (Ithaca: Cornell University Press, 1965), 1.

sciences, notably sociology, from history and the philosophy of history.[32] The attempt to place the social sciences on a firm substantive and epistemological base was itself enmeshed in a number of century-old controversies, some of which lent an enduring shape to the new disciplines. The most general form of conflict was framed in terms of positivism *vs.* idealism. This struggle appeared on the ontological level in disputes over the nature of the subject matter of the social sciences (behavior or subjective states) and in debates concerning the proper conception of causation in human affairs.[33] On the methodological plane this division was reflected in the attempt to distinguish nomothetic (generalizing) from idiographic (particularizing) sciences.[34] The question of the nature of explanation in the social sciences was linked to the legitimacy of such observational techniques as *Verstehen* (or the process of "understanding" other minds) and to the issue of which units of investigation were appropriate to the study of man and how their choice reflected the values of the investigator.[35] Mention of the course of these debates calls to mind such names as Dilthey, Menger, Ranke, Rickert, Schmoller, and Windleband, but it was men of the generation of Georg Simmel and Max Weber who sounded a distinctively modern note; they are no longer historians or philosophers

[32] See, for example, Carlo Antoni, *From History to Sociology* (Detroit: Wayne State University Press, 1959), and H. Stuart Hughes, *Consciousness and Society* (New York: Knopf, 1958).

[33] For the general relationship of idealism and positivism as rival bases for social science, see Talcott Parsons, *The Structure of Social Action* (Glencoe, Ill.: Free Press, 1949), Chap. XIII, and Hughes.

[34] The methodological issues are treated by Raymond Aron in his *Introduction to the Philosophy of History* (Boston: Beacon Press, 1961) and *German Sociology* (Glencoe, Ill.: Free Press, 1957); R. G. Collingwood, *The Idea of History* (New York: Oxford University Press, 1956); and Maurice Mandelbaum, *The Problem of Historical Knowledge* (New York: Liveright, 1938).

[35] For various formulations of the nomothetic-idiographic dichotomy see H. A. Hodges, *The Philosophy of Wilhelm Dilthey* (London: Routledge and Kegan Paul, 1952), and Heinrich Rickert, *Science and History* (New York: Van Nostrand, 1962). On the uses of *Verstehen*, see Theodore Abel, "The Operation Called Verstehen," *Readings in the Philosophy of Science*, ed. Herbert Feigl and May Brodbeck (New York: Appleton-Century-Crofts, 1953), and Murray L. Wax, "On Misunderstanding Verstehen: A Reply to Abel," *Sociology and Social Research*, LI (1967).

reflecting upon society, but social scientists committed to the creation of a discipline.[36]

The sociologies of both Simmel and Weber were compromises. They were attempts to answer the question of how generalization and systematization are possible given the infinitely varied data of history. The problem of generalization had appeared in a number of contexts in nineteenth-century German thought, beginning perhaps with the Thibaut-Savigny controversy within jurisprudence. Carl Friedrich von Savigny was the foremost exponent of the historical school of jurisprudence which, in opposition to natural law theories, maintained that the basis of law is custom and that the legal structure of a nation grows organically through usage and incremental additions by jurists steeped in the particulars of their own unique cultural configuration. Savigny developed this position in a pamphlet (*Of the Vocation of Our Age for Legislation and Jurisprudence*) published in 1814 in reply to Anton Thibaut's proposal for a sweeping codification of German law.[37] Albion Small found in Savigny's reply the awakening of a "critical" spirit and a new sense of "objectivity." Insistence on the "organicism" of social life, its "rootedness" in history, suggested an incremental conception of social change and a commitment to the study of the societal whole. Small felt that Savigny's modernity lay in his discovery of the continuity of society. "Little by little the conclusion gathered the force of demonstration in social science that, whatever may prove to be more particular principles of human relationships, *gradualism* rather than *catastrophism* is the universal manner of social cause and effect."[38]

These ideas of societal continuity and historical context inspired

---

[36] Talcott Parsons probably spoke for the majority of his colleagues when he remarked: "I for one would not hesitate to label all the theoretical endeavors before the generation of Durkheim and Max Weber as proto-sociology." "The Prospects of Sociological Theory," *Essays in Sociological Theory* (Glencoe, Ill.: Free Press, 1954), 349. Albion Small preferred to fix the beginnings of sociology in the year 1870.

[37] See H. S. Reiss, *The Political Thought of the German Romantics* (Oxford: Basil Blackwell, 1955), 38–39.

[38] Albion W. Small, *The Origins of Sociology* (Chicago: University of Chicago Press, 1924), 62.

a suspicion of abstraction or "theory" that is well illustrated by the development of German economics. During the period 1820–50 the classical economic doctrine of Smith and Ricardo was taught very much as a complete science, but in the second half of the century Germans began to introduce significant revisions. The single most important factor in these changes was the realization that Smith's science rested upon a number of cultural and psychological assumptions which were variable in time and place and not rooted in a universal nature of man. This discovery opened the way for two important developments. First, it stimulated the formation of a historical school which relied upon particularistic historical and statistical description and eschewed more formal theoretical constructs. Second, the attack on the "interest" motive of the economic man suggested that economists had to broaden the scope of their science to include much that is ordinarily considered sociological.[39] In short, the origins of attitudes and values would become part of the subject matter of economics. But whether economics were conceived narrowly as a science of the marketplace, or broadly as the study of human valuing activity, the question of generalization remained. This was the germ of the famous *Methodenstreit,* the disputes between Karl Menger and Gustav Schmoller which began with the publication in 1883 of Menger's *Untersuchungen über Methode de Socialwissenschaften and der politischen Oekonomie insbesondere,* which was answered the same year by Schmoller's *Zur Methodologie der Staatsund Socialwissenschaften.*[40]

Menger insisted that the historical school's reaction against the formalism of classical economics had produced its own sterile methodology of exhaustive description. Schmoller's reply argued for the complementary nature of theory and description and demanded that formulations of the typical required persistent modification by factual inquiry. By the close of the century, the historical

[39] For an examination of the scope problem in theoretical economics, see Talcott Parsons's discussion of Alfred Marshall's marginal-utility theory, *The Structure of Social Action,* Chap. IV.

[40] See the excellent discussion of the *Methodenstreit* in Joseph Schumpeter, *Economic Doctrine and Method* (New York: Oxford University Press, 1954).

school had developed a position similar to Savigny's. Joseph Schumpeter's summary statement of that position emphasizes its suspicion of general principles, its insistence on the unity of social life (hence the impossibility of isolating a range of economic factors), its belief in the "irrational" (noncalculated) nature of most individual behavior, its resistance to reduction of the economy to individual actions, and its acceptance of multiple causation and evolutionary change.[41] The persistence of the themes of holism and continuity are illustrated in the work of the eclectic Albert Schäffle, whose conception of economics was virtually encyclopedic sociology. Albion Small hailed Schäffle's work as "sociological economics" and added that it sought to "show that economic phenomena are something more than economic phenomena, i.e., to expand surveys of men engaged in production and consumption of wealth, into surveys of men carrying on the whole complex of purposeful activities into which they are urged by the entire range of their wants."[42]

Small thought the ideas of continuity and interconnection of social phenomena important enough to constitute the essence of the sociological vision. The continuity idea is intimately connected to the methodological problem of causation, and thus we find Small insisting that acceptance of interconnection and continuity implies multiple causation, and that this in turn implies an incremental theory of change. In a similar vein, Carlo Antoni wrote: "The problem of the relationship between all the categories, that is, of the unity and continuity of the life of the spirit, really came into prominence only after the Marxists had affirmed the dependence of all other categories upon the economic. The sociological interpretation of history is based upon the transition from one category to the others."[43] Richness, variety, and process were the terms in which cultural historians and "life" philosophers cast their opposition to the generalizing, "explanatory" procedures of the natural sciences, but, for those who would create a social scientific discipline despite their sympathy for these objections, the demand for order and gen-

41 *Ibid.*, 179.
42 Small, 303.
43 Antoni, 151.

erality could not be brushed aside. Georg Simmel was one of these, and, despite his comparative neglect by present-day sociologists, his influence in the early decades of the twentieth century in America was considerable. His work is particularly important for this study, first, because he offered a major alternative to previous conceptions of society as process, and second, because that conception was a vital element in the development of Bentley's thought.

Many people have found Simmel peculiarly difficult to read. There is an elusive quality about his writing that is remarked upon by all commentators on his work. To his critics he is superficial, unsystematic, murky, even "artistic," in the pejorative sense of that term; his admirers speak of his brilliance, versatility, insight, and sensitivity. It is probable that these varying reactions identify similar qualities, notably a subtle mind and a distaste for the systematic, that led a less than admiring contemporary to observe: "One does not come away from his lecture with too much of positive value; but it is pleasant to be offered up this and that titilating stimulation or volatile intellectual pleasure," and to conclude that Simmel was "one who operates more by wit and pseudo-wit than by solid and systematic thinking."[44] Simmel was not a "life" philosopher in the sense of a Bergson or a Nietzsche; nor could he be called a neo-Kantian or a pragmatist; but he was all of these things in some measure. Simmel remains one of those intriguing figures (Karl Mannheim is another) who stands at a major philosophical junction and looks in many directions.

Much of the difficulty in reading Simmel has its root in the central dialectic of his thought. In philosophical terms, a major effort of his thought was to reconcile being and becoming, the one and the many.

In the structure of Simmel's attitude, the poles of *becoming* and *the many* have precedence. The traits of the world which seem to impress him the most profoundly are its changeability and its multiplicity. The pre-philosophical mind of Simmel sees the world as a flux. Nothing is, nothing is still; everything moves con-

[44] Dietrich Schaefer, quoted in Lewis Coser, "The Stranger in the Academy," *Georg Simmel*, ed. Lewis Coser (Englewood Cliffs, N.J.: Prentice-Hall, 1965), 38–39.

tinuously. Yet, though all is in flux, what appears is not a single homogenous, viscous stream flowing at an unvarying pace. On the contrary, there is an attractive shimmering of a myriad different qualities; for the fleeting moment that they can be discerned, not one seems like another. Nor is the pace of the flow measured and even. It is marked by a rhythm of great irregularity.[45]

The social scientific problems involved in such a vision are illustrated by this passage: "Pitted against Simmel's vision of the instability and particularity of things is the requirement of fixity and unity. As a flux, the world is unknowable and uninhabitable. Without stability and rest, without order and structure, without being and the one, there is no objectivity."[46] The reconciliation of ordered thought with the flux of experience was a problem of major concern to both Bergson and Simmel, but while the former boldly concluded that conceptual thought can never represent the experiential reality, Simmel sought to accommodate both variety and order.[47] This is the problem to which Parmenides and Heraclitus gave their opposing answers. For Simmel, as for most modern thinkers, the craftsman must work with both permanence and change, and his task becomes, in Rudolph Weingartner's insightful phrase, "that of a sculptor who attempts to mould statues in a medium that is always on the point of melting."[48]

This image suggests that an essential tension lies at the heart of the social scientific enterprise. Simmel sought to use this tension creatively at the methodological level through his distinction between *form* and *content*. He gave this methodological dichotomy its philosophical statement by distinguishing between "more-life" and "more-than-life." The Hegelian overtones of these phrases are

---

[45] Rudolph Weingartner, *Experience and Culture: The Philosophy of Georg Simmel* (Middleton, Conn.: Wesleyan University Press, 1962), 183.

[46] *Ibid.*

[47] "Bergson contemplates duration as an observer, standing idly on a bank, might watch a river sweep by: the observer is more or less fixed, the object flows on. Simmel views it as one might examine a cathedral: while one walks outside it, around it, within it, or looks down upon it, it evolves." Matthew Lipman, "Some Aspects of Simmel's Conception of the Individual," in *Georg Simmel, 1858–1918*, ed. Wolff, 121.

[48] Weingartner, 183.

frightening to many contemporary readers, but they can be rendered in more empirical terms. The active, vital processes of human action give birth to "products" of life which then attain a status independent of the source which creates them. These products, "thrown up" as it were by the process, come to confront human action as external structures.[49] Nicholas Spykman has captured Simmel's idea in a passage that merits quotation in full.

> Life as process, continuous and essentially dynamic, creates the non-temporal forms, discrete and essentially static. These forms, once created, confront life, obstruct its free, unhampered flow, and try to shape it according to their norms. Out of this tension life's eternal dialectic is born. The processes of life create forms and embody themselves in structures. The forms of life, although the product of its processes, yet limit and define them. But life eternally transcends its self-created forms in order to find embodiment and modify the ceaseless flow of life until, no longer capable of giving it adequate expression, they are superseded in turn by other forms. This is the eternal dialectic inherent in life itself. For life is not only a continuous process and, as such, relative in relation to the forms and structures; it is also, as process, at the same time creator of these forms and therefore more than either.[50]

Forms as ordering principles do not inhabit an ideal realm, as with Plato, nor do they stand prior to experience, as with Kant; instead, they are immanent in experience, psychological, not ontological. According to contemporary theoretical usage, they might be regarded as "elements" of an action situation. On the concrete

[49] Readers familiar with the theme of "alienation" in Hegel and Marx will sense a similarity to Simmel's process product distinction. See Weingartner, 83–84n, and Kaspar D. Naegele, "Attachment and Alienation: Complementary Aspects of the Work of Durkheim and Simmel," *American Journal of Sociology* (May, 1958). Interpretations of alienation in the young or "philosophical" Marx are hotly debated. See Erich Fromm, *Marx's Concept of Man* (New York: Frederick Ungar, 1961); Robert Tucker, *Philosophy and Myth in Karl Marx* (Cambridge: Cambridge University Press, 1961); and the rebuttal by Sidney Hook, "New Introduction," *From Hegel to Marx* (Ann Arbor: University of Michigan Press, 1962). Daniel Bell's "Two Roads from Marx," in Bell, *The End of Ideology* (New York: Free Press, 1961), is a useful introduction to this debate.

[50] Nicholas Spykman, *The Social Theory of Georg Simmel* (Chicago: University of Chicago Press, 1925), 20.

level Simmel remained a consistent nominalist; men come together with other men in behaviors which, studied over time, yield patterned regularities called "institutions" or "societies." Society is sociation. Patterns may be studied in part by charting their frequency of occurrence, but Simmel regarded total reliance on an external methodology as inadequate. For him, as for Weber, the study of sociation was required to tap the actor's motives and his awareness of others; thus "conflict" must be understood both as a state of mind and as a behavior pattern.[51] Simmel differed from Weber in consigning such operations as *Verstehen* to the province of psychology. He was compelled to adopt this course because such matters belonged to the realm of content. This important distinction may best be rendered by examples. Simmel himself described content in these words:

> Content may be of an objective kind, the production of a work, the progress of the mechanical arts, the domination of an idea, the success or failure of a political combination, the development of language, or customs, etc., or it may be of a subjective nature and concern the innumerable sides of personality which through socialization find stimulus, satisfaction and development, now towards a refinement, now towards a deterioration of morals.[52]

Elsewhere Simmel referred to content as the "body" or "material" of the social process, including both material and nonmaterial culture.

The idea of form is somewhat more elusive. In Simmel's usage, form is employed to describe slavery, law, honor, the stranger, the teacher, the family, political parties, hierarchy, stability, conflict, and subordination. Contemporary sociologists might prefer to distinguish law as "structure," family as "institution," and teaching as "role," but such niceties are not relevant here. An example may illustrate the manner in which the form/content dichotomy can be applied in concrete analysis. Consider the familiar situation of dis-

---

51 See F. H. Tenbruck, "Formal Sociology," in *Georg Simmel, 1858–1918*, ed. Wolff, 69, and Theodore Abel, *Systematic Sociology in Germany* (New York: Columbia University Press, 1929), 32.

52 Quoted in Abel, *Systematic Sociology*, 21.

sident members of a community who determine to form an opposition political party. Given a certain initial success in recruitment, the party may find it necessary to adopt elements of organization and hierarchy. The resulting vertical stratification, particularly the emergence of a leadership elite with values and perceptions different from those of the rank and file, can inhibit militancy and is likely at least to alter original programmatic goals. In this case we might speak of a form product exercising a constraint upon the content process; while it would be nonsense to envision the hierarchy as "existing" without its constituent, flesh-and-blood party members, it would be a comparable folly to ignore the fact that, so long as hierarchy persists, certain other kinds of organization and values (for example, some kinds of equality) are necessarily precluded.[53] To "abstract" form in this manner is to engage in an imaginative act; as F. H. Tenbruck has phrased it, "abstracting must be understood in the radical sense of extracting from reality or extricating from reality something which is not a directly observable and common element in it."[54] The process of abstraction provides a means of reconciling being and becoming, but it also suggests a solution to the methodological problem of generalization, for one may say that, while form is general, content remains unique.

Simmel's analogies frequently liken social form to geometrical form, sometimes to artistic form, and later he drew parallels with organic forms. The geometrical analogue confirms Simmel's fascination with the spatial dimension of socialization and dominates his writing on sociological theory; the organic image appears most consistently in his use of historical materials. If sociology could be made the study of form, it might achieve the generality and power of geometry by consigning the particular and the unique to history or to encyclopedic sociology. For this reason E. V. Walter criticized

[53] The illustration is, of course, drawn from Michels's organization theory. For more detailed analyses of Michels's ideas about form, see C. W. Cassinelli, "The Iron Law of Oligarchy," *American Political Science Review*, XLVII (September, 1953), and John D. May, "Democracy, Organization, Michels," *American Political Science Review*, LIX (June, 1965).

[54] Tenbruck, 75.

the translation of *Die Kreuzung sozialer Kreise* as "the web of group affiliations"; a literal rendering would be "the intersection of social circles."

> On the contrary, an accurate rendering of Simmel's thought would convey that a "web" stretches out and connects, whereas a "circle" closes off and excludes. Simmel's sociological constructs are not clusters of organismic tissues but architectonic structures, and his "circles" are closed perimeters which separate one area from another. His social forms are not expressions of organismic vitality but mechanical structural devices which place limits on life to keep its fluctuating elements under control, and there is no point in imposing organismic prejudices on an architectonic system.[55]

Simmel's distinctive contribution to the development of the process conception was to suggest that the "becoming" dimension of historical action might be captured in part by the being of formal sociology. Thus Simmel preserved the vision of society as process of the historical and vitalist schools but denied that such material was absolutely resistant to disciplined generalization. This answer, however, does not touch on the problem of how one is to go about extricating these forms from the richness of their historical matrix. The great weakness of the geometrical analogue, as Simmel realized, is that while the geometer can offer an analysis of a crudely drawn figure and feel confident in his proof even if the drawing is flawed, "the sociologist . . . may not make the corresponding assumption; the isolation of truly pure sociation out of the complex total phenomenon cannot be forced by logical means."[56] The means he suggested for accomplishing this isolation was the "method of causal resolution." Simmel carefully distinguished this procedure from

[55] E. V. Walter, "Simmel's Sociology of Power: The Architecture of Politics," in *Georg Simmel, 1858–1918*, ed. Wolff, 153. The translation in question was rendered by Reinhard Bendix in Georg Simmel, *Conflict and the Web of Group Affiliations* (Glencoe, Ill.: Free Press, 1955). Bendix regards the literal translation as "almost meaningless."

[56] Georg Simmel, "The Problem of Sociology," in *Georg Simmel, 1858–1918*, ed. Wolff, 324.

the alternative methods of empiricism and observation, formulation of epochal configurations, and systematic conceptualization of variables within an empirical system.[57] In the method of causal resolution, "the course of inquiry depends, rather, on the particular perspective and interests of the investigator, and on the cause or causes of whatever he happens to isolate as a problem."[58] This is methodological laissez faire worthy of American pragmatism. In fact, Simmel has returned by a rather circuitous route to a position argued by Heinrich Rickert and later developed by Max Weber, namely, that interests or values guide the selection of materials, but that despite that element of personal choice objective regularities are discoverable in the flux of experience.

Whatever its virtues in other respects, Simmel's attempt to solve the dilemma of process material and ordered thought had paradoxical consequences. The tradition of social process thinking which Small saw as essentially historical and organic found its statement by Simmel in terms of timeless two-dimensional form. In a sense, Simmel's formal sociology was a gesture of resignation, a surrender to the richness and multiplicity of experience. The terms of the surrender implied the sacrifice of social scientific pretensions: the admission that order and generality must be purchased with renunciation by the admission that life has overwhelmed science. This profound tension between the vitality of social life and the rigor of the scientific enterprise was Simmel's legacy to Arthur Bentley. Bentley, too, refused to embrace either horn of the dilemma, indeed he sought as earnestly as Simmel to transcend that dualism. Bentley's developing notion of process encompasses Simmel's solution at the same time that it struggles with its dualistic legacy. Before returning to Bentley, however, one final aspect of the German background of the idea of process must be mentioned.

[57] The "formulation of epochal configurations" probably refers to the constructs of cultural historians and possibly to the Weberian ideal type to be discussed below, while "systematic conceptualization of variables within an empirical system" sounds remarkably like a description of the Parsonian theory of action.

[58] Donald Levine, "The Structure of Simmel's Social Thought," in *Georg Simmel, 1858–1918*, ed. Wolff, 24–25.

This can best be seen by a brief consideration of Max Weber's "ideal-typical" construct as an alternative to formal sociology.[59]

The ideal-type is not based on a mean, an average, or any other aggregate of behaviors, nor is it an explicitly normative device. It is instead an imaginative projection of what certain behaviors would be *if* they were pursued to their fullest realization. For example, we might try to imagine what a rational man whose sole value was the accumulation of wealth, or one who cared only for the salvation of his soul, would be like. Ideal-typical analysis is thus rooted in actual behavior, but it views concrete acts as *tendencies toward* certain states. Weber formulated his constructs in active nouns (gerundive forms) as a safeguard against reification. Ferdinand Tönnies's polar types of organization, community (*Gemeinschaft*) and society (*Gesellschaft*), would become in Weber's usage *Vergemeinschaftung* and *Vergesellschaftung*.[60] In this way Weber thought he could hold his collective constructs close to the level of observable behavior. Ideal-typical analysis resembles Simmel's method of causal resolution in that it seeks to combine empirical and conceptual elements; the investigator builds the construct by encouraging their mutual interaction. It was partly this interdependence that enabled Weber to control the conceptual element by insisting that it be based upon logically possible action tendencies. The ideal-type portrays "pure" relationships not to be found in concrete reality, but its very exaggeration illuminates that reality. Nathan Rotenstreich has cogently compared the ideal-type to formal sociology.

> In formal sociology the separated element is arrived at through an abstraction from the material context, such as the forms of rule

---

[59] Literature on the ideal type is voluminous. Weber's discussions may be found in the essays " 'Objectivity' in Social Science" and "The Fundamental Concepts of Sociology," in Max Weber, *The Theory of Social and Economic Organization* (Glencoe, Ill.: Free Press, 1947). Representative commentaries include Abel, *Systematic Sociology*; Don Martindale, "Theory and Ideal Type," in *Symposium on Sociological Theory*, ed. Gross; and Parsons, *The Structure of Social Action*, especially Chap. 16.

[60] This formulation enabled Weber to treat collectivities as emerging from certain tendencies rather than as "existing with a fixed set of attributes." See Reinhard Bendix, *Max Weber: An Intellectual Portrait* (Garden City, N.Y.: Doubleday, 1962), 476.

and obedience, and establishes itself as an independent domain, that is to say as the sociological domain proper. In this theory there is a clear-cut distinction between the material-historical domain and the formal sociological. Weber's system does not offer a clear-cut duality of this kind, however, but rather a comparison. This feature is methodologically expressed in the emphasis on the one trait of the given historical phenomenon, by way of which sociological concepts qua Ideal Types are formed. The Ideal Type is *meaning* only; the historical contents are both facts *and* meanings. The stress is not on the formal elements but on the meaningful one which is inherent in the facts themselves. The formal element as formal is merely *constructed*; the meaningful element is separated from its full context and is not sheer construction. Weber's position has a rather nominalistic touch, whereas formal sociology has in a way a more realistic bias. This difference accounts for a further one: Formal sociology stresses the clear-cut difference between the material and the formal, while the theory of the Ideal Type has rather to recognize the gradual transition from what is both fact and meaning to what is meaning only.[61]

The relative stress on meaning and form has lent an enduring dualism to the idea of social process. Hugh Duncan's discussion of communications models of society illustrates the differences between meaning and form. Interaction within a physical field, he argues, requires the location of points or agents "which are internally modified by, and in turn modifiers of, the process which affects them." If the ideal-type is constructed on "meaning" and social form on "interaction," their basic units are, respectively, "persons" and "roles." The concept of role is "positional" in that it is defined and understood in terms of a system of roles, but can we attach a dimension of "meaning" to a role? "Communication cannot be a process which somehow passes through one individual to another for in such passage the individual is meaningless."[62] If interaction is taken literally as an exchange between two or more

[61] Nathan Rotenstreich, *Between Past and Present* (New Haven: Yale University Press, 1958), 174–75.

[62] Duncan, "Simmel's Image of Society," 163. See also Duncan, *Communication and the Social Order* (New York: Bedminster, 1962).

39

concrete individuals, then their states of mind (the meaningful dimension) are a legitimate, indeed necessary, area of sociological inquiry. If, on the contrary, the patterned forms of behavior abstracted from concrete sociation constitute the subject matter of the discipline, then investigation of individual states of consciousness is unnecessary, perhaps even improper. Put another way, the question is this: If the subject matter of social science is human interaction, what interest ought the scientist to have in the entities *between* or *among* which that sociation takes place? Confronted with this problem, some social theorists adopted the heroic alternative of denying that sociology need concern itself with entities at all. Commenting on the work of Robert Park and E. W. Burgess, Duncan remarks that "interaction became process, and processes such as imitation were but 'mechanisms of interaction.'" This was later to become a major problem for G. H. Mead and John Dewey in their attempt to assert the existence of a social self.

The difference between interaction and process conceptions of society has been generally overlooked by social, especially political, scientists. In a little-known monograph published in 1901, Philip P. Jacobs wrote that the question, "What is society?" might be answered by replying that it is an aggregate of groups *or* that it is a "social process, a constantly changing equilibrium."[63] Jacobs considered Ludwig Gumplowicz the major exponent of the group-interaction school. Gumplowicz conceived of society as a universe of more or less cohesive and permanent groups formed around mutually antagonistic interests. Conflict is the means by which these groups form and develop; society is at any time a kaleidoscopic patterning of their relationships. The state, in this view, represents the organized control of the dominant minority.[64] Contemporary

[63] Philip P. Jacobs, *German Sociology* (New York: Steinman and Foltz, 1909), 30–31. Jacobs actually distinguished a third alternative he called the conception of society as a mechanical or organic unity and suggested as illustrations the theories of Albert Schäffle, Paul Barth, and Ferdinand Tönnies. This third category is of minor interest here.

[64] Compare Franz Oppenheimer, *The State* (Indianapolis: Bobbs Merrill, 1914). Gumplowicz's clearest statement of racial and cultural divisions as the basis of social conflict is *Der Rassenkampf*.

pluralists should have no difficulty in recognizing this thesis, nor would they dissent from Gumplowicz's criticism of theories of social unity. "Social science can never 'obtain a basis as real as that of natural science' until the fantastic view that 'society' is an 'organism' has been thrown overboard and all biological analogies have been cleared away."[65] Jacobs understood that the process conception was indeed different, but he was not very successful in elaborating the distinction. "It is one thing to view humanity as an accumulation or aggregation of groups, even if within the groups sufficient room for associations be allowed. It is quite different to consider it as an association, with the fundamental element in the process being not the group, but the association and the interrelation to the members of the groups."[66]

This is a perceptive statement, but the distinction it draws might be sharpened by substituting "actor" or "analytic unity" for the word "element." Can we, for example, conceive of society not as a "network" but as a "networking," or of our subject matter as "economizing activities," not as "the economy"? A more awkward but perhaps more vivid way to put this distinction might be to begin with the phrase "group interaction," dismiss the idea of "group" as an entity, and seek to envision society (and thus the subject matter of social science) as that which remains. The "what remains" in this case is the idea of process.

A major barrier to the exercise of imagining a social science of process is the metaphoric and linguistic framework with which we approach the world. "Process," we say, demands an organizing "structure"—change presupposes the permanent. But this neo-Kantian reply did not satisfy Arthur Bentley. He came to understand more clearly what was required of a social science that could accept the metaphor of society as process; he knew that such a discipline would require a fundamental revision of our language and a revolution in our conceptions of time and space.

This condensed and schematic chapter has illustrated only a few

[65] Ludwig Gumplowicz, *The Outlines of Sociology*, trans. Frederick W. Moore (Philadelphia: American Academy of Political and Social Science, 1899), 35.
[66] Jacobs, 31.

41

of the major uses of and tensions within the idea of process in late nineteenth-century European social thought. I have been most concerned with two tasks. First, I have tried to indicate the matrix of issues imbedded within the process idea: to exhibit the interplay of logical, ontological, and methodological elements involving questions about the nature of social causation, the proper use of history, conceptions of society, relationships among the social sciences, and the possibility of social science. Second, I have sought to contrast this universe of discourse with that of the American "antiformalists," among whom Bentley is often numbered. But a cautionary note is in order. Although Bentley must have absorbed much of this background, he had not—certainly by 1908—organized his thought about these issues after the fashion of my exposition. His first book, more accurately two extended essays, was primarily the embodiment of a critique of formalism and only secondarily a suggestion of alternatives. It was written in the idiom of American social science and society (despite its wealth of comparative materials), but the issues implicit in both the critique and the reconstruction lead back inevitably to the problems reviewed in this chapter. In one sense it could be said that Bentley's entire intellectual journey was an attempt to enunciate these issues in another form of his own creation—a form that would permit their resolution.

Though he did not recognize it at the time, Bentley's attempt to fashion the tool was almost the whole of his science. His remark that when the groups are stated everything is stated was not, as his disciples have read it, an injunction to proceed with an empirical mapping of the political universe; it was, instead, Bentley's attempt to identify the *conceptual* problems of "stating" as the essential difficulty of social science. But this is to anticipate. It is now time to examine Bentley's initial efforts to explicate the idea of process.

II

To Prepare the Way

> Bentley has been working, and is still working, on
> that effort to solve the problem of human beings in or-
> ganized society. . . . I can hardly believe that all this
> great concentration and devotion could have been ex-
> pended for so long a time without a production which
> someday will be more widely recognized as of value.
> —Hutchins Hapgood

> I believe that you will find the effect of your writings
> is definite, though cumulative and slow. In a few years
> you may expect to see some parts of your ideas appear-
> ing in other men's writings with little or no recog-
> nition—not deliberate ignoring, but they will have
> absorbed something so gradually they won't quite
> know the source themselves. . . .
> —John Dewey, letter to Arthur F. Bentley

THE CRITICAL BENTLEY

EVERY POLITICAL SCIENTIST knows that Arthur Bentley described
The Process of Government as an attempt to fashion a tool, but few
have noted the heading of Part One of that volume, "To Prepare
the Way." On the first page Bentley warns his readers that this attempt will take him far beyond the subject of government. "If in
this preliminary task I use many words and seem a long way from
the processes of government which are my subject matter, it is because I feel the need of making sure against misinterpretation
later."[1] In the summary of the first section he describes what he
has done in these words: "I have written the preceding chapters to
prepare the way for the chapters that are to follow. I have wished to
make it clear why the method of interpreting society which I am
about to set forth is justified, and why the irruption into it of any

[1] Arthur F. Bentley, *The Process of Government* (Evanston, Ill.: Principia Press, 1949), 3.

43

unassimilated factors of the kind I have been criticizing would only serve to distort."[2]

Between these two passages lie three chapters: "Feelings and Faculties as Causes," "Ideas and Ideals as Causes," and "Social Will." Read as a unit, they constitute a critical essay on causality in social science, and by extension they present a conception of what may and may not be expected of such investigation. "Preparing the way" is for Bentley in these opening chapters a matter of "clearing" or "sweeping away" erroneous practices and doctrine. The task appears to him not as a matter of hewing a path through virgin land, but rather as that of leveling a forest of human error; it is reconstruction, not discovery. The fashioning of the tool had, at least initially, to await completion of this essentially critical, and in that sense negative, task. But these two projects, the preparation and the fashioning, could not ultimately be kept separate, for the critique not only set forth the limitations of social theory but also suggested a possibly fruitful way forward.

We are given indications of the nature of Bentley's concerns in the first sentence: "The most common way of explaining what goes on in society, including of course the processes of government, is in terms of the feelings and ideas of the men who make up the society."[3] A few lines later we read that the "old fashioned feelings and ideas which make up the whole of interpretation much of the time" require attention "before our real work can begin." These feelings and ideas "are irresponsible and unmeasurable," and they actually block explanation; their "false pretenses" must be "annihilated" before any interpretation can be made. Bentley states his intentions so bluntly that their radical nature escapes notice. The extremism of his proposal is emphasized, not diminished, by this passage:

> I may say now as well as later that I have no care for the fine discriminations which psychological terminology draws between motives, feelings, desires, emotions, instincts, impulses, or similar mental states, elements, or qualities. If I separate such factors from

[2] *Ibid.*, 165.
[3] *Ibid.*, 3.

ideas and ideals it is solely for convenience in discussing two ill-defined types of social theory. It is not, I repeat, psychic process that I am going to discuss, but social life, which from the point of view of functional psychology appears as content. The material is the same, but fine discriminations in psychological terminology used as criteria for classifying the content are not merely useless but positively harmful.[4]

Psychologists might be offended by this sweeping disregard of their painfully created distinctions, but this is not the most important point. Bentley lumped all these elements together, proclaimed that they represented the commonest means of explaining "what goes on in society," and then almost casually announced that it is necessary to annihilate their pretensions. Other men may certainly have consciously set out to accomplish similar tasks of destruction or redirection of prior thought (for example, Marx's conception of a new role for philosophy), but it is difficult to recall one who did so with less sense of the drama and import of his intentions. One is reminded of Thucydides's casual remark that "nothing on a great scale, in war or other matters," had occurred prior to the Peloponnesian War. For Bentley the past contained something "on a great scale," and that was error and confusion.

We might well inquire how a means of explanation or interpretation in common use for such a long time could be so wrong-headed; surely there must be pragmatic justification simply in endurance. Bentley met this objection immediately by proposing a distinction which remains basic throughout his work: the distinction between "everyday speech" and the demands of scientific explanation.

> For most of us all of the time, it is quite sufficient to regard human beings as "persons" who possess qualities or motives which are phases of their character and who act in accordance with these qualities or this character, under certain conditions of life in which they

4 *Ibid.*, 4. Bentley's refusal to consider any distinctions of this sort was almost surely a mistake, for without them we are in danger of confusing various levels of explanation. This point is forcefully argued in R. S. Peters, *The Concept of Motivation* (London: Routledge and Kegan Paul, 1958).

are placed. Much of the time we subordinate the conditions or ignore them entirely. Indeed the greater conditions are never known to us. . . .

We put the main weight then upon the character, or the motives, of the actors in the social drama. A man is kind, or violent, or careless, or "smooth," or stupid, or dishonest, or tricky, or insincere, or clever, or trustworthy; or, more generally, good or bad, wise or foolish. These are his qualities. They designate "him." They are put forth not merely as habits of action, labeled by us, but as his very personality. All of this in the current life of one man, judging the others around him. Out of material of this kind we have built up many theories of the causes of man's activities in society.[5]

For our daily purposes, our immediate needs, such interpretations serve us "fairly well"; if they prove mistaken in this or that instance we revise them, "changing not their character but the proportions of their mixture." That is, we decide that this person has a little less honesty in proportion to his avarice than we had previously imagined. In these respects, Bentley says, everyday speech may be adequate, but when the practice is extended to the realm of science, when it seduces the unwary or uncritical investigator by encouraging an exaggerated sense of its explanatory power, it is pernicious.

Everyday speech habits fall short of providing a basis for scientific explanation in many ways, and it is worth our time to examine the various arguments Bentley levels against them. The first is a logical one. Imagine, he says, a situation in which, to the cheers of onlookers, a man engaged in bullying a boy is knocked down and put to flight by a stranger. "I turn to my friend and ask: 'What made him do it? Why do they praise him?' 'He's a big-hearted fellow,' he answers. 'It is sympathy for others. He's a credit to our civilization.' "[6] In this form of "explanation," Bentley continues, the stranger's *act* is observed and described as sympathetic; then a *quality* of sympathy is attributed to the person as a motive "standing behind" the overt action. The approval of the crowd and the choice

[5] Bentley, *Process of Government*, 4–5.
[6] *Ibid.*, 5.

46

of "sympathy" as the quality are immaterial; the act might be disapproved and labeled malignant in a different time or place. Bentley's point is that such "explanation" adds nothing to the original description.

The second objection is closely related to the first, but it takes a more empirical turn. What, asks Bentley, does "sympathy" mean beyond its application to this particular act? How, for example, do our friend's sympathetic qualities direct him in the matter of child labor, human poverty, or abysmal factory conditions? More generally, how can we apply these "qualities" to the multifaceted beliefs and behavior of whole cultures and civilizations? The explanation in terms of qualities breaks down when general answers are required. "What I wanted to know was why this particular kind of 'sympathy' expresses itself in this form of protecting a boy who is merely being hectored or tormented without serious hurt."[7] Everyday speech, when it cannot ignore this difficulty, solves it by making numerous ad hoc distinctions and modifications. What we need to know is why this quality manifested itself or this act occurred in this place and at this time. The answer of ordinary speech postulates an imaginary state of mind and then introduces the necessary modifications to account for behavior in a particular case. Bentley does not foreclose the possibility that a general account of "sympathy" might be given, though he is clearly not enthusiastic about the effort.

Bentley suggests the additional criticism of careless or actually corrupt application of this method through endlessly "distinguishing" ad hoc one's way out of difficulty, but this is subordinate to the more general contention. Qualities, unless we can state them in such terms that they distinguish among a multitude of behaviors throughout the culture or even cross-culturally, without reducing ourselves to selective application of the quality to each particular situation, are of no use in scientific explanation. The question to be answered is why men choose their actions (for example, displays of sympathy) in various times and contexts. Qualities of sentiment

[7] *Ibid.*, 6.

and feeling, even if they are not prey to the previous objections, are at present (and perhaps also in principle) beyond direct observation and control.

> Whenever anybody steps forward with any method by which he can show that there actually exists at one time more of one of the psychic qualities, the "stuff," than at any other time, it will be perfectly legitimate to take it into account. So long as such "stuff" is used in explanation of the forms of our social actions on no better ground than that we assume changes in the "stuff" from the mere fact of the changes in the modes of action, then it is no explanation.[8]

In lieu of establishing this measure of control, Bentley considers explanation in these terms only the roughest description at the level of everyday speech.

These arguments constitute Bentley's critique of feelings and faculties as causes, but he does not permit the case to rest there. The habits of everyday speech are not only inadequate, they inhibit development of superior forms of explanation by fostering "animism" and what Bentley calls the "billiard ball" notion of the social process. It is well to remind ourselves that Bentley meant the phrase "feelings and faculties" to include an entire range of "mentalisms," even the notion of intelligence. Intelligence, like "luck" and "original sin," promotes an animistic, or as Bentley was later to call it, a "self-actional" idea of causation. This is a variant of the circular explanation described above, but animism deepens that error by reifying the "soul qualities." "If we are going to infer a soul quality from the social fact and then use the quality to explain the fact, we put ourselves on a level with animists in the most savage tribes. A branch falls. It was the life in it or behind it that threw it down. Thunder peals. It is the spirit speaking."[9] The particular virulence of animism is the encouragement it offers to scientists and philoso-

---

8 *Ibid.*, 18. Bentley leaves open the possibility that some day such direct control of faculties and the feelings might be achieved. Despite his quite apparent skepticism, it must be understood that he does not foreclose it in principle.

9 *Ibid.*, 19.

phers to rescue everyday speech patterns by ingenious and subtle argument, despite the hopelessness of their attempts. Even the great empiricist Aristotle sought to account for the institution of slavery by referring to the psychic qualities, or soul, of the individual slave.[10] Animism, then, is both a corollary and an extension of the circularity fallacy.

The "billiard ball" idea completes this tapestry of error by providing a substantive image of social causation. Personal qualities, reified and endowed with self-actional powers, "are looked upon as a sort of 'thing' acting among other 'things' in the social world." (The billiard ball image, of course, is not necessarily connected to explanation by psychic states.)

> They are a sort of "stuff," different, or not different, as one likes, from the material "stuff" of the world, but in either case interacting with the latter in series of events that can be linked together, with each event in the series explaining the other that comes after it. For example, Tom sees the bully maltreating the boy. The bully makes Tom act in a particular manner. The bullying is stopped by the impact. Brain states, or soul states, forming this "stuff"—it is all one in the practical explanation.[11]

Bentley was later to distinguish the self-actional from the interactional in considerably sharper terms, and to contrast both with a "transactional" viewpoint. It is important here that we be sensitive to Bentley's use of words like "environment" and "process" in relation to notions of causality.

Before passing on to an examination of what Bentley might call "the errors at work," we might pause to review what he does *not* say. He does not contend that no such things as feelings "exist," nor does he maintain that men do not differ in intelligence and character. "I am not insisting that there is no difference in 'brain power,' if that phrase may be used, between men. I am not saying that such differences can never, in some respects at least, be taken into ac-

[10] Bentley was later to locate in Aristotle's logic the root of an even more fundamental error.

[11] Bentley, *Process of Government*, 17.

49

count; it would be foolish indeed to erect a verbal barricade against the future."[12] It is as explanatory tools that the psychical qualities of individuals must be found inadequate and pernicious; Bentley does not present himself as a materialist, nor even as a debunker of the efficacy of ideas. His criticism seldom strays from its central concern about any hypothesis—namely, how adequate is it as an account of collective human behavior? Bentley might have conceded some legitimacy to motive-state explanations and urged that they be supplemented by other forms, but he consistently adopts the extreme position of rejecting them almost completely. A possible reason for this immoderate stance was that he associated motive-state explanation with the vagaries and vulgarities of "ordinary" discourse. In this respect his argument might be said to run against "bad" motive-state explanations. This is not the point at which to begin a discussion of what Bentley thought a fully satisfactory account would be, but that question may profitably be kept in reserve.

The writings of Albion Small, especially his *General Sociology* (1905), provided Bentley with his first example of the misuse of psychical qualities in social analysis. This criticism is particularly interesting because *General Sociology* was strongly influenced by Gustav Ratzenhofer, whom Bentley admired. Bentley's determination to distill and salvage what he considered Ratzenhofer's genuine value presents in embryo an enduring dualism of his social theory. Small's preface announced a proposition that Bentley must have warmly embraced: "Our thesis is that the central line in the path of methodological progress, from Spencer to Ratzenhofer, is marked by gradual shifting of effort from analogical representation of social structures to real analysis of social processes."[13] The idea that human association might be seen as a process, he continues, had been familiar to philosophers from the time of Hegel, "but hardly in a realistic sense."[14] For Small, the task of sociology was

12 *Ibid.*, 15.

13 Albion W. Small, *General Sociology* (Chicago: University of Chicago Press, 1905), ix.

14 *Ibid.*, 3n. Presumably, it had been familiar as an "analogical representation."

the study of the social process as a whole rather than of fragments selected for particular analysis by more specialized social sciences. On occasion sociology and others of the sciences of man may study the same phenomena, and in these instances the difference is one of emphasis.[15] The terms of the relationships within the process become the forms of the integrated science, but these relationships are not simply those of proximity in time, space, or series: "They are relationships of working-with, of process."[16]

So far we might imagine that Bentley would have thought that Small was treading the path of rectitude, but soon he slips and falls heavily: "All action that goes on in society is the movement and counter-movement of persons impelled by the particular assortment of these feelings which is located in each."[17] Sociology begins with individual feelings, wants, or desires; it takes men and wants as "finished products," as opposed to biology and psychology, which are concerned with their "making." "Before science that is properly social begins . . . analysis of individual traits must have taken into account all the peculiarities of individual action which betray the individual impulses or springs of individual action which are the units of force with which social science must deal."[18] The "push," the dynamic element in collective behavior, lies "in" the individual's want, desire, or interest, which, projected into a human environment and multiplied by the number of other individuals present, accounts for social action. Social arrangements and institutions are results of the operation of these individual wants, and to further explicate this relationship Small composed tables of individual desires, which, raised to the power of social forces, could lead to the "arrangements" of society. Starting with individual endowment plus physical environment, he proposed to "construct" society.

The nature or number of personal wants or desires listed by

[15] Thus Small accepted what Germany knew as "encyclopedic sociology," which, with individual variations, regarded sociology as the master, generalizing discipline. In this sense, it was also the view of Comte and Spencer. See Aron, *German Sociology*, 1.

[16] Small, *General Sociology*, 18.

[17] *Ibid.*, 480.

[18] Small, quoted in Bentley, *Process of Government*, 31.

Small is immaterial here, as is the propriety of including any one or more of them in a "basic" list. The issue is not the familiar query about the possibility of environmental modification of fundamental human drives; Bentley argues that any attempt to "go behind" collective behavior in search of individual desires or motives is useless as a means toward a deeper understanding of society. Small's enumeration of "subjective" individual desires is "matched" by a corresponding number of "objective" satisfactions or situations which might be viewed as their result.[19] These satisfactions are described in highly generalized terms, and there is an enormous range of variation. For example, the "social instincts" may be satisfied by situations ranging "from wolfishness to brotherhood." Sociological investigation, in this view, would proceed to a parallel examination both of the situations and of their instinctual "causes."[20]

> At all events the appropriate order of procedure, from a sociological point of approach, is analysis of social situations, in connection with analysis of purposes of the persons involved in the situations, to the end of arriving at generalizations of regularities and uniformities of sequence between types of social situations and types of human volitions.[21]

When individual drives are matched with their situational consequents, the tool is complete as far as classification is concerned, but it will still lack analytical power. Small was aware that a society in the real world is a complex of situations and drives existing in diverse intensities and degrees of development. To remedy this deficiency, Small proposes to assign coefficients to the drives in order to measure quantitative variations among them; these variations, taken as a particular compound or configuration, produce a

19 Bentley referred here to the lists of personal wants and satisfactions which appeared in Small and Vincent's *Introduction to the Study of Society* (New York: American Book Co., 1894); see *Process of Government*, 28–29.

20 I do not distinguish here between "drive," "motive," "volition," or "desire," though I am aware that much controversy attaches to the use of any of these terms. Bentley's criticism did not distinguish, and this account attempts to follow his usage where possible. See my reference to Peters.

21 Small, *General Sociology*, 476.

qualitative change in the satisfactions. This method of measurement is variously called an "algebra" and a "calculus" of desires.

There is no need to repeat Bentley's general critique of the use of psychical faculties in social exploration; the result of their application to such an unwieldy apparatus is quite clear. More interesting is the fact that Bentley's conception of social theory was at this time so similar to that of Albion Small. If this is true, we must look with some skepticism on Bentley's assertion that he offers a criticism of Small purely, or primarily, on "sociological grounds."[22] It is Small's theory of social causation which is under attack, but it is a relatively minor segment of his social theory that is questioned—specifically, the use of the individual and his drives as causal agents. It is unprofitable to dispute Bentley's use of the term "sociological," but it is not without purpose to contend that his objections to Small's "individual" as fictitious, to the use of that individual's faculties in causal analysis as tautological, and to the very conception of social forms as capable of analysis in individual terms are at least as much epistemological or philosophical as purely sociological.

If we consider *The Process of Government* and *General Sociology* from the specifically sociological perspective, several interesting parallels are apparent. Both Bentley and Small speak repeatedly about "social processes" and make serious efforts to distinguish their intended and recommended procedures from those of predecessors and contemporaries. This similarity finds expression even in their respective analogies. For example, Bentley: "If we take all the men of our society, say all the citizens of the United States, and look upon them as a spherical mass, we can pass an unlimited number of planes through the center of the sphere, each plane representing some principle of classification. . . ."[23] Compare Small: "Human desires are not so many mathematical points. They may rather be represented to our imagination as so many contiguous surfaces stretching out from angles whose areas presently begin to overlap each other, and whose sides extend indefinitely."[24] In their

[22] Bentley, *Process of Government*, 476.
[23] *Ibid.*, 207.
[24] Small, *General Sociology*, 446.

developments of the process theme both men found it useful to criticize Spencer, though Small is the more restrained. Another point of similarity is the centrality both accorded the idea of "interest"; the concept is ambiguous, and we certainly would not be justified in ignoring the differences in their respective usages, but it should not be forgotten that interest was not then the almost commonplace in social theory that it has come to be in our time. Closely related to interest is their common emphasis on the "group" as a tool of analysis. This is dominant in Part Two of *The Process of Government* and almost as pronounced in Small, particularly when he attempts to shift attention from study of *the* social process to that of "social process*es*." Finally, both men were strongly influenced by Gustav Ratzenhofer: Part Four of *General Sociology* is devoted to an extended commentary on Ratzenhofer, and Bentley remarks that Small's formulations are "frequently a decided improvement on Ratzenhofer himself."[25]

More detailed analysis would confirm and add to the similarities indicated above, and would, consequently, invite the question of why Bentley felt it necessary to criticize Small so extensively. Part of the answer probably lies in Bentley's desire to avoid empty "verbalism" and to emphasize always the working value of any theory; the question he invariably addresses to a construct is, "What can you accomplish with it?" This conviction, that sociology must be firmly anchored in practice, might have been weakened if presented without reference to existing theory. But there is a deeper reason, the full implications of which can only be indicated at this point—namely, Bentley's commitment to what might be called a methodological monism.

The preliminary but unmistakable introduction of this conviction appears in Bentley's discussion of the subjective-objective dichotomy in Small's tables of "desires" and "satisfactions." We have already seen that a causal account based upon this sort of dichotomy is worthless because circular, but Bentley is anxious to extend his critique further: "There are no desires nor interests

25 Bentley, *Process of Government*, 476.

apart from content. There are no nerves which carry feelings inward without at the same time carrying ideas . . . ; there are none which carry ideas without at the same time carrying feelings. You never can make a feeling all alone explain an act—not even in the simplest case imaginable. *And the ideas bring the whole outside world into the reckoning.*"[26] The last sentence is of supreme importance: if one sentence could be selected to illustrate both Bentley's objection to traditional social theory and the greatest obstacle to its reconstruction, it would be this one. He emphatically does *not* say that there are no such things as "ideas" or "feelings" (although he does consider these words "crude"), nor does he claim that they are in some way reducible to physical expression as "electrochemical impulses" or whatever. (He later specifically rejected that possibility.) The argument is that there is no way to take mental constructs, isolate them from their physical, biological, or social context, and then set them over against or behind the milieu that remains.

This is not the same as the tautology argument, for it suggests a substantive conception of the phenomenal world which does not permit certain kinds of bifurcation of nature. Indeed, the argument implies that, if mental-state descriptions can achieve this full, integrated statement, they may serve an explanatory function. That world, if not quite a seamless web, exhibits continuity, and—for lack of a better word—interpenetration of phenomena. The fundamental mistake of Small and other sociologists is their introduction of a false sense of "boundedness," of planes of cleavage or separation that possess no demonstrable relation to the natural world. Bentley's polemics are repeatedly directed against thinking in terms of what he variously calls "bunches," "bundles," "clots," and "stuff," and against that destructive dichotomy, "subjective" and "objective." This argument is put most clearly in Bentley's analysis of Rudolph von Jhering's two works *Der Zweck im Recht* and *Geist des romischen Rechts auf den verschiedenen Stufen seiner Entwicklung.* In contrast to his view of Small and Herbert Spencer,

---

[26] *Ibid.*, 37. (My emphasis.)

Bentley considered von Jhering's thought to be "patiently power-ful" and free of the more obvious confusions.[27] Precisely because of this regard for von Jhering, Bentley found his ultimate failure the most damning indictment of this approach to social theory.[28]

Jhering set himself the task of explaining the possibility of so-ciety by linking individual action to social utility through the concept of *"Zweck."* (Bentley regarded this word as untranslatable and continued to use it in his analysis. He offered these imperfect substitutes: "purpose," "aim," "end," "object," "intention," "tele-ology.") *"Zweck"* does not mean, indeed is specifically distinguished from, "interest" *(Interessen)* in order that it may serve as a vehicle for the transcendence of "interest" narrowly construed. *Zweck* is used by Jhering to apply to a variety of conditions or situations; for example, it indicates the satisfaction which the action gives to the individual actor. In this usage it might be considered a "cause" of that action or a "need" for which the action is a fulfillment. Thus, although *Zweck* is not identical with *Interessen*, there is always some element of the latter in any action. In addition to this meaning Jhering also speaks of the *Zwecke* of institutions such as the church and the state, and even of the society itself. The problem of social theory is to understand how individuals can be linked to each other and to institutions, and ultimately to society. In Bentley's words:

> We have found "Zwecke" (and "Interessen") scattered through all the individuals in the society, where they are, so to speak, on a common level, that is alike in quality or kind. We have found "Zwecke" also running in an ascending series—on different levels, so to speak—becoming ever more and more objective. The prob-lem is to harmonize them in all three lines: to harmonize the "Zwecke" with the "Interessen"; to harmonize the "Zwecke" and the "Interessen" of many individuals with one another; to har-monize the objective "Zwecke" with the subjective.[29]

27 "Der Zweck im Recht must be reckoned with, page for page, by everyone who seeks to understand the process of government and the function of law in social life." *Ibid.*, 57.

28 The following account is a summary of Bentley's interpretation of von Jhering. The point is less whether Bentley read him correctly than how he read him.

29 Bentley, *Process of Government*, 65.

"The foundation," and, one might add, the problem, "of society lies in the process by which one man's 'Zweck' is bound up with the interests of all."

The subjective-objective distinction is not the same as that between the individual and society. There are classifications of individual *Zweck* which may be considered "objective," and social *Zwecke* can be interpreted "subjectively," for example, as individual motives. Individuals possess both egoistic and social *Zwecke*, and these are distinguished by the test of whether a person has only himself or others in mind as he performs a particular act. When this involved classification has been set out, it remains that for Jhering there was some more general sense in which the subjective-objective dichotomy corresponds to the individual-social, or individual-institutional, division. In brief, he regarded the collective *Zwecke* as more objective and the various individual *Zwecke*, considered perhaps as motives, as more subjective. The more inclusive, the more general *Zwecke* appear objective almost in the sense of being "projected out from" man.

This detailed examination of von Jhering's conceptual apparatus is a necessary preliminary to a full illustration of Bentley's criticism. Jhering's difficulties begin, he argues, with the separation of *Zweck* from action.

> It is the "Zweck" indeed that is the main thing; the action is merely the means to the "Zweck," which means—at this stage of his progress—the satisfaction. This is radically different from asserting that all action is purposive, with purpose strictly as process, because of the very separation which he establishes between the action and the purpose. It is on this separation that his system is built up. It is in this separation that his unsolved, and insoluble, puzzle problems lie.[30]

Much of the speculation about Bentley's use of the terms "interest," "activity," and even "group" could be terminated by a reading of this passage. When he speaks of understanding "purpose strictly as process," he is arguing that any attempt to distinguish between such

30 *Ibid.*, 63.

words as "interest" and "activity" leads necessarily to an analytic chasm which swallows up all our energies in our attempt to bridge it. Jhering's error is akin to Small's attempt to "match" a table of interests or drives to their social "results" or "satisfactions." Just as there can be no "form" apart from "content," "purposes" may only be known as they appear in and as action. What we have is an "attempt to state life in terms of 'Zweck,' instead of 'Zwecke' in terms of life facts."[31]

The subjective-objective dichotomy is the direct result of this initial error, as is the individual-social division. Jhering's ultimate failure is the presentation of a "fictitious and hence insoluble problem." Individual and social might properly have been taken as points of view and the subject matter examined in its entire range from both, but if they are taken as concrete entities they prove impossible of reconciliation. Instead of finding the activities of men somehow a puzzle, and seeking a concealed solution, Jhering ought simply to have asked *how* men do things in certain ways. In a revealing paragraph Bentley insists upon "how," not "why," questions. To ask the latter, he argues, is to ask why gold is gold and not silver, when the proper procedure is to study all available appearances of gold itself. For Bentley, at least at this time, "fact" was not something to puzzle about; it was simply *there*. Inquiry was, so to speak, "confined" by the necessity to take its departure from brute existence. "Scientific" enterprise begins its inquiry with the word "how," rather than with the "why" of speculative discourse. "How" introduces queries demanding responses which will provide us with knowledge about the state of our subject matter, that is, description. When we have answered the "only scientific question," we will have offered a complete description. There is nothing more science can do.

Fairness to Bentley demands that something more be said about this matter of description, lest his position be rejected out of hand as trivial or superficial. When he talks about offering an account

---

[31] *Ibid.*, 89.

of how men and groups function together, he is proposing a difficult undertaking, because his conception of description is so demanding. A full account of what Bentley means by "description" must await a discussion of the concepts and vocabulary he developed later, but his expectation far exceeds our contemporary abilities.

Jhering and Small fell prey to a common error, which, because it was so basic, resulted in a misdirection of all their subsequent efforts and also enshrined that fundamental mistake—the separation of feelings from content.

> The trapdoor that lets the sociologist through into this pit is to be found at the spot where the complicated interest groups, differing in individual adherents as we actually find them in society, intercept one another. Tom the miser, and Jack, the spendthrift, go into partnership, and therefore the partnership is *an outside thing* caused by miserliness in one and extravagance in the other, and the metaphysics begins.[32]

In fact, Bentley continues, Tom and Jack are members of numerous interest groups, through membership in which they reflect "phases" of the social world about them. In the partnership those groups intersect one another, and this is all that need be said. What a science of society must do is uncover and trace the interests "across" society. There is no room or necessity for any conception of an outside or inside, subjective or objective, "realm" apart from Tom and Jack. The trap consists of two mistakes which follow from one basic error. First, the sociologist introduces a "vertical" division in which social action appears as the result of deeper-lying forces, motives, or drives; second, the conceptual separation of the partnership from the actions of Tom and Jack invites what Whitehead called the fallacy of misplaced concreteness. Both mistakes result from the temptation to segment the "stuff," the raw material of sociation— the process.

Contemporary readers have understood and accepted Bentley's argument against reification, but they have not remembered that

---

[32] *Ibid.*, 37. (My emphasis.)

59

he *also* warned of the opposite mistake. His analyses of Marx and Ludwig Gumplowicz illustrate both points.[33] Bentley rejected Marx's use of "class" as a descriptive tool: "Marx's theory of classes, then, *was poorly representative of what was happening,* because he made his classes too 'hard and fast,' or in other words because the particular groups which he called classes were abstractions."[34] The point is not simply that Marx ties "class" to a program of political action (although that itself was a disability) but that his classes are far removed from the operational level, too rough a measure, "too crude a form."

Gumplowicz's notion of groups is more versatile and varied, and thus a superior descriptive tool. For example, his "classes" do not come into being until one group has been conquered and subjugated by another; once these classes are formed, Gumplowicz uses a number of indices for their description. These characteristics marked, for Bentley, a distinct theoretical advance, but he was far from satisfied. While Gumplowicz's groups "are concrete in the sense that they are composed of so many different people who can be gathered together in physical separation from other groups," they are, precisely for this reason, *too concrete* for Bentley's taste. "They are not groups as I have used the word in early chapters."[35] Perhaps because he was preoccupied with more primitive group antagonisms, especially those in which violent conflicts occur, Gumplowicz was inclined to see his individuals as occupying spatially discrete spheres, specifically the national enclaves of Eastern Europe. The failure in Gumplowicz's system is that he found men acting in certain ways which he was content to specify as group action; what he should have done was "to make the further analysis into the underlying specific interest groups which they represent."[36] Bentley would have made his point less ambiguously if he had simply referred to the "underlying interest" instead of "interest

[33] Bentley thought that the group interpretation of society originated in the nineteenth century; its "starting point for practical purposes" he thought to be the work of Karl Marx.

[34] Bentley, *Process of Government,* 469. (My emphasis.)

[35] *Ibid.,* 470.

[36] *Ibid.*

groups," for what he means is that observable activity is the clue by which we may discover the underlying interest. Once that has been done, we may then proceed to talk about a concrete "group" advancing an "interest." Unless we take this additional analytic step, we become prisoners of mere appearance, because our concepts are frozen into a static universe in which each individual is assigned to and circumscribed within a spatially distinct group sphere.

Bentley's determination to be clear and to avoid mentalisms and ghosts probably defeated him on this point. He would not risk the appearance of discussing an interest "ghost" separated from activity. "The interest is just this valuation of the activity, not as distinct from it, but as the valued activity itself."[37] In his concern to guard against one misinterpretation, he invited another no less damaging, namely, the impression that he would be guided entirely by appearance. Concrete historical groups might mislead, might fail by inclusion or exclusion to inscribe the activity that is the interest. Shared attitudes, characteristics, or behaviors might be necessary to the existence of interest, but their existence does not necessarily imply the presence of an interest. If this were the case, Bentley could not distinguish group classifications based upon such incidental physical characteristics as hair color from political groups, nor could he warn against accepting a group's statement of its own intentions or values as definitive. To proceed in that manner would be to abandon reason and analysis in favor of pure experience, and that, despite some of his interpreters, is not at all what Bentley had in mind. Appearance, words, and even deeds can deceive, and the mind of the investigator must remain alert to that possibility. But to say that observable activities or behavior are not of themselves sufficient does not mean that they are not necessary, indeed indispensable. Activity, behavior, is the raw material, but Bentley, no more than any other serious student of history or society, believed such materials capable of speaking entirely for themselves. When we find the interest, it will be through its manifestation as activity; in this sense we may refer to "interest,"

[37] Bentley, *Process of Government*, 213.

61

"group," or "activity" as the same phenomenon stated in different ways. Against Gumplowicz's empiricism, Bentley's discussion of phases or aspects of phenomena maintains the necessity of abstract or analytic elements to social analysis.[38] Much of the difficulty in understanding Bentley's idea comes from his strenuous exorcism of ghosts, which led him to write as if the universe exhibited chunks of activity bearing the labels "farm bloc" and "minority vote."

> If we cannot take words for our test, and if we cannot take "bedrock truth," one may say we are left swinging hopelessly in between. Quite the contrary. The political groups are following definite courses. They may appear erratic, but hardly ever to anyone who is in close enough contact with them. The business of the student is to plot the courses. And when he does that—it is the course of only a single step, not of a whole career, that he can plot—he will find that he has all together, the group, the activity, and the interest.[39]

In addition to "over-concreteness," there is a second failure in Gumplowicz's theory: its inadequate treatment of "psycho-social phenomena," which are distinguished from the purely "social."[40] The former category includes language, religion, and law, and is set against group processes per se. The trouble, from Bentley's point of view, is that psychosocial phenomena are not treated or conceptualized in terms of social phenomena; rather, they occupy "an awkwardly nondescript position" as it were "between" the concretely sociating group and the concrete individual. These psychosocial phenomena are not given adequate ontological status; but more importantly, they are not accommodated methodologically within Gumplowicz's system. The result is that ideas continued to intrude

---

38 For the important distinction between "concrete" and "analytic" components, see Parsons, *The Structure of Social Action*, Chap. 1. Such a distinction could answer the criticism of Vernon Van Dyke: "The other problem to which the Bentleyan type of definition leads is that it apparently rejects the view that anyone other than the actor has a basis for identifying the actor's interests." "Values and Interests," *American Political Science Review*, LVI (September, 1962), 575.

39 Bentley, *Process of Government*, 213-14.

40 Gumplowicz, *The Outlines of Sociology*, especially 155-62.

into group analysis, sometimes as causal agents, sometimes as "undigested lumps of matter in his system." "When Gumplowicz gives the 'idea' itself such potency as he does, he merely indicates one spot at which his theory is not adequately elaborated."[41] This second criticism by itself should suffice to forestall the careless judgment that Bentley dismisses the potency of ideas; instead, he rejects Gumplowicz's conceptualization precisely because it does not deal with ideas when they are important. "He [Gumplowicz] gets around them [ideas] for the most part mainly by rejecting them as unimportant products of group action on the individual, and when he finds cases in which he cannot thus reject them, he has trouble in handling them, or rather he makes no pretense of handling them, but swallows them raw."[42] Gumplowicz's theory is "cold and remote" in its failure to get beyond the surface or appearance of the Austrian group alignment at the same time that it remains "focused too closely" on the existential groupings as they appeared at one moment of historical time.

The line of criticism Bentley advances recalls Georg Simmel's dichotomy of form and content. In those terms we might say that Gumplowicz confused the categories; this may explain why Bentley found him simultaneously "remote" and yet too "concrete." Bentley was well acquainted with Simmel and had read him with considerable admiration. He praised Simmel's "mental power" and "delicacy," comparing both qualities favorably to those of Gumplowicz; Simmel's studies are characterized as "brilliant" and "of the greatest value." But with all this appreciative comment, in 1908 Bentley found Gumplowicz's work superior in "its main practical value in the matter of group interpretation." "Practical," as should now be apparent, was a word of praise for Bentley, but it assumes, especially in its application to Simmel, richer connotations. Simmel's analyses were deprecated as "psychic" and "thin"; his interpretation of the lie was "stated more as a psychic curiosity than as a piece of powerful pushing human life," and his notion of society

41 Bentley, *Process of Government*, 471.
42 *Ibid.*

63

failed to show "its tremendous cohesiveness as a mass of immense human pressures."[43] It is this sense of power, movement, and the surging, striving aspect of human life that is lacking. This is the Bentley of the Progressive movement and the group-struggle school, who insisted that reality is hard, mean, and dangerous—perhaps even brutish. It is almost as if he found the delicacy of Simmel aesthetically incongruous with his view of reality.[44] "Curiosity," however accurately that word might describe Simmel's quality of mind, is not usually associated with the "practical."

The psychological roots of Bentley's reaction cannot be divorced from the substance of his critique. Some years after the publication of *The Process of Government*, he expressed his objections more specifically: "One thing Simmel seems to lack, the forcefulness, the energy, pointed to by Ratzenhofer's interests, by Durkheim's exterior constraint."[45] The absence of the "practical" in Simmel is a consequence on the methodological level of his failure to incorporate a sense of constraint or power into his vision of society. Gumplowicz, for all his bluntness, indeed perhaps because of it, comes closer to a grasp of reality. But, despite their obvious differences, stylistically and otherwise, Gumplowicz and Simmel balk at the same obstacle, ideas. Bentley, in 1908, saw Simmel's difficulty as an inability to keep his psychology distinct from his social analysis. "Simmel has traced the group lines, and endeavored to make clear many of the typical forms in which group relations occur. But here is his defect. He has done this in terms of a psy-

---

43 Bentley, *Process of Government*, 474–75.

44 Bentley's own language is far from elegant: groups "grind together," and ideas refuse "to lie down together." The crudity of his prose may be complementary to the examples of social man he adopts: street brawls, prostitution, machine politics, and the corruption of urban government are favorites. Sometimes these subjects are introduced as an attack upon grossly optimistic notions of man's progress, but even here Bentley's contempt for the hypocrisy implicit in such comfortable judgments is apparent. Bentley's passion, his anger and scorn, are manifest on several levels: they are directed against the organization of society as well as against the discipline that pretends to study it, and his prose style reflects, in its very crudity and forcefulness, his rejection of the niceties and inhibitions of convention.

45 Bentley, *Relativity*, 165. This passage might serve to illustrate Bentley's casual regard for the construction of the English sentence.

chology which is itself not simple process, but is too often a content which intrudes with crude persistence into all his analysis. . . ."[46] In this passage Bentley seems to agree with the criticism common among sociologists that Simmel could not, in his empirical work, maintain the form-content distinction. Theodore Abel subsequently made exactly that point.[47] However, in a paper published in 1931, Bentley rejects this line of criticism as it had been applied to Simmel, insisting that the form-content dichotomy has been misunderstood.[48] This is an important shift in attitude, but Bentley's point in 1908 was that Simmel used words like "hatred," "envy," and "desire" at a point in his social analysis comparable to that at which Gumplowicz resorted to a similar usage when he was in need of causal or explanatory agents. This required that Simmel introduce ideas as entities, "undigested mass," predicates of individual actors —in sum, that he repeat Gumplowicz's error.

Bentley's concluding comment on Simmel in *The Process of Government* provides a further hint of what a social science of process might be like.

> Taken as a bit of the general social activity itself, Simmel's work then represents the social world more as it appears to the individual engaged in the process than as it appears from a point of view which gets away from that of the acting individual and looks upon the process as proceeding through him. Even his analysis of the crossing of the social groups was more a by-product of his investigation of personality than a direct interpretation of social process.[49]

---

[46] Bentley, *Process of Government*, 472.

[47] Abel, *Systematic Sociology*, 33.

[48] This has also been contended recently by F. H. Tenbruck in his article, "Formal Sociology," in *Georg Simmel, 1858–1918*, ed. Wolff. Bentley's repudiation of this particular criticism may have been addressed to Abel, since he refers to "a series issued by one of the greater universities," and Abel's volume is one of a series published by Columbia University. A comparison of Bentley's remarks with those of Tenbruck is interesting. See Arthur F. Bentley, "Sociology and Mathematics," *Inquiry into Inquiries*, ed. Sidney Ratner (Boston: Beacon Press, 1954), 86ff. This paper appeared originally in the *Sociological Review*, XXIII (July, 1931) and (October, 1931), about two years after *Systematic Sociology*.

[49] Bentley, *Process of Government*, 475.

The meaning of this passage is not entirely clear. Bentley appears to argue that a distinctly sociological perspective requires the achievement of a sense of distance from the flow of activity. One cannot accomplish this by beginning from a psychology, introspective or otherwise. There is the further suggestion that the sociological perspective requires not only detachment but a certain passivity, a conscious suspension of certain human activities on the part of the investigator. The observer must see process proceeding through him and "out" along society. This detachment separates the scientist not only from the individual as a unit but from at least certain kinds of involvement. It would be sheer speculation to press this point much further; from the few sentences Bentley devotes to the subject here we cannot divine the full meaning he assigned to certain key words, but it is not unfair to suggest parallels to Bentley's life. His own retreat to Paoli, Indiana, following academic and journalistic careers, his essential withdrawal from the mainstream of American intellectual life, present obvious examples of detachment in both senses. There is an element in Bentley's writing, echoed in what we know of his life, that might be described as "renunciation." One is reminded of Nietzsche's remark that science involves the capacity to care deeply and work diligently for something which is not of direct, personal benefit.

Gustav Ratzenhofer is the last group theorist considered in the closing pages of *The Process of Government*, but this section merits little attention. Bentley considered Ratzenhofer's work a retrogression from that of Gumplowicz, and it is not clear why he deserves the attention he receives. Bentley accorded him the damnation of faint praise implicit in the statement, "His categories . . . must be taken into account by all students of the field."[50] Albion Small's *General Sociology*, essentially an elaboration of Ratzenhofer's categories, probably lent a currency that Bentley could not dismiss lightly. Ratzenhofer imagined himself "advancing beyond Gumplowicz," but he was actually losing himself and the group-interpre-

[50] *Ibid.*, 476.

66

tation idea in a metaphysical haze. Not content "to take the facts as they paraded themselves before the exceptionally well-located window which his position in life afforded him through which to observe them, [Ratzenhofer] instead felt impelled to swathe them in an exceedingly wearisome and maladroit metaphysics."[51] The metaphysics, the retrogression, was Ratzenhofer's introduction of "inherent interests"—racial, individual, social, etc.—behind actual group forms. He was then tempted to assign personalities to groups and to describe society as in this or that "phase" according to the dominance of a particular personality.

Most of this was, for Bentley, quite unnecessary. Ratzenhofer did not escape Gumplowicz's difficulty, the tendency toward freezing group concepts at too concrete a level, because his inherent interests were not only mystical but static. The criticism common to Gumplowicz, Simmel, and Ratzenhofer is that they are unable to treat ideas except as discrete bundles of "stuff" functioning outside the social realm. Their systems fail, in this respect, to give an account of the world. The nexus of the problem, in terms of the group-theory approach, lies in the relationship of the words "interest," "group," and "activity." Recent literature in political science abounds with analyses and evaluations of "what Bentley really meant" by these words, and the proposal to indulge in still another such discussion would appear to require some justification. The relationship of these terms constitutes Bentley's alternative to the criticisms he leveled against previous formulations of the group-interpretation school and against traditional notions of causation.

INITIAL RECONSTRUCTIONS

There is, initially, a distinction between political or interest groups and what might be called "classification" groups, for example, the class of all left-handed American men born on February 29. The basis of both types of groups, the criteria of inclusion, must involve commonality, the possession of some similar feature, but

[51] *Ibid.*

Bentley was interested in "political and other groups that function in the specifically social process."[52] The key word here is "function"; the class (group) of left-handed men born on February 29 is not salient; it "exists" as a collectivity only in a mind and has no social counterpart in the real world. The commonality in this instance does not create cohesion or a sense of belonging on the part of the members. They do not think or act in any manner connected to this shared feature, which is what Bentley means by the "functioning" of a group.

Another way to approach this point is through the notion of the "potential" interest group. In terms of the previous example, we might say that a piece of legislation which proposes to visit inconvenience upon a group defined as "all left-handed American men born on February 29" could activate a latent similarity. The individuals concerned would suddenly perceive that a previously insignificant personal predicate has become a shared characteristic which "makes a difference."[53] This perception that something "makes a difference" is the vehicle by which the social world is individuated, "broken up" into patterns. Since the number of such characteristics and of their combinations is infinite, there is no logical or a priori way to limit the number of "latent" categories which may become activated. If we look at our rich and varied world from the perspective of a search for similarities, or more properly, for various bases of commonality, we come closer to Bentley's thinking than if we begin with "interests." The interests are, as it were, already a step removed from the basic thing—commonality. Bentley's insistence on the necessity for an empirical conception of interest confirms this interpretation. "The interest I put forward

---

52 Bentley, *Process of Government*, 212. The realist-nominalist difference as it applies to classification is tangential to my discussion here. "For in every classification, we pick out some one trait which all the members of the class in fact possess, and therefore we may call it natural. All classifications, however, may also be said to be artificial, in the sense that we select the traits upon the basis of which the classification is performed." Morris Cohen and Ernest Nagel, *An Introduction to Logic and Scientific Method* (New York: Harcourt, Brace, 1934), 223.

53 Bentley specifically warns against conceiving of "interest" in the narrow sense of economic self-interest, *Process of Government*, 212.

is a specific group interest in some definite course of conduct or activity. It is first, last, and all the time strictly empirical. There is no way to get hold of one group interest except in terms of others."[54] This last sentence is particularly significant, since Bentley continued to discuss the means of "isolating" an interest group from its milieu. He is not, as has sometimes been claimed, asserting a belief in the necessity of group conflict, nor the antagonism of interests, but rather he is striving to present an epistemological problem: namely, how may interest groups be isolated from, and at the same time related to, their environments? "No group has meaning except in its relations to other groups. No group can even be conceived of as a group—when we get right down close to facts—except as set off by itself, and so to speak, made a group by the other groups."[55] (In the hypothetical instance of an isolated tribe, its very separation could be an identifying feature. Within this universe, interests would be studied just as they are in more complex societies. It might, of course, be that the tribe's interest activities would be fewer, or "simpler," but this would be a question open to empirical determination.)

Viewed from this perspective, interest is a commonality factor that has social consequences, that is, it "makes a difference." "Activity" enters through Bentley's insistence that the difference be observable or somehow open to empirical investigation. We can speak of activity as a manifestation of interest, but only if we add the qualification that interest is not some kind of entity standing "behind," or in any way bringing about, the activity. Each is a phase, an aspect of the same thing, and it is absurd to imagine one as more "basic" than the other.

> In the political world, if we take the interest alone as a psychological quality, what we get is an indefinite, untrustworthy will-o'-the-wisp, which may trick us into any false step whatsoever. Once set it up and we are its slaves, whatever swamp it may lead us to. If we try to take the group without the interest, we have simply nothing at all. We cannot take the first step to define it. The group is

54 *Ibid.*, 214.
55 *Ibid.*, 217.

activity and the activity is only known to us through its particular type, its value in terms of other activities, its tendency where it is not in the stage which gives manifest results. The interest is just this valuation of the activity, not as distinct from it, but as the valued activity itself.[56]

In this passage Bentley adds the notion of the group. Groups, unlike interests or activities, have no independent ontological basis; while the latter terms indicate the two aspects of human valuation, "group" is simply a verbal economy, a summary of certain activity complexes. Instead of referring to the "valuing activity of the oil industry," we say "oil interest group." Ironically, it is precisely this conventional usage which leads Bentley into trouble, for to speak the language of entities, even if they be understood as possessing no identity apart from their constituent elements (that is, activities), is to introduce a sense of boundedness into the social realm. It is to suggest a world of discreteness and discontinuity in which one group, or complex of activities, is identifiable as belonging together. Bentley's own remark that an interest can be known only as it is distinguished from others is an oblique recognition of the need to create "space" among distinct activity groups. This spatial requirement may be conceptualized in terms of several dimensions and does not, therefore, forbid overlapping memberships or coincident activities among interests.

But how are we ever to get hold of unifying principles, of what I have called the "commonality factors with social consequences," that constitute and illustrate the pattern? We are denied recourse to a priori determinations of "objective interest," for this would be speculative and beyond empirical reference; nor can we be satisfied with an interest's definition of itself. If we shift our inquiry to a more empirical level and permit formal organization or "structure" to define the "group" or activity pattern, we emasculate our efforts as Gumplowicz did his; the categories are fixed at the purely formal level. This would leave us in exactly the position from which group interpretation promised an escape.

---

[56] *Ibid.*, 213.

[Political science] is a formal study of the most external character-istics of governing institutions. It loves to classify governments by the incidental attributes, and when all is said and done it cannot classify them much better now than by lifting up bodily Aristotle's monarchies, aristocracies, and democracies which he found sig-nificant for measurements of all sorts and conditions of modern government.[57]

Some modern versions of these classifications had, Bentley thought, lost "all sight of the content of the process in some trick point about the form." The entire purpose of group interpretation is to get behind the incidental characteristics of appearance, but in order to do so the "formal" or "structural" unities must be reduced to simple activity. When we have arrived at a conception of the social realm as homogeneous, continuous action, we must then find differentiat-ing principles, ways to reintroduce discreteness—in short, new units of investigation. But Bentley had by this time rejected so much, closed so many doors, that he was unable, within the confines of *The Process of Government* at least, to recreate them. This must appear an odd conclusion since group theory vociferously contends that it has discovered *the* meaningful social units; its critics give tacit recognition to this claim by their espousal of "individuals" or "classes" as alternatives.

To see precisely why this is the case we need to put aside the troublesome word "group" entirely and speak simply of valuing ac-tivities. The investigator is to "plot the course" of these across the society. The image of a continuum implicit in this phrase must be taken literally, as the following quotation demonstrates:

The raw material we study is never found in one man by himself, it cannot even be stated by adding man to man. It must be taken as it comes in many men together. It is a "relation" between men, but not in the sense that the individual men are given to us first, and the relation erected between them. The "relation," i.e., the action, is the given phenomenon, the raw material; the action of men with or upon each other. We know men only as participants in such activity. These joint activities, of which governmental activi-

[57] *Ibid.*, 162.

71

ties are one form, are the cloth, so to speak, out of which men in individual patterns are cut.[58]

Bentley does not talk about "constructing." Indeed, he specifically tells us that the relationships are not "erected"; they are there to be "traced." "The activities are interlaced. That, however, is a bad manner of expression. For the interlacing itself is the activity. We have one great moving process to study, and of this great moving process it is impossible to state any part except as valued in terms of the other parts."[59]

Two examples would probably be helpful here. The first statement of what this "tracing" operation might be like comes from *The Process of Government.*

> Take the indictments against the Standard Oil Company. The only way we can state them adequately is in terms of eighty million people, more or less; and indeed that even may not be a sufficiently comprehensive statement for purposes of study. The meaning of the indictments, their values, extend to the activities of people who live far beyond the confines of one country; extend, indeed very nearly to all parts of the world.[60]

This statement yields some idea of the scope of inquiry Bentley envisions, but it falls short of clarity in those key words "adequately," "sufficiently comprehensive," and even "activities." By 1926, Bentley was ready to suggest a more detailed example. It is a rather lengthy passage, but we must add some meat to the rather abstract bones of the argument as presented thus far. Bentley is talking about the Volstead Act, and he begins with the question, "What do we have? A set of words, an enacting clause, many printed copies."

> When we have said that, have we said anything? Hardly, unless we carry with those words a great unexpressed background of reference. Let us set down some of those background references, not

---

[58] *Ibid.,* 176. Exactly how and whether this task can be performed must await later discussion.

[59] *Ibid.,* 178. Compare Simmel's view that "society" is "sociation," "The Problem of Sociology" and "How Is Society Possible?" in *Georg Simmel, 1858–1918,* ed. Wolff.

[60] Bentley, *Process of Government,* 178.

by way of being complete or by way of discussing the Volstead Law, but merely for illustration of the material.

A vote of Congress. The signature of the President. Many days of debate in Congress. Many weeks of committee hearings. Very, very many man-years of lobbying for and against.

A constitutional amendment. All of its attendant efforts. Its submission to the states.

State and community law and ordinance experiences, local option and prohibition.

A generation or two of writing, speaking, organization, public meetings, addresses, editorials. Temperance societies, prohibition societies, political parties and platform planks. Brewers', distillers', and retailers' organizations. Chemists' investigations.

Circles of discussion widening out into principles of government and rights of man.

A changed industrial system, division of labor, machinery, motors.

A changing food complex.

A cross-section of the courts, judges, attorneys, marshals.

A welter of private attorneys, legal points, technicalities, relations to other laws and to the constitution, and the supreme court at last.

A new staff of investigators in the treasury department.

A new mass of law-breakers, differently law-breaking.

Some new reaches and magnitudes of corruption.

A change in expenditures and in lives, in durations and experiences of men's lives. Disease changes, jail changes.[61]

The heterogeneity of this assortment of factors removes any illusion that Bentley was thinking in terms of "concrete" or physically interacting groups. Indeed, the word "group" does not appear in the entire passage, though there are several points at which we might expect it. Instead Bentley chooses to speak of "circles," "cross-sections," "reaches and magnitudes." Each of these expressions has mathematical relevance; "cross-sectional activity" is particularly suggestive. A few pages earlier Bentley defines it as "any activity in its characteristic appearing across a group of men. It is definable

[61] Bentley, *Relativity*, 95–97.

only in terms of a number of men, but not in terms of any or all those men, qua individuals."[62] A little later he indicates the reason for preferring it to the more customary "group."

> In the definitions the word group has substantially the meaning of cross-sectional. It would have been here used by preference for cross-sectional, had it not such concrete reference to a total of individual men, that it tends to divert attention from the common activity by which alone the group is characterized. It has been much used in recent sociology though without sufficient definiteness of meaning, and it will very possibly prove to be the term which sociology will adopt for the type of fact under consideration.[63]

Presumably Bentley has found the effort to purge the word "group" of its overly concrete connotations unrewarding. But we may as well talk about a "slice of life" as a "cross-section" for all the distance either term advances us toward attaining an analytic unit. Bentley, through his critique of causality, was prevented from turning to the "interest" aspect and using it as a determinant of a type of activity. Such an attempt would risk losing all clarity by restoring the "idea things" to their place "behind" or "below" the level of action. A Weberian ideal-typical analysis, insofar as it could be considered to accord primacy to its idea components, is clearly excluded. David Truman's concept of the "potential interest group," a second attempt to build a unit of analysis, is dubious for the same reason.

Truman tries to escape the limitations of concreteness by using "shared attitudes" as the defining characteristic of interest groups; he is, by this means, able to speak of "interests that are not at a particular point in time the basis of interactions among individuals."[64] After conceding the necessity of reference to observable data, Truman adds that "even the most insistent defenders of the scientific position, however, admit that, although activity is the basic datum of social science, a 'becoming' stage of activity must be recognized as a phase of activity if any segment of a moving social situation is

---

62 *Ibid.*, 91.
63 *Ibid.*, 91–92.
64 David B. Truman, *The Governmental Process* (New York: Knopf, 1951), 34.

to be understood."[65] He sought support in Bentley's term "tendencies of activity" and endorsed Gordon Allport's definition of "attitudes": "An attitude is a mental and neutral state of readiness, organized through experience, exerting a directive or dynamic influence upon the individual's response to all objects and situations with which it is related."[66] There are several difficulties with this definition, particularly when it is linked to Bentley's "tendencies of activity."

Bentley does suggest the word "potential," but in the same passage he draws an analogy to the case of molecular (unobservable) motion and molar, "palpable or external activity." It might be possible to distinguish "bodily motion" from tendency as "interior brain motion," but Bentley was skeptical of our ability to avoid the error of everyday speech or of "treating these brain motions concretely as feeling things, making them crude causes of outside happenings." "We are driven back to a statement in which we give the brain motions value *only in terms of bodily motions*, which they mediate, and which are themselves (taken in the social mass) the creative or constructive phase of the whole world, social and physical, as we know it."[67] This is the point at which Bentley's critique of theories of social causation and his search for analytic units meet. Truman is entitled to enlist Bentley in his support only if he clearly and consistently denies his "shared attitudes" or "potential interests" any independent, causal status. It is difficult to imagine how Allport's phrase "exerting a directive or dynamic influence" could escape Bentley's objection. He would not accept "feelings" as in any way more basic, or more "interior," than actions, for this would bifurcate the unity of experience and of the world. Inquiry must proceed along temporal and spatial dimensions, but always at the level of valuing activity. Thus, the experience of anger would be analyzable as a complex of observable activities. "If we should follow this anger activity backward in time, we should find it a complex of certain other activities, which, when stated with sufficient

65 *Ibid.*, 35.
66 Quoted by Truman, *Governmental Process*, 35.
67 Bentley, *Process of Government*, 185. (My emphasis.)

completeness, would state the anger activity itself with no need of any soul-plus to add to it."[68]

From what has been said it should be apparent that Bentley hoped to escape his own critique of causality and satisfy the stringent empirical requirements he placed upon social theory by a much more extensive and complete description than he thought had ever been proposed. That is, in fact, what he found lacking in previous group interpretations, but in 1908 he did not see clearly that the complete description he demanded could not be accomplished by, perhaps required the rejection of, the group as an analytic unit. What he thought necessary, and what he began to grope toward in *Relativity in Man and Society*, were new conceptions of time and space. There are indications of this in his early rejection of the subjective-objective dichotomy, but especially in his remarks about "environment." It must not be conceived as "something external 'plus' the acting man," but rather it should be stated in the same terms as the activity itself. For example, mineral deposits become important elements in social behavior when they are discovered and prized, but then they are already a part of the valuing activity of man. To describe and classify activity in this way requires that our everyday, common-sense experience with space and time yield to new formulations, just as was the case with our everyday speech patterns. It is entirely appropriate, then, that *Relativity in Man and Society* opens with a discussion of the new physics, particularly its space-time concepts, by analyzing the meaning of the term "Einstein." Bentley demonstrates how one might go about describing a man, a system of thought, a group of workers and experimenters, past and present, and so on.[69] His review of physical theory emphasizes the disparity between the certitudes of experience and of scientific knowledge and concludes by relating this hiatus to the

---

[68] *Ibid.*, 188. It should perhaps be re-emphasized that the words and their meanings spoken during the state of anger are themselves analyzable as activities.

[69] Bentley, *Reliability*, 6–15. It is probable that Bentley was caught up in the enthusiasm and mystery surrounding relativity theory, and he perhaps did not fully explore the resources of ordinary discourse and a Euclidean universe. Whether or not he underestimated that conventional resource, Bentley obviously found the language of Einstein's physics more appropriate to the articulation of his vision.

need for "units" and "limits." After listing the number of constants now known and extending the table of elements to ninety-two, he observes: "Needless to say there is at present no such remark to be made relating this status to the study of society. If anybody believes that the individual man, such and such a clot of hands, feet, muscle cells and nerve cells, feelings and ideas, is such a unit, he is entirely free to prove it."[70] Physics, he argues, has been able to conceptualize its subject matter as "events," as "living, moving process," a combination of perspectives identified by such words as velocity, energy, and mass. "Properly speaking the whole process is the primary fact they observe of which the duration, distance, energy and mass are measurements. The word is Action. Action is the event in the studied world, in combined terms of space and time and work, all varying with reference to one another."[71] Social science must begin to develop similar conceptualizations, and since scientific thought, as all of knowledge, is ultimately social, the language employed must undergo a concomitant adjustment. Linguistic dichotomies such as mind-matter, conscious-unconscious, man-society, and actor-environment are especially dangerous. Thus, as the reformulation of social science proceeds, there must be constant recognition that thought and language operate "on" the world but are simultaneously themselves "of" it.[72]

---

[70] *Ibid.*, 54.

[71] *Ibid.*, 47. Contrast Frederick J. Teggart's use of the term "events," "objects," "situations," and "conditions."

> The most cursory observation of the world makes us aware of the objects, entities, things, as well as of events. Science deals with objects, entities, things, and their relations; history concerns itself with events. Now events, as we say, "happen," but things undergo change. Things do not "undergo" events, though they may be affected by them. It is of importance to notice that our everyday, common-sense judgment associates change with events. On the other hand, extraordinary as it may seem, scientific investigation during the last two centuries has maintained the view that the study of change in objects, entities, and things must be carried on independently of the study of events.

Theory and Processes of History (Berkeley and Los Angeles: University of California Press, 1960), 77–78.

[72] The insistence that the realms of thought and knowledge must be viewed in their social dimension, i.e., as behavior, is well known through *Wissensoziologie* and

Bentley offers the example of an editorial concerning regulation of food additives to illustrate how description in the new terms would liberate inquiry:

> Put our editorial writer and his activities in this [Euclidean] space. His head is in one cubic foot, his body in certain other cubic feet adjacent, his typewriter in another one near by, his editorial supervision in certain cubic feet not far away, his printing presses in still others, and his readers in still others. His behavior is in space at any rate, even though we have our private ideas as to where his mind may be under the terms of the old puzzle split. But at any rate if he has his mind and another man his, then they present themselves in different parts of that space, and their relation to one another is across that space.[73]

This kind of description has already posed insurmountable problems. How is causality to be introduced through these empty spaces and between the realms of matter and mind? What is the spatial locus of "editorial policy"? How is the "actor" to be reunited with his "environment"? Our inquiry, Bentley insists, is over before it is fairly begun. The focus of description has been *the* editorial writer, John Smith, writing under certain direction for certain other individuals, "with each factor so emphasized taken as capable of independent definition prior to the attempt at interpretative relation."[74]

Under the activity form we would emphasize food processing methods, practices of representational government, certain language specifications as represented by editorials, "and the presses

---

the more recent work in philosophical anthropology. Less often noted are the somewhat similar contentions of two quite analytically oriented philosophers, C. S. Peirce and Ludwig Wittgenstein. "Our idea of what belongs to the realm of reality is given us in the language that we use. The concepts we have settle for us the form of the experience we have of the world. . . . The world *is* for us what is presented through these concepts." Winch, 15. "What is thought to be known is simply specialized and universalized construction on the part of man." Nathan Hakman, "Bentley's Transactional View of Politics: An Approach to Social and Political Analysis," *Social Science* (January, 1958), 136.

[73] Bentley, *Relativity*, 131–33.
[74] *Ibid.*, 135.

of the newspaper and magazine proprietors (who now present themselves as loci of phenomenon examined, not as unit facts), and
passing across this or that reading public (these publics again as
loci of investigation)."[75] As to the editorial and its writer, we might
note certain characteristics of shading, particular skills or devices
that would themselves require statement in terms of the writer's life
experiences, the activities of his teachers and colleagues. In this example the writer, qua individual, is only an intersection of a chain of
activities which are focused "through" him and funneled out again
to his audience via his prose. This stream of activity represents not
only a spatial distribution but also a temporal dimension, for, as
the writer is joined to his audience, that bond connects both to those
prior influences and experiences which molded his literary taste and
skills. No a priori limit can be placed on the extension of the description. One is reminded of Wittgenstein's remark that "to give
the essence of a proposition means to give the essence of all description, therefore the essence of the world."

In the example cited, "writer-audience" is a particular configuration of the "man-society" complex, and it is, of course, only an
aspect of John Smith that is involved in the description. This must
not be understood as an "unreal" abstraction, however, for Bentley
insists that it is the notion of a complete individual Smith, taken in
Euclidean space, that is the abstraction. In reply to the criticism of
his method as somehow belittling or degrading to the worth or
stature of man, Bentley had argued some years earlier that the individual "can be banished only by showing a plus of existence,
not by alleging a minus," and he added that there could be no
derogation from a reality which did not exist.[76] In phrases strikingly reminiscent of Simmel, Bentley suggested that the "real life"
of men is "too rich" for the notion of the individual; through his
action man "transcends" any definition of himself as discrete entity.
Unlike Dilthey, who believed that the unit of investigation in the
cultural or social sciences is given in experience, Bentley found that
appearance belies reality.

[75] *Ibid.*, 135–36.
[76] Bentley, *"Knowledge and Society,"* in *Inquiry*, ed. Sidney Ratner, 4.

Relativity in Man and Society, as the title suggests, is centrally concerned with physical and mathematical analogies and with the inadequacies of the Euclidean spatio-temporal descriptive frame. But this work also contains a second strain, only momentarily muted and strangely suggestive of the life philosophers. Giving a somewhat different stress to his criticism, Bentley argues that the Euclidean universe cannot accommodate the stuff of life.

> We can picture the whole society so cut into individuals. But we cannot do it without arresting for the moment the whole action, that is, the whole life, of our society. We cannot do it without "staining" our tissue. We cannot do it without finding that our product is morphological in the least helpful way; it is "dead," "stained," and capable of observation under the form of individuality, but with no good evidence that this form of individuality is the morphological form best to be chosen for knowledge of the living society.[77]

These words appeared in 1910, two years after the author of *The Process of Government* had expressed his preference for the vigor, if not the crudity, of Gumplowicz over the elegant but formal contribution of Simmel. By 1926, Bentley could still criticize the lack of a sense of force in Simmel's sociology, but he also expressed the conviction that "today, . . . when Euclidean geometry is absorbed into physics, for Simmel's sociology what is manifestly needed is that its statement too should pass into one of energy, of activity, or of interests or pressures."[78] The two strains are not, however, as easily reconcilable as Bentley's casual analogy seems to indicate.

Relativity in Man and Society is probably the most loosely written of Bentley's books. He remarks halfway through that the plan of his "essay is however not to specify as far as possible, but to hold back from specification as much as possible, in order better to get the feel of the process."[79] Relativity and quantum theory are the dominant but by no means the only themes. It is probably more correct to say that they provide a powerful stimulus, but Bentley

77 *Ibid.,* 9.
78 Bentley, *Relativity,* 165.
79 *Ibid.,* 179.

clearly believed that there were trends toward convergence in a number of physical and social sciences. His remarks about these, especially his evaluation of sociology, will lead to his more rigorous theoretical formulations, but some general observations about the significance of the rather generalized analogues described above are necessary here.

Bentley's description of this book as an "essay" is quite accurate, certainly as compared to *The Process of Government*. Beyond this, and in terms of its subject matter, it might be described as a transitional effort. He devotes a chapter to political matters, but the focus of attention has clearly shifted away from substantive discourse toward the kind of inquiry undertaken in Part One of *The Process of Government*. The desperate need for "observational coherence" is a recurrent theme, and that requirement is intimately linked to the search for satisfactory units of investigation, a demand not adequately met in the earlier book. It is tempting to believe that Bentley had not, in 1908, fully realized the magnitude of the task he had set for social science. The group universe suggested in *The Process of Government* was abandoned, as Bentley turned to the notion of process as a way of conceptualizing the wider and radically altered perspectives of man, space, and time requisite to the development of adequate descriptive techniques. The voluminous appendices of *Relativity in Man and Society* contain elements and evaluations of trends in various of the social sciences as they might be helpful to or congruent with Bentley's efforts. It is clear that he was making an effort to relate his general concerns to narrower work in sociology and psychology. Despite Bentley's belief in convergence, the dissatisfaction with available theoretical tools felt by many sociologists was not to issue in a willingness to follow him in his excursions into the universe of process.

American sociological and political theory remained for some time fascinated by the notion of the "group," but it was not to be drawn into a confrontation of those issues which might have led to a new conception of the universe. The first review of *The Process of Government* in the house organ of American political scientists failed to discern in it "value as a contribution to the literature of political science."[80] With the exception of individuals like Charles Beard, the profession accepted this judgment until Charles Merriam and his graduate students at the University of Chicago "discovered" Bentley.[81] Merriam was interested in the application of scientific methods to microscopic study, and the tough-minded empiricism of *The Process of Government* had an obvious appeal. In his *History of Political Theories in Recent Times* (1924), Merriam praises Bentley's theoretical contribution, and another contributor, Harry Elmer Barnes, records his estimate of Bentley's importance. Barnes's *Sociology and Political Theory* expresses the dominant interpretation of Bentley which placed him firmly in the pluralist, group-conflict tradition of Albion Small and Gustav Ratzenhofer.[82] As a contribution to American pluralism, *The Process of Government* was mentioned in a number of text and reference books, such as those of Merle Curti, Herbert W. Schneider, William Y. Elliott, and Margaret Spahr, all published during the 1940s.[83] This acknowledgment reflects Bentley's inspiration of a number of classic monographs and case studies completed in the late 1920s and the 1930s. "Since the publication in 1908 of A. F. Bentley's pioneering book, *The Process of Government*, academicians have given increasing attention to political groups."[84] To mention the authors of these works, such as Peter Odegard, Pendleton Herring, E. E. Schattschneider, Belle Zeller, Oliver Garceau, and Dayton McKean, among many others, is to remind anyone familiar with American

80 James Garner in *American Political Science Review*, III (May, 1908), 457.

81 Eulau et al., 7.

82 (New York: Alfred Knopf, 1924), 33ff. and 101. Bentley is discussed in similar terms in two other essays by Barnes: "Sociology and Political Science," *The Social Sciences*, ed. William Fielding Ogburn and Alexander Goldensweiser (Cambridge, Mass.: Riverside Press, 1927), and "Sociological Contributions to Political Theory," *Twentieth Century Political Theory*, ed. Joseph S. Roucek (New York: Philosophical Library, 1946). See also Barnes's extended treatment of similar themes in *Historical Sociology* (New York: Philosophical Library, 1948).

83 Curti, *The Growth of American Thought* (New York and London: Harper and Brothers, 1943); Schneider, *A History of American Philosophy* (New York: Columbia University Press, 1963); Elliott and Neil McDonald (eds.), *The Western Political Heritage* (New York: Prentice-Hall, 1949); and Spahr (ed.), *Readings in Recent Political Philosophies* (New York: Macmillan, 1935). See also Crick, 120n.

84 Truman, *Governmental Process*, 46.

government and political parties of a large portion of the scholarly literature.[85]

These case studies were relatively narrow works, and deliberately so; they were written by professional political scientists seeking to establish a basic factual inventory. There are undoubtedly many factors, apart from the particular influence of *The Process of Government*, that directed American political science through what Harold Lasswell and Abraham Kaplan have called the "empirical revolution." David Easton's remarks should be kept in mind:

> For American political research the factual conception of science had its birth in the period following the Civil War. Prior to that time the building of factual inventories was practically unknown; after that time there sprang up a view of science that became the basis for modern political research. In this view the essence of science lay in the collection of objective data, the hard facts, about political life. Fundamentally it arose in revulsion against the speculative kind of system-building prevalent in the nineteenth century, especially in Europe and specifically in Germany where most prominent American social scientists either were trained or drew their inspiration.[86]

[85] Peter Odegard, *Pressure Politics*; Pendleton Herring, *Group Representation before Congress* (Baltimore: The Johns Hopkins Press, 1929); E. E. Schattschneider, *Politics, Pressures and the Tariff* (New York: Prentice-Hall, 1935); Belle Zeller, *Pressure Politics in New York* (New York: Prentice-Hall, 1937); Dayton McKean, *Pressures on the Legislature of New Jersey* (New York: Columbia University Press, 1938); Oliver Garceau, *The Political Life of the American Medical Association* (Cambridge, Mass.: Harvard University Press, 1941).

[86] David Easton, *The Political System* (New York: Knopf, 1953), 68–69. Interest in establishing a reliable literature did not end with the early efforts listed above. Compare Stephen K. Bailey, *Congress Makes a Law* (New York: Columbia University Press, 1950); Fred W. Riggs, *Pressures on Congress* (Ithaca: Cornell University Press, 1952); Earl Latham, *The Group Basis of Politics: A Study in Basing Point Legislation* (Ithaca: Publication for Amherst College by Cornell University Press, 1952); Bertram M. Gross, *The Legislative Struggle: A Study in Social Combat* (New York: McGraw-Hill, 1953); Gilbert Y. Steiner, *Legislation by Collective Bargaining: The Agreed Bill in Illinois* (Urbana: University of Illinois Institute of Labor and Industrial Relations, 1951); *Public Administration and Policy Development: A Casebook* (New York: Harcourt, Brace, 1952); George L. Grassmuck, *Sectional Biases in Congress on Foreign Policy* (Baltimore: The Johns Hopkins Press, 1951); Julius Turner, *Party and Constituency: Pressures on Congress* (Baltimore: The Johns Hopkins Press, 1951); David

The drive toward "hyperfactualism" in political science is as old as this century, and by the 1920s it had received the imprimatur of its professional association.

> Early in the twenties, under the inspiration of a Committee on Political Research of the American Political Science Association, although not under its auspices, a series of meetings was held in 1922, 1923, and 1924 called the National Conference on the Science of Politics. The basic conceptions running through the reports of these meetings reveal that those most keenly interested in developing a science of politics assumed that the task of political science at that stage was to gather new information. The brief reports of the Conference indicate that the participants devoted themselves to identifying what they considered to be "important" problems upon which research could be undertaken and to devising techniques, statistical and otherwise, for obtaining accurate knowledge about these problems.[87]

Factual knowledge was the necessity, whether it related to legislative, executive, or judicial actions on national, state, and local levels, or administrative procedures, or the activities of private pressure groups; a glance at the titles of the studies cited above reveals interest in all of these. Certainly the intellectual tide was running favorably for an endorsement of a vigorous, no-nonsense research program. Bentley had added to *The Process of Government* an appendix in which he gave as examples of research in politics his own studies of a Chicago municipal referendum, of the 1905 session of the Illinois legislature, and of the proceedings of the Chicago city council. He could thus be read both as a pioneering methodologist and as a theorist about politics.

Bentley, through his most famous book, had a profound though delayed impact on the professional political scientist qua researcher and, in a more general way, on American thinking about politics.

Truman, *The Congressional Party* (New York: Wiley and Sons, 1959). See the bibliographical accounts of Jean M. Driscoll and Charles S. Hyneman, "Methodology for Political Scientists," in Eulau et al., and Charles S. Hyneman, *The Study of Politics* (Urbana: University of Illinois Press, 1959).

[87] Easton, 75.

Bernard Crick's view that *The Process of Government* was primarily (and properly) received as a recommendation of particular research programs has a good deal of merit, as does his remark that "a particular methodology becomes a way of stating what is alone thought to be significant political experience."[88] Presumably he means to say that substantive notions about politics underlie and interpenetrate ideas of method. In 1951 a volume appeared which combined an appreciative professional view of the research monographs with a more generalized theoretical conception of politics and government. This was David Truman's *The Governmental Process*; it was, in a sense, the rediscovery of Bentley.

Early in his preface, Truman states the importance of the interest-group studies: "More important for purposes of this book are the academic monographs on particular interest groups, of which there have been a considerable number over the past three decades. These monographs have scrutinized techniques utilized by those groups in connection with the enactment and administration of particular public policies."[89] A little later he acknowledges his indebtedness to Bentley:

> Among these many items [of indebtedness] there is one book, however, that deserves special mention because it has given the subject much of what systematization it has so far received. That is Arthur F. Bentley's *The Process of Government*, first published in 1908. As the title of the present volume suggests, Bentley's "attempt to fashion a tool" has been the principal bench mark for my thinking. In fact, my plans for this study grew out of my experience in teaching from Bentley's work.[90]

The "plans for this study" to which Truman refers are in essence the project of updating Bentley. This is in no wise intended to minimize the importance of a book which in a little over a decade established itself as a modern classic for the instruction of researchers and the education of students. Truman's intent is quite plainly to write a synthetic work which would gather relevant data under

88 Crick, 120.
89 Truman, *Governmental Process*, vii–viii.
90 *Ibid.*, ix.

Bentley's categories and to offer a summary of the state of our knowledge in these areas. A perhaps unintended consequence was that, in reinforcing Bertram Gross's reminder to contemporary researchers of their predecessors' contribution, Truman implies a more continuous and conscious tradition than actually existed.[91]

Another, though quite deliberate, achievement of *The Governmental Process* was to place these summary research findings within the context of a substantive theory of politics supported by the empirical data. Truman, and a year later Earl Latham, give perhaps the most clearly articulated versions of the theory which had been implicit in much of the monographic work on political parties and public opinion; it was, of course, the version of pluralism known as "group theory."[92] The theoretical framework called "pluralism" is so much a part of American political experience, as well as of its science of politics, that by far the greatest part of it lies beneath the articulated surface.[93] The degree to which American political thought and analysis has been and is a creature of our history and institutions is a vast and intriguing question to which a number of recent scholars have addressed themselves;[94] at this

---

[91] See Gross's review of the second issue of Bentley's classic, *American Political Science Review*, XLV (March, 1950). *The Governmental Process* is somewhat like Robert Lane's *Political Life* (Glencoe, Ill.: Free Press, 1958), but because Lane does not write within or in reference to a particular theory or theoretical work, his book assumes a more bibliographical character. A closer parallel is Lewis Coser's *The Functions of Social Conflict* (Glencoe, Ill.: Free Press, 1956), which attempts a rather rigorous reformulation of some of Georg Simmel's propositions in the light of recent sociological evidence.

[92] Earl Latham, "The Group Basis of Politics: Notes for a Theory," *American Political Science Review*, XLVI (June, 1952). The literature on group theory is too voluminous to be meaningfully sampled here, but, of books already cited, Bertram Gross's analysis might profitably be examined.

[93] For a suggestive account of Madison's victory over Paine and its impact on the course of American political science, see Jacobson.

[94] Henry Kariel, "The Norms of Social Research," *The Decline of American Pluralism* (Stanford: Stanford University Press, 1961), and Louis Hartz, *The Liberal Tradition in America* (New York: Harcourt, Brace and World, 1955), are two such accounts. So pervasive is the notion of pluralism that Hartz was led to disregard the considerable comparative material that Bentley urged in support of his interpretation and to insist that a group approach was somehow uniquely American: "The Bentley group analysis, which was to have so great an influence on our political science, was

point my interest is primarily to indicate the manner in which *The Process of Government* became absorbed in the mainstream of political science.

In summary, it may be helpful to recall the appendices of the two essays centrally considered in this chapter. The standard commentary on *The Process of Government* is surely correct in recognizing Bentley's hostility toward the formal and institutional mode of political analysis. Those research strategies recommended in the appendix (essentially observation, roll call, and ballot analysis) are, though primitive, suitable illustrations for the political science of that day. Informal groups and "raw" activity could define a process approach as a welcome alternative to constitutional law. Had Bentley been content with this formulation, the traditional interpretation of his role in and contribution to the discipline would not need revision—but such was not the case. Neither the second part of the book nor the methodological appendices could sustain his deepened understanding of the initial critique. Broadly considered, Part One constitutes an argument against segmentations (inner-outer, subjective-objective, psychological-sociological, cause-effect, etc.), whether employed for purposes of description or for causal analysis. It was not that Bentley objected so vigorously to mental or nonmaterial factors in social inquiry—it was rather that they were treated as qualitatively distinct substances, "held apart" from the phenomena they were presumed to illuminate. The fact that Bentley chose causality as the ground upon which to conduct his polemical assault has obscured the fact that he did not return to it as a central concern. The questions which become most urgent at this point are not causal but descriptive, e.g., how is activity to be conceptualized and stated without "clothing"?

It became apparent that "group" and even "person" were no more justifiable "clothing" than "nation" or "law." In terms of his appendix example, Bentley must have come to wonder why he

a variation of the same process: the projection of irrational 'Americanism' into the study of America. It was not, to be sure, a political weapon, as the Beardian analysis was, but its elevation of peculiar American phenomena into absolute categories of political analysis was of the same kind as we found there" (30).

was observing something called "Chicago city council" at all; surely, if such a phenomenon did exist, it could not be captured within the walls of a meeting room. The appendices of *Relativity in Man and Society* confirm that Bentley is no longer looking for methodologies which can tap informal political behavior. He is now in search of analogues from the literature of physical science which will yield a clue to the form of adequate statement. His effort is now much more conceptual, more "philosophical." Despite his renewed insistence that we must begin with the "something doing," it is apparent that he now finds that first step more difficult than he previously imagined. His example of a process description of the Volstead Act is an intimation of the fantastic demands he would later place upon adequate description.

At this point Bentley had already left behind the group universe rediscovered by mid-century political science. Perhaps somewhat sobered by the difficulties of his own thinking, he began to search the literature of theoretical sociology for possible avenues of advance. American sociology at this time had a good deal to say about the process concept, and some of its major formulations and their relationship to the development of Bentley's thought must now be examined.

III

Process in American Sociology

> Our life is a process signalized by events. Succession
> is transition, a one-way road from the past to the future.
> The road has no breaks in it. The discontinuous sign-
> posts, the events of experience, merely reveal the con-
> tinuity of passage.
>
> —R. M. MacIver

> Etymologically, "process" merely means "the fact of
> going on or being carried on."
>
> —Read Bain

> The main trouble with my scheme is that I have never
> been able to state it so that anybody knew what I said—
> which is some considerable defect. . . .
>
> —Arthur F. Bentley

PROCESS AS EVOLUTION

ALBION SMALL is widely credited with the most forceful as well as
one of the earliest American formulations of the process approach
to social phenomena. His *General Sociology* is an extended commentary on the work of Gustav Ratzenhofer, and thus we would
anticipate the prominence of group-struggle notions. These are
certainly present, but Small wanted to express a broader, though
perhaps less substantive, idea. He saw the central line of methodological progress in post-Spencerian social science as the change
from a structural to a process viewpoint. The possibility of conceiving of human association as a process is, he said, as old as
Hegel, but "hardly in a realistic sense."[1] Sociology is a study of the
social process, a whole of knowledge, and this idea of the process
view of events requires that we conceive of relationships not simply

---

[1] As I will argue later, Hegel represents an important addition to the process
conception, but its origins are as old as Western speculative thought. Small himself
credited E. C. Hayes and E. A. Ross with the earliest, presumably "realistic," formulations of the idea. See *General Sociology*, 3.

89

in terms of proximity in time, space, or series, but also as "relationships of working-with, of process."[2] Small's notion of "working-with" is elusive; it seems to involve temporal proximity though it is not reducible to that alone.

> We do not see the real fact in a simple, familiar episode of today—
> like a teamsters' strike in the stockyards, or a merger of railroad
> systems—unless we see it as a transient phase of a permanent whole,
> which not only fills the present, but which shades off gradually into
> an invisible past, on the one hand, and into an impenetrable fu-
> ture on the other. In a very real sense, the life which we live is one
> with all the life that has occupied the earth, or will occupy it
> hereafter.[3]

It is the temporal dimension of the "permanent whole" that is emphasized in this Burkean passage, and Small continued to stress the continuity of the process: its incompleteness and openness. We cannot describe "an absolute terminal for the social process," nor refer to an association as a finished affair; we can, however, "discover a definite content of the social process, a work which it is always doing, and which in the nature of the case, so far as we can see, it must always continue to do, so long as the process persists."[4] This "definite content" is linked substantively to Small's tables of drives or desires, and methodologically to the teleological implications of "becoming." "Nothing is ever described properly unless it is described with reference to the end which it is supposed to be fitted [*sic*], serve or to the process in which it occurs."[5]

The requirement that becoming be seen as a whole ("around it, and along toward the outcome of it") puts on sociology a burden previously borne by the philosophy of history, namely, the search for coherence in human experience. Philosophers of history had suggested various one-sided views of that experience, such as the great-man interpretation of history, later to be superseded by a

2 *Ibid.*, 18.
3 *Ibid.*, 32.
4 *Ibid.*, 34.
5 *Ibid.*, 33–34.

belief in collectivities as the bearers of culture. These exaggerations produced sociology, a balanced perspective.[6]

Small defines this advance primarily as a recognition of previous distortions, but not as a new vision or even as a synthesis of partial truths. He does not, for example, suggest that sociology has found a way to combine or otherwise more successfully relate the units of individual and collectivity; instead he suggests that an increased number of categories might be applied to an object or situation. Comprehension of "reality" consists in thinking these classifications through the concrete situation.[7] The sociologist's advantage over older disciplines seems to lie largely in his increased awareness of possible classifications, an awareness that leads him to accept a different notion of reality. If this injunction suggests a pluralistic universe of descriptive categories, it also favors a theory of multiple causality. Sociology should focus on precise problems and employ more scientific methods toward their solution. Presumably, once an adequately defined problem area is given, the appropriate classifications would, if not immediately suggest themselves, at least prove identifiable. In the absence of a given starting point, we can speculate about which classification or combination would prove the most enduring or yield the maximum information about what goes on in society, but Small's implication is plainly that speculation is the appropriate term. In this sense, the advance represented by the emergence of the sociological perspective is a kind of suspension of belief, a reluctance to characterize finally the universe of human association.[8] Small's concept of society as process extended

---

[6] *Ibid.*, 52. "The several one-sided views have thus been merged into a many-sided inquiry."

[7] *Ibid.*, 73–74. It is interesting to compare Small's remark with Bentley's circle analogy in which the sphere (or society) is intersected by countless possible planes (classificatory principles); *Process of Government*, 207. Note especially Bentley's remark: "No one set of groups, that is, no set distinguished on the basis of any one plane, will be an adequate grouping of the whole mass."

[8] Of course, this kind of analysis might simply move the argument back one step. Instead of asking, "What classifications of sociation are most important?" we could ask, "What problems are most important?" Pursuit of this line of inquiry would move us to another level in which the social and psychological determinants of knowledge would have to be considered.

the parameters of inquiry in both space and time and placed definite though unspecified limits on the depth and permanence of social knowledge.

The alternatives presented to us by the philosophy of history are possible classifications of reality, and the task of sociology is to narrow our choice through posing and analyzing relatively smaller problems and situations. Small suggests these questions as examples: What forces join men's actions? What are the conditions or laws of action? How may we distinguish between constants and variables? How should an "equilibrium" be described?[9] Queries of this kind can scarcely be described as narrow, but they do provide a focus for thought and can probably yield subpropositions of manageable proportions. Yet precisely because sociology as the master social science must speak to the largest issues, this narrowing method is perilous. Small writes of the danger this way: "Regarding human experience as a whole, how may we mentally resolve it into factors, and at the same time keep effectively in view the vital interaction of the factors in the one process?"[10] He did not find a satisfactory answer, but his efforts to suggest the means through which this total view might be attained do take us quite a distance toward our contemporary situation. Before examining those efforts in more detail, it is well to recall that Small, unlike Bentley, did not purge his idea of process of its fixed points, such as drives or instincts. Because he retained some substantive conception of what is "there" in sociation, he had a means of identifying and locating recurrences. This is how he was able to speak of a "definite content" and to assert that some kind of "work" must, in the nature of things, be done by this or that particular process.

Small tried to illustrate this content by incorporating the contributions of Herbert Spencer and Albert Schäffle. Spencer's conception of society as an entity composed of discrete units which are formed into aggregates through performance of necessary services was to Small a structural view. "The essential idea in the concept

9 Small, *General Sociology*, 105.
10 *Ibid.*

92

'structure' *is parts of a whole at rest in relation to each other.*"[11] Spencer uses the word "function" to describe those services, and thus in some sense structure could be said to follow function.[12] He was interested in these structures, and primarily in their larger more formal manifestations. Small accepts a structural point of view not simply as a stage of sociological thought but as a perhaps enduringly necessary perspective.[13] Yet he leaves us in no doubt that the structural viewpoint has been exaggerated and "dynamic" inquiry comparatively ignored. For Small, Schäffle's work represented a trend away from the structural perspective—"Spencer is chiefly interested in demonstrating *that* functions are; Schäffle is chiefly interested in demonstrating *what* functions are."[14] To Schäffle, the "initial fact of structure becomes the device for work," and large organizations represent increasingly complex "agencies for work."

Welcome though this corrective to Spencer's teaching was, Schäffle did not investigate causal or consequent states before and after

[11] Small, *General Sociology*, 131.

[12] There is a sense, of course, in which this would be true analytically, since "structure" as a particular aggregation is not something else in addition to activity. It is well to be aware of this tautology, but such an interpretation of the relation between structure and function or service is not necessary. We might, for example, so define the structure of the family as to keep it in view while the services it performs evolve; we might expect altered services to transform the structure eventually, but the short-run structural modifications might be imperceptible. See, for example, Barrington Moore, "Thoughts on the Future of the Family," *Political Power and Social Theory* (Cambridge, Mass.: Harvard University Press, 1958). The literature on the logic of functionalism, especially the question of tautology, is extensive. These are a few citations of particular interest: Carl G. Hempel, "The Logic of Functional Analysis," in *Symposium on Sociological Theory*, ed. Gross; Ernest Nagel, "Teleological Explanation and Teleological Systems," *Vision and Action: Essays in Honor of Horace Kallen on His Seventieth Birthday*, ed. Sidney Ratner (New Brunswick, N.J.: Rutgers University Press, 1953); Robert K. Merton, "Manifest and Latent Functions," *Social Theory and Social Structure* (Glencoe, Ill.: Free Press, 1957); and Marion Levy, *The Structure of Society* (Princeton: Princeton University Press, 1952). A stimulating essay on closely related matters is Ernest Gellner, "Holism versus Individualism in History and Sociology," *Theories of History*, ed. Patrick Gardiner (Glencoe, Ill.: Free Press, 1959).

[13] Small, *General Sociology*, 114.

[14] *Ibid.*, 148.

the function; Schäffle described but did not explain. An additional difficulty with Schäffle's method was the circularity involved in identifying a structure and assigning a function to it. Small found this serious enough to require a denial that functions are identical with the operation of structures. In support of his argument Small offers several examples of the failure of structural operations to fulfill functions. We might, he suggests, say that the operation of the medieval church did not fulfill a religious function but that the Protestant reformers did.[15] "Functions," Small concludes, "are parts of processes, not parts of machineries." Hoping to combine the perspectives of Spencer and Schäffle while at the same time avoiding their respective distortions, he subordinates both structure and function to the concept of process and asks it to sustain the study of aggregates through time. One great weakness of this attempt was Small's failure to be clear about the relation of structure and activity on the methodological and ontological levels. Does Small mean that "static" analysis of institutions is the result of an investigator's choice of what stress he will give to a uniform process, or is he saying that institutions or structures are "there" alongside "functions"?

Small presents this paradigm of two types of sociological investigation:

Static[16]	*Dynamic*
Contemporary relationships	Historical background
Classification	Process analysis
Institutional study	Informal group study
Institutional analysis	Causation
Description	Explanation

If, as Small said, sociology was moving toward a process view, are we to understand that process analysis belongs to the dynamic classification, or does it somehow transcend both? Small was reluctant to dispense finally with structural analysis, but he clearly felt that the study of development, the way in which structures come to be,

15 *Ibid.*, 175.
16 *Ibid.*, 113.

94

was more significant. This is a preliminary definition Small offers of the social process:

> The social process is a continuous rhythm of the *individualization* of structures arising anew out of others already in existence—i.e., the reappearance in the social realm of the biological phenomena of the propagation of organisms; and on the other hand, of the *socialization* of social structures already existing—i.e., the reappearance in the social realm of the physiological phenomenon of the somatic upbuilding of organisms.[17]

Aside from its awkward language, the most striking characteristic of this passage is the pluralism in its notion of realm. There is nothing particularly new in the conception of a phenomenal world composed of vertical realms, the "biological" underlying the "psychological and the social," but it is interesting to find Small incorporating a "continuous rhythm" into this universe. His process, describable either as socialization or as differentiation, goes on within the social realm, but it is yet in some way a reflection (a "reappearance") of what has gone on or is going on at a physiological or biological level. The process itself seems to operate on the social level rather than running vertically through several levels. As such, the social process is set in motion by some yet unnamed mediator operating between the levels.

The concern to distinguish the social from other, lower-lying spheres is obvious in Small's second definition of the social process:

> While we must hark back constantly to the traits of individual persons, the philosophy of social action can never long at a time leave out of sight the affinities that work in groups of persons. In other words, *the social process is a continuous formation of groups around interests, and a continual exertion of reciprocal influence by means of group action.*[18]

We are back to the "relationships of working-with," the term Small used earlier, but now we are in a position to understand that phrase in greater depth. The "concrete elements" of the social

[17] *Ibid.*, 191.
[18] *Ibid.*, 209.

95

process, Small tells us, are these: environment, interests, individuals, social structure, social functions, and social purposes. It is the "incessant workings of reciprocal cause and effect between [*sic*] these elements" that comprises the social process.[19] What we call "society" is the activity of individuals, but it is a special aspect of that activity that constitutes the social process. Whatever the multiple determinants of that activity—biological, physiological, geographical, etc.— they reach the social process at or perhaps through the mediating link of interest. The psychological dimension of interest is "subjective," but at the point of emergence as collective action it is "objective."[20] At that time we may speak of "rivalry," "competition," and "conflict"; they occur through individual interest, which arranges activities into fixities or structures. In this sense, any motion of the social process is an index of the interest behind it, and our study of visible motions "is merely a means of approaching the view-point from which it will be easy to inspect the spiritual reality that impels the motion."[21]

In interpreting society as a process, we must see the initial thrust of the interest as it emerges from the subsocial realm and "out along it" to its fulfillment. "That is, we are bound to schedule associations in accordance with our judgment of their relation to the scale of the ends at issue in the particular situation in which these associations function."[22] To grasp the "real process" carried on in structures and activities, we must discover "the deep undercurrents of energy in all association."[23] This insistence on inquiry in "depth" seems to strain the conclusion reached earlier in this chapter: that Small's notion of "thinking" classifications through reality implies acceptance of a certain tentative or conditional character in knowledge of the social. The tension might be resolved if we distinguish between the relative depth of possible analyses of

19 *Ibid.*, 212.
20 *Ibid.*, 282.
21 *Ibid.*, 284.
22 *Ibid.*, 217.
23 *Ibid.*, 234.

interests at the psychological level and those at the social level. Interests form the classifications which may be thought through society, and they are determinate—possessing one character or set of characteristics and not another. They can be grasped firmly for exactly what they are, but, when projected onto the social level and incorporated into the social process, their multiplicity and complexity precludes attainment of the same depth and precision of knowledge.

We might, for example, be able to delineate the biological and psychological roots of a "wealth" drive, trace its emergence as an interest in the social process, and conclude by describing the arrangement of activities we call a banking system together with the purposes it serves. It would be a very different matter to describe the society in which the banking system exists from the point of view of the wealth interest, by placing those concerns at the center of our analysis and treating any others as dependent or secondary institutions and structures. In the latter case we could, if we chose, adopt the wealth perspective, but only with the knowledge that we were making a selection, and perhaps (though this is not certain) only after thinking through a number of alternative interpretative principles. At this point Small's methodological dictates parallel his ontological conception of a universe of multiple causality.

The basic unit of the social process is the group, though only the constituent individuals have ontological reality. But to have arrived at this point is not to have given the social process any *content*. Small speaks of the arrangement of interests when they are congealed into groups, but is there anything that can be said about that of which the stuff of this succession of occurrences, the "congealing," is composed? Of course, interests considered psychologically, in the presocial stage, have content; Small's six interests— health, wealth, sociability, knowledge, beauty, and rightness—are substantive, but it is not at all clear what they will look like in the specifically social realm. This point was troublesome, and Small specifically warned against conceiving of the social process entirely as the operation of psychic machinery. Still, in a general survey, "we must describe the social process very largely in terms of the mechanism of the process rather than of the content of the process."[24] Later Small seemed to suggest that the social content is psychological interest differently viewed. It is discoverable, he says, in qualities and relations of persons "considered as the ultimate terms rather than as factors in an ultimate cultural process."[25] Unless Small means simply that psychology need not concern itself with "social" phenomena, this passage is unclear: he does, however, continue to view the notion of conflict as vital at the social level. Because he built his entire notion of the social realm upon an individual psychology of need in a universe of scarcity, Small was led to envision the social process as predominantly a conflict area.

Social organization, with the state considered the most inclusive manifestation, progresses to a condition of relative civilization from one of relative barbarism through the resolution of conflict. Conflict takes place not only among the various private interests, but between the idea of private interest (the sum of all private interests) and the achievement of the common good. "The tendency of the social process is thus in sharp anti-thesis with the essence of the struggle incidental to the process. Yet, as a matter of fact, the process goes on by means of this unsocial and even anti-social spirit."[26] The state suppresses conflict, but it also promotes cooperation (and thus civilization) by expanding the area of the common good—for example, by encouraging "functional equality," or the right of a man to be treated as a person rather than as a commodity. The task of sociology is to state the existing conflicts within a society, but Small was reluctant to prescribe or even characterize the nature of the social process.

> Our present thesis anticipates nothing with reference to the nature of the social process, or its mechanism, or its results. We are concerned at the start merely with the empty, formal conception that, so far as it goes, whether taken in its minutest fragments or in the

24 *Ibid.*, 284.
25 *Ibid.*, 350.
26 *Ibid.*, 332.

largest reaches which we can contemplate, human experience is a congeries of occurrences which have their meaning by reference to each other.[27]

Here is the familiar holistic theme—the insistence that occurrences must be understood less for themselves (as their content of nature) than in their juxtaposition to the remainder of the congeries—but a vague note of uncertainty has entered. Sociologists must no longer maintain the presumption of historical philosophers that they can discover final meanings in the nature of events. Earlier Small had urged the need to seek out connections between and among processes, but, he insisted, "at the same time, we are freed from all assumptions that bind us to theories of likeness or other relation, if it does not exist."[28]

We would not expect to be bound to theories of demonstrably nonexistent relationships, but surely Small has more than this liberation in mind. He is asking for the freedom to think through possible classifications as they might apply to this or that situation of the social process. Freedom in this sense means being without prior commitment to one or another classification. "We do not represent human experience to ourselves as it is, unless we think every portion of it as a factor in a process composed of all human experiences."[29]

As to precisely how such an analysis might proceed, Small offers the example of the French Revolution. A process analysis of this "event" would begin with the recognition that all the activities of the period accomplished some part of the realization of essential human interests, and the first task would be to achieve an over-all view of the entire movement. This is how Small would make such an initial appraisal:

> The French, from lowest to highest, had become conscious of wants which the traditional social system arbitrarily repressed. The Revolution is in part a spontaneous, spasmodic effort, and in part a

[27] *Ibid.*, 514.
[28] *Ibid.*, 185.
[29] *Ibid.*, 513.

reasoned plan, of the French to release themselves from those inherited restrictions, and to achieve a social situation in which the
wants of which they are now conscious, or semi-conscious, will be
free to find satisfaction.[30]

The second step would identify the specific wants of particular
portions of the French population. Presumably, it is at this second
stage (though possibly also at the first) that Small would undertake
the exercise of thinking about possible classifications of the population. Once these steps are completed, the specifically dynamic
conception of process analysis begins, as we "follow out the details
of analyzing the several classes of wants" down to concrete demands
of specific interests, tracing relations of "each occurrence worth
noting" to the "whole complicated interplay of these desires
throughout the complex movement."[31] The "dynamic" quality of
this inquiry consists in its encompassing prior and subsequent
states in the idea of a single developing interest and in its refusal
to erect conceptual partitions between these evolutionary chains of
interests. The tracing of these interests does not need to "bump
into" or "flow over" a law or an institution. Finally, the whole of
the situation, the post-Revolutionary society, should be reconstructed and the degree and direction of change recorded.

Throughout this example, the dominant idea is the broadening
of analysis. In part this is so because Small neglects to mention an
entire range of subsidiary questions about his procedure; in particular, we are left without a clue as to the means of identification
of interests on the social level. Specifically, the questions are these:
How are we to determine the "several classes of wants" whose details
are to be followed out? What links some occurrences together in
such a fashion as to distinguish them from others? In Small's terms,
what is the nature of the principle of classification? Does it, for example, lie on the surface of human activity, open to our sight and
comprehension?

To put the query in these terms is to raise the central difficulty
of *General Sociology*, a difficulty which Arthur Bentley locates and

[30] *Ibid.*, 515.
[31] *Ibid.*, 516.

dramatizes with considerable accuracy but insufficient generality. Small's sociology is teleological, as he admits in many different contexts. The great stumbling block is that Small cannot formulate his purposive ideas in a *social* statement. He wanted to stress movement and becoming, but this led him to remove the content from his notion of process. Had he been a speculative philosopher like Hegel, he might have offered us a metaphysic in which the dialectic, or some comparable predicate of the process, would be invested with substantive purpose. Alternatively, he might have adopted some distinction akin to Simmel's form-content dichotomy, however much difficulty he might have had in getting them together in one universe. Finally, he could have swallowed any nominalistic objections and openly built purpose into existing institutions instead of tortuously introducing it from the biological or psychological realms. In fact, Small does almost exactly this, but he is not completely frank about what he is doing. As noted above, Small's universe of human experience is hierarchical, composed of vertically conceived realms. The interchange of psychical influences within the biological, social, and physical contexts is human association, and "the interpretation of the social process which has been projected is what we know as 'social psychology.' "[32] "The psychologist and the sociologist are trying to tunnel the life-process from opposite sides; the one from the individual, the other from the associational side; but there is no way for either of them through the life reality, unless it is a way in which they meet at last."[33] The study of society begins where psychology and physiology stop, where they would stop if they adhered to a rigid, schematic program, "or where they would stop if our mental processes occurred in the lineal and serial order in which *we have to represent them in speech*."[34] For Small, apparently, intelligible discourse could not transcend sequences and entities, but "thought" might in some fashion do so.

This point forcefully illustrates the differences between Arthur

---

[32] *Ibid.*, 622.
[33] *Ibid.*, 506.
[34] *Ibid.*, 447. (My emphasis.)

Bentley and Albion Small. It is little exaggeration to say that the main thrust of *The Process of Government,* and the corpus of Bentley's later work, is the denial of any such necessity, together with a determination to formulate alternative language patterns. A corollary of this is the obvious difference between their views of the connections which obtain among thought, science, and language. Bentley's point against Small's plural realms and use of drives or interests was that, as vehicles of scientific analysis and ultimately as the very basis of thought, their linguistic forms lead to imprisonment, not liberation.

Most of Bentley's specific critique of *General Sociology* is a polemic against Small's belief that we can think one way but that we speak in another. The immediate theoretical consequence is that Small's social process goes on in the social realm which holds an "interchange of psychical influences" with other spheres, while Bentley's process runs transactionally through *the* realm of human experience. In this sense, Small's arbitrary joining of the terms "social-psychology" appeared to Bentley as a concise confession of bankruptcy. It was the joining of two nonexisting "halves" of experience into a fictitious whole. For Small, on the other hand, this union was vital, since the only way "definite" content could find its way into the social process was through psychology.

> That is, after human experience is formulated in terms of structure, and of function, and of process, we have only formulations of effects. The causes of these effects, so far as we can trace them, are the volitions that register the resultant of purpose and feeling and choice. *The restatement of the social process in terms of purpose and choice is social psychology.*[35]

Finally, it is through individual purposes that Small gets to the teleological principles underlying those classifications he wished to introduce into the social process and which he needed to conduct any kind of analysis at all. The difficulties in which Small was enmeshed by this procedure are legion. In the end, the old ambiguity of methodological and ontological levels remains. Is the "restate-

[35] *Ibid.,* 637.

ment" referred to above simply another perspective, as Small sometimes seems to intend his social classifications to be? If so, are we
then precluded from assigning causation at the specifically social
level? If not, does a social psychological statement represent a richer,
more complete conception of the universe of experience? Neither
alternative seemed to satisfy Small, nor do they satisfy us today.

But to conclude that Small's formulation of the process idea is
unsatisfactory in many respects is not to give unqualified assent to
Bentley's criticism of him. Small is important for a number of reasons, primarily because of his determination to get on with the work
of sociology while at the same time developing a methodological
foundation for the enterprise. His desire to do both made him reluctant to embrace totalistic solutions or to discard any sociological
weapons. Small believed in a sociological tradition, which he saw
as an evolving one, and he was much less prepared than Bentley was
to dismiss his predecessors as incompetent or mistaken. For this
reason the compromises, the patchwork, and the stopgaps that Small
employed are more likely to reflect the course a discipline will
pursue in the short run than are the more profound, but also more
ruthless, resolves of an Arthur Bentley.

My intention has not been to compile a catalogue of vagaries or
outright inadequacies which might be charged against Small. The
structure of this inquiry has necessarily stressed the differences
among writers in the process tradition, but, apart from the admittedly fundamental divergences discussed above, there is a wide
area of agreement between Bentley and Small. This is especially true
on the metaphorical level; passages from the works of one author
could readily be exchanged for those of the other without violating
either text. And Bentley's detailed critique even notes with considerable approval certain of Small's "social" formulations of interests. To a degree, this is a consequence of the metaphorical use
of the word "process," but metaphor, simile, and analogy are as
surely means of communication as is symbolic logic, and they are
much more widely employed and employable. Bentley pursued his
inquiries into the idea of process much more deeply than did the
author of *General Sociology*, but Small's statement is still repre-

sentative of important aspects of that idea. His admiration for Ratzenhofer and his drive and instinct theories, wherever they are placed in a conceptual scheme, provide a link to contemporary theories of the group process. For many American political scientists the phrase "group process" is still the totality of the "theory." Small's clear perception of the need for unity, expressed in his desire to break down false divisions among the social sciences, and his demand for continuity in our study of human activity lent to the idea of process a holistic inclination which it still retains.[36]

Closely associated with the sense of "connectedness" in continuity and holism is the notion of the social process as a "becoming," with all the teleological overtones of that word. This temporal dimension of becoming has inclined at least one scholar to classify Small's entire approach to process analysis as "evolutionary," as opposed to later "analytical" approaches.[37] This interpretation has merit, and will be explored more fully later, but there is another connotation of "becoming" that is worth at least as much attention, namely, that of "richness." For Aristotle and Hegel, and certainly for Small, *something* was becoming. The analogies that come to mind at the mention of the word are organic relations, and we think immediately of complex interconnections, multiple causes, and variety. Small thought very definitely in terms of human experience when he wrote about "becoming"; he was not thinking about the austere geometrical analogues which appeared to Georg Simmel. And yet Small then proceeded to a conception of the social process in which it is extremely difficult to accommodate any "content," or familiar human concerns and characteristics, which remained the province of psychology. In fact, Small's process had become much closer to Bergson's sense of passage, and in one respect it was as empty of content as Simmel's form. Despite his passionate insistence on the dynamic analysis of the social process, Small poured all content into the subsocial realm and then forced it "up"

---

[36] We are more likely to express this today by talking about "systems," but the equivalence is evident.

[37] Earle E. Eubank, "Relationship of Social Process," *Social Problems and Social Processes*, ed. Emory S. Bogardus (Chicago: University of Chicago Press, 1932).

to the surface of collective action through the funnel of interest. When he came to discuss ways of tracing interests through the social process, there was no path for him to pursue; he had to "think" all kinds of hypothetical patterns through the process as if it were the analogical sphere of Bentley and Simmel. Simmel had charged sociology with the task of abstracting general form from the rich content of ongoing process of sociation, which was neither simply individual nor simply collective. By locating causal factors in the subsocial realms, Small put himself in the position of examining a becoming process from which he had drained the content and dynamism. The social process "passes"; could one say more? This is a curious termination for a historical, evolutionary version of the idea of process.

Central to these remarks about Small and Simmel is the difficulty of making statements about social phenomena in terms of social process. In large part, the problem was one of bringing methodological constructs into harmony with ontology—for example, in maintaining a consistent treatment of the idea of a "social relation" on both levels. Small's formulation is definitely nominalist in that, whatever unit of investigation he commends to sociology, he insists that "society," the social process, is composed at bottom of acting individuals. In this respect Small represents a conception of the ontologically real that has dominated recent American sociology and political theory. However, a belief in individual action as the ultimate basis of society does not require that sociology accept a particular methodological unit (although it may exclude some). What, after all, is a "social relation," and what connection does it have to activity per se? Simmel's reply to the question was the form-content dichotomy, but this alternative has been distasteful to the mainstream of American social science.

THE SOCIOLOGY OF FORM

One of the most interesting and detailed attempts to establish a theoretical foundation in this treacherous ground, without following Simmel into the speculative realm, is that of Leopold von Wiese and his associate Howard Becker. Their most complete exposition of this approach in English is *Systematic Sociology*, published in 1932.[38] Wiese is especially important here because Bentley praised him for making the most striking advance in systematizing our technical knowledge of society.[39]

By comparison to Small, Wiese gives at least the initial impression of rigor. "Society," he asserts, is a purely verbal expression for the sum of "happenings," but it does not follow from this that "structures" are adequately stated when their component parts are enumerated. It is the particular configuration of parts that constitutes the structure. On the troublesome question of "purpose" Wiese is more cautious than Small; he concedes a need to understand the contribution of the parts to the whole, but he remains skeptical of the teleological method as scientifically acceptable and distrusts the conception of actions as "functions" of something else. In response to the direct question, "What is the 'social'?" Wiese gives this answer: "The specifically 'social' or interhuman consists in an involved and entangled network of relations between men; each social relation is the *product* of one or more social processes; the human cosmos will find its ultimate explanation in the social processes."[40] The social, as distinct but not isolated from the realms of body and soul, is a "chain of occurrences flowing along with time," and therefore "a dynamic conception of the interchange will be more adequate."[41] The social relation, a product of the social process, is "a station or halting place in the vast stream of occurrences." "We will always find in dismembering the social occurrence that it consists only of processes but never of substances existing independently of the individual men."[42] If we were to halt the "constantly flowing stream of human activity" for just a moment, we would find an "apparently impenetrable network of lines

38 (New York: Wiley Inc., and London: Chapman and Hall, 1932).

39 Bentley, *Relativity*, 344. Bentley retained some reservations, and we will need to look very carefully at these, since they provide a clue to the later development of his own idea of process.

40 Leopold von Wiese, *Sociology* (New York: Oscar Piest, 1941), 23. (My emphasis.)

41 *Ibid.*, 29.

42 *Ibid.*, 38.

between men." A "static" analysis would consist in "dismemberment and reconstruction of this system of relations."

Thus far we seem to be on relatively firm ground, but, as Wiese
recognized, we are not. "Relations" might be considered as analogous to the rapid motion of magnitudes which create a stream of
energy-bearing atoms from one molecule to another.[43] The molecules ("individuals") and "crystals" ("plurality patterns") were
probably (although this question is beyond science) historically
coexistent, but as concepts they are inseparable. "Hence the analogy
might with some justification have been reversed. We might have
postulated an 'energy-stream cosmos,' within which there come to
exist large and complex structures that reciprocally influence each
other until as a result of this activity molecules, atoms, etc., are
detached."[44]

Sociology focuses upon the "socius," the "spatial locus of sociation"; in Charles Horton Cooley's phrase, "a man may be regarded
as the point of intersection of an indefinite number of circles representing social groups, having as many arcs passing through him
as there are groups."[45] If either the energy-stream analogy or the
circle analogy is acceptable, why choose the former? The answer
is that terms like "society" and even "socius" refer to relatively
advanced stages of complexity, and in a temporal dimension the
first analogy enables us to follow an historical development from
the simpler to the more complex. Wiese and Becker argue that they
have achieved a secure epistemological foundation in the individual
actor, but, following Simmel, they concede that, though reciprocity
is all that is "out there," the complexity of human institutions is
such that we are "compelled" to speak as if there were substantial
social unities at a supra-individual level.[46] The point at which

43 Von Wiese and Becker, 25.

44 *Ibid.*, 29.

45 Quoted from Cooley by von Wiese and Becker, 25. The persistence of the arc
and circle analogy in the work of social-process theorists is remarkable.

46 "It must be remembered that the object of the world of ideas as a whole is not
the portrayal of reality—that would be an utterly impossible task—but rather to
provide us with *an instrument for finding our way about more easily in this world.*"

sociology begins to disentangle this web of interrelationships is entirely a matter of convenience and utility. As to the "depth" aspect of human experience—the various physiological, biological, and psychological and purposive elements—these should be examined by the appropriate special social sciences.[47] This position excludes any consideration of "inner" states. "Sociology must consider as 'real' what manifests itself in action. Often it must take mere appearances for truth as long as it wants to give surveys or to develop a frame of reference; only later in its individual analyses can it reach the 'reality' of inner relationships."[48] Contentions of this sort prompted Theodore Abel to view Wiese as the prototypical heir of Simmel, as contrasted to Alfred Vierkandt, in whose phenomenological alternative the *Verstehen* approach to inner states becomes the dominant method.[49]

For Wiese, no predicates of psychological or individual states, instincts, interests, etc., can be determined a priori or "deduced" from existing social arrangements and then installed as principles or classifications by which to analyze society. How, then, does analysis proceed? "What is a social process? It must be some kind of occurrence which can be shown as a basic happening in the whole interhuman sphere."[50] Wiese begins this vital phase of inquiry with a very simple suggestion. Social processes, he says, do one of two things: either they bring men "closer," induce them to "approach" one another, or they separate them, "create a distance." This formulation gives Wiese's analysis an enduringly spatial emphasis in contrast to Small's temporal, sequential stress. But what might such a conception of "closeness" or "apartness" mean? Could it be made to include "social" distance? Wiese argues that spatial distance might, to an extent, "illustrate" social interconnections. We should be concerned with the direction and the degree of move-

---

Hans Vahinger, *The Philosophy of "As If"* (London: Routledge and Kegan Paul, 1952), 15. Compare Small's suggestion that the choice of classifications of the social process could be determined by the selection of problems.

47 Of course, this exclusion comes very close to Simmel's purely formal sociology.

48 Von Wiese, 36.

49 Abel, *Systematic Sociology.*

50 Von Wiese, 30–31.

ment of social processes, the former understood as "toward" or "away from" and the latter understood as a comparative measure. We would begin with simple occurrences, select a "thread," an original and primal process which leads to a relation, and follow its course through possible or probable interconnections with other processes to the formation of a social structure.[51] Social processes, as we have noted, create social relations which are relatively stable, that is, repetitive; these are social structures "which in a static study must be defined as a number of social relations so bound together that they are understood as units or substances in daily life."[52] The constituent individual processes might be divided according to a simple scheme: "A" or associative processes, comprising advance, adjustment, accordance, and amalgamation; and "B" processes including competition, opposition, and conflict. On the same conceptual level, provision could be made for "M" or mixed processes.

The realm of the social is "external," and is thus more easily expressed in physical terms of distance. But to avoid the criticism that this view is overly "naturalistic," we can define "sociologically relevant action as the 'projection' of mental phenomena into the world of physical space by means of sensually perceivable modes of expression."[53] In this sense social phenomena would not be equivalent to the social as a category.[54] Wiese contends that, once we have attained some measure of agreement on the categories applicable to "perceivable modes of expression," the theory of relations would become "primarily a theory of the procedure (method) of observing the phenomena of the social sphere in a correct manner."[55]

If at this point Wiese had proceeded to specify sociology narrowly as a theory of relations, he might have found his way to a position very like that of Georg Simmel, but instead he took a step which closed that door. The general method of analysis, he continues,

---

[51] *Ibid.*, 42–43.
[52] *Ibid.*, 40–41.
[53] Von Wiese and Becker, 70.
[54] The language is Dewey's, but the point might well be Simmel's.
[55] Von Wiese, 51.

can be expressed in the formula, P[rocess] = A[ttitude] × S[itua-tion]. This is a formula for uncovering "process" and not simply "relation," for "if we were interested in mere relations we should not care whether they were caused by human influences or by mechanical forces and chemical processes, or whether they were dynamic or static."[56] If it were simply a matter of saying that so-ciology should concern itself with the external manifestations of attitude or motive states, Wiese might have let this formula stand as a heuristic device, but he continues to assert that men's inner states are not independent of the social realm. Thus "A" must be itself a product of "I," or "innate pecularities," and "E," experi-ence. The "S" component then must be subdivided into "C," the nonhuman environment, and "AS," the attitudes of other men in-volved in a particular social process. Situation would then be rep-resented as "S = C × AS." The original formula as modified would then read: "P = A (I × E) × S (C × AS)."[57] Instead of a conceptual scheme like Small's, in which the individual and the psychological lie "behind" (in a temporal sense) or "beneath" the social, we have elements of both realms interacting on the same phenomenal and conceptual level. In order to disentangle them an-alytically Wiese introduces the methodological device of "orders" of processes. Those which take place between or among individuals ("interhuman processes") he calls "processes of the first order"; processes of the second order are occurrences among men when the existence of a social structure must be taken into account, and there is yet a third category of processes among structures themselves.[58] The latter two orders presuppose a theory of social structure on a conceptual level comparable to the theory of social relations in order that the ideas of social process and distance can remain basic to both. Wiese suggests that such constructs as "crowds, groups, and abstract collectivities" could be distinguished by determining the degrees of distance between the individual and the collectivity. In part, "distance" seems to rest on the degree of

[56] Von Wiese and Becker, 54.
[57] Von Wiese, 58.
[58] *Ibid.*, 63.

freedom or proscription enjoyed by the individual "within" the structure.[59]

These remarks indicate Wiese's willingness to enrich and broaden his plan for a systematic sociology, but as he proceeds he strays farther from the strict formalism with which he has begun. Elements of psychology become increasingly prominent as he refers to the "perceptions of group" by its members and to the "principal desires" of the membership. At the other end of the scale we find him introducing a notion of "force," similar to Durkheim's constraint, as a predicate of structures.[60] The attempt to reassert a rigorous formalism becomes strained when we are told that the "power" of a plurality pattern is the mental influence it wields over its members and that the state is real because men define it as such.[61]

The two forms of sociation (association and dissociation) are to be analyzed by the following sets of concepts:

Dynamic	*Static*
Motion	Distance
or	or
Action Pattern	Action *Pattern*
or	or
Process	Relationship[62]

The second of these paired concepts, "*Action* Pattern" and "Action *Pattern*," is strikingly similar to Arthur Bentley's "inter*action*" and "*inter*action," with the difference that Bentley was not willing to rest content with a dualism.[63] For all their labors, the conceptual

59 *Ibid.*, 71.
60 *Ibid.*, 75–77.
61 Von Wiese and Becker, 88–93.
62 *Ibid.*, 53.
63 Another parallel might be Franklin Giddings's discussion of "form pattern" and "action pattern" in *The Scientific Study of Human Society*, quoted in von Wiese and Becker, 54–55n.

framework of Wiese and Becker is not satisfactory. They do, however, manage to clarify difficulties which are obscured in Small's work. In an important footnote, they explicitly recognize the central tension in the process tradition; "with Ross," they proclaim, "we choose the social process as the unit of the present system—not the group, not the single human being, not the family nor anything similarly static, and finally not even the institution."[64]

We have at last arrived at an unequivocal assertion that the process unit is not necessarily the group. We do not yet have much idea of how to identify and work with the process unit, and unhappily Wiese did not seem to either. His empirical and comparative method depends entirely upon determining the direction and the intensity of the process, but movement in spatial terms must be relative to some system of coordinates. Even the fundamental notion of association and dissociation is qualitative, and Wiese's attempt at "ranking" those processes, as Theodore Abel points out, does not provide a parallel unit basis for quantification.

Bentley located the source of the difficulty with his usual astuteness. He recognized that Wiese's *Beziehungen*, or relations, were essentially Simmel's forms, with an important modification; they were "not merely logical relations, but 'something doing,' something going on, Handeln, activity."[65] Bentley describes Wiese's system, particularly its treatment of relations and institutions, and notes that "Beziehungen showed signs of going all the way up and Gebilde of coming all the way back." At this point, continues Bentley, Wiese discovered that any social situation appeared as process from some point of view in reference to other situations. To accommodate this insight Wiese introduced the term *Prozesse* between *Beziehungen* and *Gebilde*, but "almost at once the Prozesse identified themselves with the Beziehungen; there was no way to hold them apart."[66] Recognizing this, Wiese made the terms virtually equivalent but continued to distinguish them for "analytic purposes." As he proceeded to an analysis of concrete situations, "some-

64 *Ibid.*, 55–56n.
65 Bentley, *Relativity*, 345.
66 *Ibid.*, 346.

thing surprising happened": "The Gebilde began to appear in between the technical Beziehungen and the technical Prozesse, without waiting for their due time to appear later on in his system."[67] Wiese "grudgingly" recognized this, "calling them by preference Zustende, which we may translate as situations that are going to be." This entire difficulty, Bentley maintains, was caused by the notion of distinct stages of psychology, that is, the individual, psychosocial, and social psychological levels. This notion retained too many of the mentalistic trappings of German philosophy and led Wiese into his tortured formulations.

Despite all this, however, Wiese stood fairly high in Bentley's estimation until he came to the old obstacle of the subjective-objective dichotomy. Wiese had regarded William McDougall's instincts, or some comparable formulation, as necessary to a full comprehension of human experience, even though such areas were external to his idea of the social. Because he distinguished the instinctual, mental realm from the external or social, Wiese was forced to "see" his stages from these different viewpoints.[68] This, Bentley argues, introduced a familiar division into the realm of human experience, the old boundedness of phenomena that renders the world in two incomplete spheres awkwardly conjoined. Wiese stressed the externality of social behavior because his analytic procedure rested upon detecting and measuring spatial movement. Presumably, he envisioned these terms to be much more operationally acceptable than any he could devise to examine the internal or psychological state. Unlike Alfred Vierkandt, who represented an alternative development of Simmel's social thought, Wiese chose action and the observable as the basis of sociology. Vierkandt's phenomenological sociology insists that the objective or external manifestations of interaction are trivial in comparison to the inner states of individuals in sociation. The former are but "sediments" of the latter. Both Abel and Bentley regarded Vierkandt's phenomenology as a departure from the most fruitful lines of Simmel's thought, and Bentley went so far as to call it a destruction of Sim-

---

[67] *Ibid.*, 347.
[68] *Ibid.*, 351.

mel. Bentley's criticism of Wiese is not that he conceded the "inner state" phenomena a place in social analysis, but rather that he conceived of it as distinct from "external" phenomena. The difficulty lay in the reintroduction of dichotomous realms.

Howard Becker's reply to Bentley centers around a concept closely related to the subjective-objective dichotomy, namely, the "self." Becker begins by affirming (as opposed to Vierkandt, for example) the impossibility of apprehending an essential self when it appears always in a state of flux. The self so considered is "in actuality nothing more than a temporary focal point of mutable relations," and thus: "Should not everything fixed, permanent, and indissoluble, or in other words, substantial, be completely decomposed into interhuman processes and the relationships and plurality patterns arising from them?"[69] This Becker describes (correctly, I think) as Bentley's position, and he continues to make the conception of the self the essential difference between them. Despite the elusiveness of the self, and despite a measure of agreement with Durkheim's dictum that one social fact must be explained by reference to another, "we nevertheless regard the self as the point of initial and fixed focus in any genuine science of interhuman behavior."[70] From this it follows that Bentley deals with only half of the sociological problem. "[Bentley's] road avoids the morasses of over-hasty judgments and crude single-factor fallacies but finally confuses and dismays us by the multiplicity of its facts and branches, by the indistinguishably intricate maze of social occurrences that flashes by."[71] We must, Becker argues, have system, a sense of relative priorities, or we flounder and are drowned by our factual knowledge. "At bottom the question is whether sociology can dispense with an Archimedean point," which for Wiese and Becker is the individual, "the loci of sociation."

The issue is now joined at the Archimedean point. For Becker the individual self was necessary as a unit by which the multiplicity of plurality patterns and their intersections could find a focus; it

69 Von Wiese and Becker, 102.
70 *Ibid.*, 103.
71 *Ibid.*, 103–4.

would also serve as a locus of the inner states, the dimension of psychology and motivation. It is apparent that Becker, despite his inclination to defend retention of the self concept as a heuristic principle, believed that the individual had a more secure basis in reality than simply that of a conceptual convenience. We must imagine that Bentley would have conceded the possibility that under some specific circumstances the self might appear as a useful unit of analysis, but he unquestionably rejected a vision of human experience in which the individual self and the social self formed two "halves" of a whole, if that is what Becker intended. Wiese and Becker present the case against Bentley's radical version of a process universe more clearly than Small. How, they ask, can one avoid being overwhelmed by pure, undifferentiated happening? Their reply to Bentley constitutes a forceful critique of the position advanced in *Relativity in Man and Society*, and it is probably this argument that accounts for the refusal of American sociology wholly to accept Bentley's science. But Wiese and Becker failed to accomplish two important tasks. First, they did not answer Bentley's criticism of the inability of systematic sociology to accommodate the event, dynamic, or process half of its universe to the form, static, patterned portion. Second, their countercriticism of Bentley did not take account of the later development of his thought, in which he attempted to meet the central difficulty—namely, how can there be a science of process?

There is a great degree of similarity between the Bentley and the Wiese-Becker positions, a similarity which seems to have been recognized on both sides. The systematic sociology of Wiese is close to that of Simmel, even with respect to their process/relation and content/form dichotomies. Bentley's social science was a radical attempt to cut across that dichotomy by expanding the concept of process to eliminate distinct realms or spheres within human experience. In an over-all view, Wiese and Bentley are closer to one another than either is to Albion Small. American sociology has dealt rather gingerly with the methodological and theoretical differences among these various approaches, but there did develop what might be loosely designated "schools" of process analysis which emphasized the historical or becoming phase on the one hand and the analytic or systematic on the other. Political science in America has been less conscious of the strains and discontinuities within the process tradition, and because of its largely uncritical acceptance of Bentley's version, one of the richest and most complex, it has been able to accommodate a wide variety of differing approaches. Political scientists, placing the group unit at the center of their analyses, began to explore the notion of process in terms reminiscent of the "becoming" variant, and only recently have they begun to take a more analytic turn, for example, in their concern for political "systems."

OTHER FORMULATIONS OF SOCIAL PROCESS

The 1931 annual meeting of the American Sociological Society was devoted in large part to analyses of the idea of social process.[72] The papers presented a variety of approaches—case studies, historical accounts, and conceptual analyses. Evaluations of the term "social process" also varied widely, from provisional if cautious approval to outright dismissal. Emory Bogardus sounded an uncertain note with his remark that, although the term "social process" had long been prominent in the sociological vocabulary, it had often been "swallowed whole" and "has never achieved a commonly accepted meaning, nor has it been sharply enough defined to give it status as a reliable scientific tool."[73] He continued to call it a "generalization of concepts," useful in referring to all social processes, but he cautioned against its use as "a concrete working tool in the study of social problems."

He thought "interaction" the best illustration of process.

> The term, a social process, as representative of many social processes, has scientific import. . . . Objectively, a social process is a series of social changes. Structurally, it is the mode which the social changes of a given series follow. Subjectively, a dynamic social process is found in the changes in attitudes and values of those persons who figure in any series of social changes. Intrinsically,

---

72 A number of the papers were published the following year in Bogardus.
73 Bogardus, "Introduction," in *ibid.*, ix.

a social process is a dynamic moving equilibrium of human energy.[74]

This is not remarkably helpful, but it does indicate the degree to which the idea of social process had retained its association with notions of dynamism, motion, and change.

C. M. Case echoed this theme and added the idea of the study of wholes. Read Bain remarked: "The social process concept was a protest against both static, descriptive sociology and the normative implications of progress and social evolution."[75] He assigned the non-normative implications to the methodological realm and added that, as a philosophical concept, "process" indicated the "relative on-going-ness" of social phenomena. As a natural science concept, it was "useless and meaningless." "Social interaction," "socialization," "organic social growth," "social evolution," "social organization," "social dynamics," "social change," or the normative "social progress" were all possible substitutes. Bain viewed social process primarily, it would seem, as an evocative phrase. If, he argued, we adopt plural phrases such as processes of competition, conflict, accommodation, and so on, we will be talking about observable, possibly measurable and classifiable, conceivably even scientific concepts, but the phrase "process of" is mere tautology, "so we must render a verdict of pseudoscience alike for the singular and plural form of social process."[76] Process is, he concluded, harmless in its tautological usage but pernicious when it suggests that *it*, and not the specific activity, for example conflict, is the concept. In this form the use of process is "pseudoscientific jargon" and "an attempt to make a natural science concept out of a methodological or philosophic concept."[77]

Bain's criticism of careless usage certainly merits attention, but on the whole his colleagues did not endorse this hard line. Of primary interest is his list of equivalent terms, which echo Small's version of process analysis: "growth," "organism," "evolution,"

[74] *Ibid.*, xi.
[75] Read Bain, "The Concept of Social Process," in *ibid.*, 105.
[76] *Ibid.*, 107.
[77] *Ibid.*, 110.

and so forth. Florian Znaniecki, with customary care, contributed a more convincing discussion of process and science. "In modern science, every process is referred to some static or dynamic *system* of interconnected events"; this system "furnishes the set of conditions under which a cause produces its effect and the causal law applies to the process in the very measure in which the system is *closed*."[78] Social life does not contain this kind of system; instead, it offers innumerable systems and systems without structures, which are therefore "open." Znaniecki preferred to use "social process" in "the abstract generic sense (like chemical process)" to denote "a certain general class of facts."[79] Earle E. Eubank contributed an interesting historical account of various uses of the term by American sociologists. He concluded that the kind of dichotomy we found emerging in German sociology and illustrated in the twentieth century by Small and Wiese had persisted in the United States.

C. M. Case applied the term social process to "characteristic social change," a repetitive or recurrent activity, as opposed to the historians' concern with the unique. L. T. Hobhouse used it to denote sequence, especially growth, development, evolution, and, implicitly, progress. E. C. Hayes, among the first to use the term, intended the whole, ongoing life of society, especially causal relationships, and for C. H. Cooley it meant "adaptive growth." Cooley gave the term a distinctive organic meaning; his version of process stressed the interaction of organism and environment, and to this he added the ideas of holism and multiple causation. "If you insist that there is a centre from which the influence comes, all flowing in one direction, you fly in the face of fact. What observation shows is a universal interaction, in which no factor appears antecedent to the rest."[80] Cooley represents probably the best example of the evolutionary, historical tradition of process analysis. In his work the diverse strands flow together so naturally, in what must appear to a more self-conscious generation as ingenuous prose, that he is,

[78] Florian Znaniecki, "Analysis of Social Processes," in *ibid.*, 126–27.
[79] *Ibid.*, 123.
[80] C. H. Cooley, *Social Process* (New York: Charles Scribner's Sons, 1918), 45.

if anything, too rich a source. Charles A. Ellwood also thought in terms of "reciprocal progressive adaptation," but he imagined the process to be going forward among individuals within a group. W. I. Thomas and Znaniecki viewed process as stages or sequences of behavior in individuals or groups.

These examples belong more or less to the evolutionary conception, which, according to Eubank, passed through three distinct stages. The first image was one of universal process, a general, cosmic unfolding of which social life was a part; its connections to the philosophy of history and to philosophy proper were intimate. The second stage stressed the specifically societal process itself, and the third period was more analytic, intent upon studying the "multitudinous constituent processes" composing the larger process.[81] This evolutionary approach was largely descriptive and was particularly concerned with social origins and their relation to nature. The first, the universal process phase, claimed such sociologists as Comte, Spencer, and Ward, who were writing under the influence of the biologists Darwin, Lamarck, and Huxley. Sociologists of the second or specifically social process period were Ratzenhofer, Small, Kropotkin, Keller, Thomas, and Hobhouse. The final stage included the later Small and many others. Eubank correctly perceived that Simmel belonged to a different classification of process analysis, a branch he called "analytical." E. A. Ross, Robert Park, and E. W. Burgess were American representatives of this third stage. This approach concerned itself with timeless form, with the typical rather than the particular, and was little interested in historical context or chronological sequence.[82] Ross, in *Foundations of Sociology*, paid tribute to Simmel, and in the chapter entitled "Unit of Investigation in Sociology" he suggested the study of relations as complementary to that of groups.[83] Park distinguished between the "realist" and "nominalist" perspectives in sociology, arguing that the former accepted collective behavior as its starting point

[81] Eubank, 114.

[82] *Ibid.*, 113.

[83] E. A. Ross, *Social Control and the Foundations of Sociology* (Boston: Beacon Press, 1959), 148.

while the latter began from individuals; he indicated his preference for the former.[84] In the text he wrote with Burgess, social
process was used as "the name for all changes which can be regarded
as changes in the life of the group."[85]

Eubank considered their text, *Introduction to the Science of
Society* (1921), and Ross's *Principles of Sociology* (1920) to represent a decisive step in the direction of the analytic approach. A few
years later the use of the term "relations" by Park and Burgess was
to be the subject of a debate between E. C. Hayes and Floyd House
which raised a fundamental problem. Before examining that exchange, we should note Eubank's point that the choice of approaches
has consequences for the units of investigation adopted by the
sociologist. This has been mentioned above in discussion of Bentley's critique of "vertical" or hierarchical theories which segregate
social "results" from their personal or psychological causes; Eubank
took a somewhat different tack. He explained the difference between Small's causal use of the interest concept and the more
formal approach which preferred descriptive study of activity itself,
on its own level. Eubank found this difference illustrated in the
work of Park and Burgess, who had listed four "social processes"
(historical, cultural, political, economic) and contrasted these to
four fundamental types of interaction, which, they asserted, were
"of much greater value for analytic purposes." These were competition, conflict, accommodation, and assimilation. E. C. Hayes
disputed this classification, finding assimilation, for example,
much too broad a term, and proposed instead a list of thirteen
subtypes. More important, however, was his argument that assimilation was itself a result and not a process. The difference he
suggested distinguishes between a social relationship and a type
of activity.

> This raises the question as to the best use of the phrase "social
> process." That phrase is widely used as a technical term in so-
> ciology and by some is regarded as its most important technical

84 Robert Park, *Society* (Glencoe, Ill.: Free Press, 1955), 226.
85 Quoted by Eubank, 112.

term. Yet at present considerable confusion attends its use. The question raised is whether the term "process" should not be restricted to *activity* and *change* in *activity*. A social process would then be an activity or change in activity that is causally affected by the fact that it stands in relation to other activity by another actor.[86]

The distinction is, he continued, difficult to maintain, for his thirteen relationships (for example, "imitation," "conflict," "cooperation") could accommodate many varied activities. For Hayes, it was the relationship that gave "unity to the class of facts and meaning to the term by which the class of facts is designated."[87] "If we restrict the term 'process' to activity and change in activity, as distinguished from relations between activities then the social process is the total tide of causally interdependent activities that are impossible to individuals in isolation. It is the life process of society."[88] It is called a process because it is composed of activities, and "because it is characteristically a changing reality, a becoming," whose inner essence is psychic. Social explanation, Hayes concluded, is description of an event which extends to the conditioning relations—environmental, geographic, genetic, etc.

Hayes's article was answered a few months after its publication by Floyd House. House's reply stressed the need for concepts in making any determination whatever about activity. He correctly perceived that Hayes's argument revolved around labeling "assimilation" a result. House posed this question:

Is this [distinction between interaction and relationship] however, anything more than the distinction between the substantive or static abstraction of the reality of immediate experience, and the abstractions of the same reality which we make in terms of function, process, or activity? There can be "relation between activities" only

[86] Edward C. Hayes, "Some Social Relations Restated," *American Journal of Sociology*, XXXI (November, 1925). Hayes's sympathy for Small is apparent in his essay, "Albion Woodbury Small," *American Masters of Social Science*, ed. Howard Odum (New York: Henry Holt, 1927).
[87] Hayes, "Some Social Relations Restated," 342–43.
[88] *Ibid.*, 343.

if the persons or other elements which are thought of as the actors are interacting.[89]

One answer, and an answer House seemed to accept, is Bergson's dictum that we must choose what distortion we will accept by selection of necessarily static categories of conceptual discourse. "If our abstraction is to preserve the active aspect of the experienced datum, it must apparently tend to assume one of two forms: that of an ongoing change conceived in time, or that of a process of interaction between factors conceived as fixed at points in space."[90] Sociology, more than psychology, appeared unable to escape spatial configurations and dimensions because of the nature of interaction; sociology conceived of interaction as forces moving through space rather than time. In this spatial dimension the events which are unique in time become universal and transferrable in space. In such a construction, Comte would appear in the temporal camp and Spencer in the spatial. Naïve experience reveals a reality of continual change, and sociological method should use the term social process "to refer to the interaction of elements, factors, or forces, which are conceived from logical necessity as located at points in space."[91] House rejected Hayes's claim that science must study the conditioning relations, for this would be to follow Comte and study "history." If we focus on "interaction" instead of on the antecedent and consequent dimension, we would adopt, with Spencer, a spatial and sociological perspective. In House's terms, we would not be studying the "that" of becoming, but rather "how" one form of relationship and activity succeeds another.[92]

The Hayes-House exchange was a direct confrontation between the evolutionary and the analytic versions of social-process thought, but it was by no means the only expression of that tension. R. M. MacIver, writing on his favorite subject of social causation, distinguished the study of pattern from that of dynamics. "Patterns

---

[89] Floyd House, "Social Relations and Social Interaction," *American Journal of Sociology*, XXXI (March, 1926), 630.

[90] *Ibid.*, 631.

[91] *Ibid.*, 632.

[92] *Ibid.*

are formations, not formative processes," he argued; the former stand to the latter as fabric stands to weaving. "The weaving is a time-process, a becoming; patterns are congealed moments in this time process."[93] MacIver further distinguished two types of causal investigation; the first was the explanation of events considered as "salient concrete occurrences for some reason distinguished in the flux of change." In the second type, the explanation of processes conceived as "modes of social change," "we are concerned with the flux itself, not in its multitudinous totality, not conceived as an endless series of unique historical situations, but as a nexus of type-factors and type-situations related in a necessary or at least an understandable sequence."[94] Social science is concerned with the second, with the study of "interaction, development, reconstruction, and dissolution of social forms"; it studies particular situations to uncover their nexus, the relations among them, not the concrete situation as a whole.[95] MacIver was close to the German sociological tradition, and, although these facile distinctions pass over the heart of the difficulty, his thought is clearly opposed to that of House.[96]

Earle Eubank presented what is perhaps the most self-conscious discussion of the idea of process in American sociology, and his effort to maintain a consistent dualism between evolutionary and analytic versions constitutes a transition to such contemporary theories as structural-functionalism. Reality, said Eubank, is granular, ultimately composed of particle units clustered together in structures. Our experience with this reality includes enduring substance presented in three-dimensional space and temporal duration,

[93] R. M. MacIver, "Causation and Social Process," in Bogardus, 145.
[94] *Ibid.*, 147.
[95] *Ibid.*

[96] We might note in passing that the very words in which House, Hayes, and MacIver presented their thoughts were echoed by an English sociologist, W. J. H. Sprott. In distinguishing social processes from social relations, he contended that "the latter denotes the field in which the processes are exhibited, and it is obvious that for the purpose of explaining social change an analysis of social processes is of the greatest importance." W. J. H. Sprott, *Sociology* (London: Hutchinson University Library, 1959), 12. See also K. William Kapp, *Toward a Science of Man in Society* (The Hague: Martinus Nijhoff, 1961), especially Chaps. X and XI, and Donald McRae, *Ideology and Society* (London: Heineman, 1961), Chap. 4.

change in that substance, and causation, the link between the two.[97] While all substance is in perpetual flux and movement, and change never stops, some "results" emerge as they arrive at some kind of completed or finished state. These Eubank called "products."[98] The substance of sociology is people, alone or in human plurals called groups. Change appears as action and involves a shift in relationships. Causation Eubank described as "force," and he located it in the biopsychic realm of wants and desires.

Comte initiated the practice of building a sociology upon the physiological or psychological needs of the individual, and it had persisted until the twentieth century, when this hierarchy was challenged by C. H. Cooley and Franklin Giddings, who insisted upon the associative character of the individual and the "socius." Closely allied to this development was the idea of multiple "personalities" created by social status and social role. Psychologists were at first hostile to this movement, preferring to extend their inquiries into physiology (within the boundaries of the organism), but the year 1908 marked a decided shift in the direction of a "social psychology." E. A. Ross's *Social Psychology* and William McDougall's *Introduction to Social Psychology* contributed to the convergence of sociology and psychology into the "field" of social psychology and the idea of the socius as a unit of analysis.[99] But, whether the hierarchical or the socius approach was employed, the group remained the visible form that association was presumed to take.

97 Earle Eubank, *The Concepts of Sociology* (Boston and New York: D. C. Heath, 1932), 75.

98 *Ibid.*, 76. See chart, p. 77.

99 Evron M. Kirkpatrick's essay, "The Impact of the Behavioral Approach on Traditional Political Science," *Essays on the Behavioral Study of Politics*, ed. Austin Ranney (Urbana: University of Illinois Press, 1962), notes the coincidence of the Ross and Bentley volumes, together with Graham Wallas's *Human Nature in Politics*. The coincidence of Wallas and Bentley has been interpreted by Kirkpatrick, and by Heinz Eulau and his associates, as an early articulation of the behavioral approach to politics, Eulau et al., 8–9. In view of the Ross and McDougall volumes, it would appear that the currents of convergence should be interpreted more broadly. Of simply historical interest, perhaps, is the fact that the first private congress of psychoanalysts was held at Salzburg in 1908.

The "first conscious beginnings" of sociology, according to Eubank, were considerations of the form and appearance of human groups, "rather than of the interactions which were taking place within these groupings."[100] "Structure" entered human association through relations and form, for, it was argued, no human organization is without a coherent arrangement of parts. At this point Eubank states the case for the dualism that appears to have won the implicit endorsement of contemporary social science.

> There can be no processes, no activities, except in terms of some *thing*; there can be no forms that are not made and kept so by some sort of *process*. While the philosophers and the natural scientists dispute as to whether or not matter is "real," we must live in a seemingly substantial world, and must act as if it is composed of structural forms.[101]

Despite the Einsteinian revolution, he argued, we live and perceive in the sense data world of Newton; a new reality may lie behind it, but the world of space and substance is ours.

It is questionable to assert that we do perceive social "structures" or that we must think in Newtonian constructs; even if this is true, it does not follow that a social science must be framed in these terms, but this is not the place to raise such questions. The most interesting contribution Eubank made to the idea of process lay in the subtle but important shift illustrated in the following quotation:

> The difference—and the likeness—between structure and process is expressed in Dewey's conception of structure as process slowed down and regularized. Conversely, process is structure in action. They are merely the static and dynamic phases of the same reality, comparable to a moving picture, which is made up of a rapidly blended succession of instantaneous photographs. The one reveals the parts in the seeming inactivity of a given instant; the other reveals them in the activity of successive instants. Thus structure in its true nature is seen to be not only a relatively permanent

100 Eubank, *Concepts*, 121.
101 *Ibid.*, 124.

arrangement of parts, but an arrangement in which there are continuous modification and activity of these same parts. All societary forms include both.[102]

Eubank might have had in mind Dewey's lecture "Experience," in which the latter remarked, "To designate the slower and the regular rhythmic events structure, and the more rapid and irregular ones process, is sound and practical sense."[103] Eubank's first statement seems to argue for the impossibility of conceiving either process or structure in isolation from the other; that is, both things and change must be present "in" reality. But the passage by Eubank quoted above suggests that they are "phases" of the same reality. It sounds as if the investigator simply chooses to take a static or a dynamic view of his experience; it is a matter of perspective. Kimball Young managed to suggest both interpretations simultaneously:

> In fact the study of social processes is but one manner of viewing society while the study of social order and culture constitutes another way of looking at the same thing. . . . When we analyze the social processes we are concerned with the social functions, the interactional patterns of individuals and groups. When we analyze social organization and culture we are dealing more especially with the framework or structure of society.[104]

But, he concluded, both structure and function must be studied together.

If we say that the universe exhibits structure and function, thing and change, at the same time, and further that one presupposes the other, then we encounter the whole series of problems involving definition of object, conceptualization of change, causation, etc., to which Bentley devoted so much of his critical effort. We would also need some means by which to judge whether a given concrete situation calls for emphasis on its static or dynamic aspects. Conversely, if we accept the alternative, a kind of comple-

---

102 *Ibid.*

103 *Experience and Nature* (New York: Dover, 1958), 71.

104 *Source Book for Sociology* (New York and Cincinnati: American Book Co., 1935), 347.

mentary principle emerges; we then simply choose the perspective, the phase of reality we wish to see, but the choice of one would necessarily exclude the other. The choice would be arbitrary in the absence of a determination of the relative degree of change present in the situation under scrutiny, but this determination could be made only through, and thus after we were committed to, a functional or process perspective. "Structure" would then appear as Dewey's slowed-down processes, or the lower range of the change index. The choices appear exclusive in that the investigator cannot lay claim to simultaneously viewing structure and process; either structure or process becomes a residual category as measured in terms of the other. To reply that one or even several men may conduct inquiry from both perspectives leaves the results dualistic, and the difficulty of bringing them within a unified vision remains unresolved. This second interpretation approaches the Bergsonian dictum that reality is necessarily distorted by conceptual thought; it does not, however, commit itself to a determination of what, in fact, social reality is like. Both formulations are problematic, although the former seems to have won the allegiance of most contemporary social scientists, at least as far as the two positions can be distinguished in their work. Unfortunately, the distinction is all too frequently obscured, as in the case of Kimball Young. This difficulty emerged when what Eubank called the analytic version of social-process theory became dominant over the evolutionary view, because a tension had been recognized between the subject matter of activity and the science of form and relation. We must abstract, House had said in answer to Hayes, and we abstract through the concepts we choose. Eubank was less prepared to accept such a hiatus between knowledge and reality; he tried to preserve both the universe of activity and a science of structure. The problem was that which Wiese and Becker had encountered, the distinction between Giddings's form pattern and action pattern. When the evolutionary version of the process idea declined, the dualism was expressed within the analytic interpretation in terms such as those Giddings used.

Intimately related to this problem was the question of the unit of sociological investigation, which was, in turn, connected to the nature of explanation. If emphasis was placed upon becoming, change, activity, and succession, then groups of various sizes were appropriate units, and explanation was permitted to extend "down" or "back" to the individual, his drives, his motives, etc. If a more formal, structural, stress was the choice, then interrelations became the units, and explanation was confined to the purely sociological level; social fact explained social fact.[105]

There have been two principal versions of the process idea in American sociology, and Bentley diverged from both. Small represents a continuation of the process approach of the Austrian conflict sociologists, especially Gustav Ratzenhofer, while Wiese's systematic analysis extended the analytic perspective of Georg Simmel. Small's notion of process analysis sought to extend the scope of sociological inquiry both backward and forward in a temporal dimension and to connect the appearance of various forms of sociation at the level of behavior to prior, internal biopsychic states through the teleological use of the "interest" concept. Wiese's systematic sociology followed formal sociology's attempt to distinguish content from the patterned activity of forms and to provide operational means for the identification and classification of the latter. Bentley objected to both fundamentally because of their desire to introduce boundaries into the subject matter and consequently into their science. His own thought inclined toward the procedures of the formal version, but he was held back by the apparently unresolvable difference regarding individuation. Bentley's refusal to grant a bounded "self" is an illustration of his dissatisfaction with the static results of both formal and systematic sociology, and this kept Bentley from divorcing himself entirely from Small's temporal emphasis. He would not accept a system put together from individual interests and societal teleology, but he wanted to preserve the temporal connectedness

105 See George E. G. Catlin's comment that the term "social structure" might be a substitute for "social fact." "Introduction," Emile Durkheim, *The Rules of Sociological Method* (Glencoe, Ill.: Free Press, 1958), xvii.

128

and the sense of ongoing activity promised by the historical version of process.

Arthur Bentley's idea of process cut across, or transcended, this dualism. He sought to preserve activity and flux as his subject matter, but to avoid the introduction of false boundedness he saw in group as unit and to eliminate hierarchical conceptions of causation.

Insofar as American sociologists who have employed the process concept believed the term to be something more than a metaphor, they adopted either the evolutionary or the analytical version, both of which have their roots in German and Austrian sociologies. The choice has important consequences which affect such questions as these: What is the subject matter of social science? What are the boundaries of the field? Which units are appropriate to its exploration? What is the structure of causality? In what does a product or output of the science consist?

Not surprisingly, Bentley did not find these sociological formulations helpful. He continued his search for a medium through which social phenomena could be stated without encountering the paradoxes of the Hayes-House debate. He needed a means of stating form dynamically. The enormous difficulties of this task must have become apparent to him, for he ceased to use complex examples like the Volstead Act. Instead, he moves toward microphenomena and undertakes description of simple events, a two-person conversation, for example. Not only does Bentley's scrutiny narrow in terms of the phenomena he takes as his subject, his agenda of inquiry becomes correspondingly focused. The range of epistemological and methodological issues raised in 1908 are either forgotten or subsumed as parts of the overriding question: How is statement of social phenomena possible?

IV

Process as Transaction

In philosophy, the theories of Whitehead and Alexander in England, of Husserl and Hartmann in Germany and of Bergson in France have "placed" the nisus or the process of things at the very heart of the explanation of experience; and this is to give emphasis to the confessed incompleteness of theory.

—C. Delisle Burns

The complications that result from conceiving our subject matter as that of a society of opposed processes in a state of equilibrium, breaking up the unity of the whole into balanced process, presents a logical problem of the first importance. It has arisen again and again in every science that has reached a certain stage of development where mechanical description is inadequate and the task of describing a collectivity in a process of change was seriously attempted.

—Richard L. Schanck

My God, what a long road to travel, and how many twistings.

—Arthur F. Bentley

CRITIQUE OF PSYCHOLOGIES: "THE CONTINENTS GO, AND THE ISLANDS"

A PROCESS conception of the universe is as old as Heraclitus, but there is value in considering the nineteenth and twentieth centuries as uniquely concerned with that idea. Preceding chapters have suggested several reasons why this should be the case. The nineteenth century was the great period of the philosophy of history, especially in Germany, and of the emergence of an historically based social science. Comte, Hegel, and Marx, their differences aside, shared a fascination with the search for continuity and meaning in historical experience. But the idea of process cannot be so simply or readily identified with this tradition, for beside the names of these founders of modern social science must be placed those of its more implacable critics.

Perhaps the best examples of the latter can be drawn from the so-called life philosophers, especially Henri Bergson. His profound conviction that life was vital, a continuous flow of energy and event, would not admit the clumsy hand of analysis. Knowledge of the process that was human life and experience could be achieved only through an exercise of intuition that would grasp as essence a meaning simply there, not to be synthesized or reconstructed after dismemberment of the given. Wilhelm Dilthey felt impelled to struggle with Bergson's contention and to find a way to save analysis without rejecting the central conception of history and life as process. Nietzsche, like Bergson in this respect, was no friend of the fledgling social science, whether it was based on "becoming" or not. Concern with process, especially insofar as it implied change, is central to Nietzsche's work, but it was his critical genius—what I will somewhat inadequately call his "antiformalism"—that constituted his most interesting relation to the idea of process.

One can hardly speak of any important nineteenth-century idea without mentioning the name of Darwin. Darwin's writings, perhaps more correctly "Darwinism," have provided a cloak, a rationale, and an inspiration for the most diverse and bizarre intellectual currents and social movements imaginable. It is exceedingly difficult to develop a rigorous connection between Darwinism and process, but certain affinities immediately suggest themselves. Central, perhaps, is the notion of evolution with its concomitant or corollary associations of development, continuity, and change. The organic metaphor, long a favorite of the Romantic school of historical and social theory, found unexpected support from the realm of empirical science, and the very notion of struggle itself, lying at the center of Darwin's theory of survival, was congenial to the conflict school of process analysis.

These currents fed the idea of process in ways sufficiently similar to permit us to speak of an emerging vision of the universe as process.[1] Central as they were, however, there was a more powerful

---

[1] The text discussion of some elements in the process cosmology can but indicate some sources of particular interest, for the relevant literature is limitless. Two books especially helpful to the themes of this chapter are: Milič Čapek, *The Philosophical*

agent waiting to give the idea of process its decisive twentieth-century direction. That force was the new physics. It is difficult to overstate the impact of such physical theories as special and general relativity and quantum analysis upon Western thought. Not only was the stronghold in reality that science had so laboriously established now imperiled, the very structure of thought and the validity of perception were called into question. Something comparable might have been experienced had Hume been read widely and seriously, and had Kant not provided a means of arguing one's way around the great skeptic. But now the science of physics had betrayed its trust. Many thought it necessary to reconstruct epistemology, to reconsider logic, and to accommodate to a universe of relativity and possibility.

Even before 1905 there had been dissatisfaction with the state of scientific philosophy. Philipp Frank has remarked upon the intense interest in Henri Poincaré's conventionalism and Ernst Mach's attempt to purge scientific explanation of nonempirical ("metaphysical") elements, but the discoveries of physics lent an additional impetus and an enduring direction to the search for new foundations. A primary point of convergence between theoretical physics and the more humanistic or biological influences was the rejection of what is usually called mechanistic explanation. There were, of course, several versions of mechanism, but it usually involved postulation of a chain of events set in "motion" at some "point" by a "force." Change, development, causality were held to take place through the agency of one bearer of force coming in contact with a second, more passive entity which in its turn became an active agent, and so on. This is the billiard-ball notion of causality which Bentley, among many others, denounced. The mechanical or causal chain might be seen to extend from the present moment back to a whim in the mind of the Creator, as is suggested by the lines, "And the first morning of Creation wrote / What the last dawn of reckoning shall read."[2]

Impact of Contemporary Physics (Princeton: Van Nostrand, 1961), and Errol Harris, *Foundations of Metaphysics in Science* (New York: Humanities, 1965).

[2] See William James, "The Dilemma of Determinism," *Essays in Pragmatism* (New

But mechanical explanation was more than this. The Newtonian laws of motion had relied upon states of rest, bounded entities, absolute space, and fixed points. Action occurred when entities at rest were impelled through space by force, and it was detectable and measurable in relation to the known constants. Most of us are at least superficially acquainted with the replacement of mechanism by field theory that occurred with the advent of Einstein's theory of relativity. We have already noted Bentley's enthusiasm for what might be called combined measures, for example, space-time, mass-energy, and the intimate new relationship between physics and geometry, and it should be clear that he would welcome experimental support for his philosophical critique of mechanism.

In a paper entitled "Sociology and Mathematics," published in 1931, Bentley began in earnest to develop language and concepts capable of framing statements about man in society which would be congruent with the spirit of the field theory of physics.[3] Before that paper is considered in detail, something more should be said about the relation between mechanistic and field concepts in physics. The statement in the preceding paragraph which suggests an antithesis or at least opposition between them is something of an oversimplification. There have been, for example, continuous and discontinuous mechanistic theories as well as field theories employing mechanistic categories such as force, velocity, or stress.[4] Even Einstein's general relativity theory retained elements of mechanism. "Both the electromagnetic and the gravitational theories are dualistic theories. In both of these theories, we have sources of the field (charges, particles) and the field itself. Thus we see in both theories a mixture of two concepts: matter and field."[5]

These combinations or dualisms are now viewed as unsatisfactory

York: Hafner, 1954), for the important distinction between "hard" and "soft" determinism.

[3] *Sociological Review*, No. 2 (July, 1931), and No. 3 (October, 1931); reprinted in *Inquiry*, ed. Sidney Ratner.

[4] I am indebted to A. D. D'Abro, *The Rise of the New Physics* (New York: Dover, 1951), I, Chap. X, for this discussion of field theory.

[5] Leopold Infield, "Albert Einstein," *Makers of Modern Science* (New York: Charles Scribner's Sons, 1953), 117.

hybrids. For example, Einstein's unified or pure field theory was an attempt to eliminate mechanistic elements and to derive material phenomena from field conceptions alone. The following passage is perhaps as succinct a summary of the difference as is available:

> A field theory is a theory whose aim is to study the peculiar condition, or field, which is thought to pervade the ether of space in certain cases. Formerly, the ether was viewed as an elastic medium, having many of the properties of matter, and so a field theory did not appear to differ essentially from a mechanistic theory of the continuous type, such as the theory of elasticity. But according to modern views, the two kinds of theory are totally different, for the ether is now assumed to have no mechanical properties and hence its field is sharply distinguished from the field of mechanical stresses which pervades an elastic body.[6]

Field theories are thus to be distinguished from their continuous mechanistic counterparts, in that the former do not contain references to substantive categories, and from noncontinuous mechanistic theories, on the additional ground of the field's continuity as opposed to the discreteness of matter viewed atomistically.

The importance of this difference in theoretical physics does not fully indicate its significance here. The emergence of the dispute in contemporary physics is a dramatic illustration of a much older problem which Charles C. Gillispie has described:

> The historian finds a dialectic informing successive resolutions of the great dilemma in which science oscillates between the unity of nature and the multiplicity of phenomena, the one and the many. Is the universe a single continuum, to be described in a geometrical physics? Or is it a congeries of discrete entities?—atoms, bodies which, in Clark Maxwell's straightforward definition, "cannot be cut in two." Is the world, as Bertrand Russell somewhere asks, a bucket of molasses or a pail of sand? The issue divided Einstein from most of his fellow physicists at the end of his life. And since this problem, though ever more fruitful, is no nearer solution after

6 D'Abro, 72.

2,500 years than when it was discovered in Greece, it seems safe to say that its merit lies in the discussion, not in the answers.[7]

In Hellenistic times, Stoic philosophy and physics spoke for a dynamic nature, for activity, the Heraclitean flux, and becoming. For the Stoics there could be no boundaries in nature, and combinations could arise only from the blending of principles.[8] Against them stood the great school of Leucippus, Democritus, Epicurus, and Lucretius, which maintained the existence of atoms moving through the void in obedience to general laws, where change and process "consist not in flux or penetration by soul or realization of the goal of life, but in the physical rearrangement of varied particles of specific shape and size which do have objective existence."[9]

This is not the place to review the interesting interpretation Gillispie presents in support of this thesis, but his remarks about the scientific aspects of the revolt of Romanticism against the Enlightenment are valuable. Eighteenth-century chemists, he tells us, saw themselves as scientists of the internal, of essences, as contrasted to the "superficiality" of a physics concerned with crude location and

---

[7] *The Edge of Objectivity* (Princeton: Princeton University Press, 1960), 95. Gillispie's book was written with Arthur Koestler's *The Sleepwalkers* (New York: Macmillan, 1959) very much in mind. While Koestler wrote to celebrate the irrationality and mysticism of Kepler's genius against the "objectivity" of a Galileo, Gillispie would reverse that judgment (Gillispie, 43–44). In view of this, it is interesting to note the degree of agreement between the authors as to the lines of conflict within the history of science. Compare the text quotation with this passage from Koestler, pp. 28–29.

> The Ionian philosophers had been materialists in the sense that the chief accent of their inquiry was on the stuff from which the universe was made. The Pythagoreans' chief accent was on form, proportion, and pattern; on the *eidos* and *schema*, on the relation, not on the *relata*. Pythagoras is to Thales what Gestalt philosophy is to the materialism of the Nineteenth century. The pendulum has been set swinging; its ticking will be heard through the entire course of history as the blob alternates between the extreme positions of "all is body," "all is mind"; as the emphasis shifts from "substance" to "form," from "structure" to "function," from "atoms" to "patterns," from "corpuscles" to "waves," and back again.

Compare also the classifications of Northrop.

[8] Gillispie, 182–83.

[9] *Ibid.*, 99.

dimension. This is the Faustian idea that "nature has an inside." "It is the physicist who brutally pulverizes, ignites, and destroys. The chemist does not analyze. He divines."[10] Goethe's ideas on botany and biology illustrate, perhaps better than any other example, the desire to find "destiny and necessity indwelling in flux and process, in the organismic, and not the mechanistic universe."[11] For him, even the classifications of Linnaeus would violate a continuum not of geometry but of sentience.[12] In Gillispie's view, Romanticism appears as the despairing attempt to defend a qualitative science against a measuring, numbering science which totally objectifies nature.

> For physics romanticism would substitute biology at the heart of science. For mechanism as the model of order, romanticism would substitute organism, some unitary emanation of intelligence or will. Romanticism might take any form in politics, art, or letters. But in natural philosophy there is an infallible touchstone of romantic tendencies. Its metaphysics treats becoming rather than being. Its ontology lies in metamorphosis rather than atomism. And always it wants more out of nature than science finds there.[13]

My purpose is not to define or characterize Romanticism, nor even to suggest that it is possible to trace a consistent "process" view through the course of Western speculation. It is, however, to demonstrate that such concepts as process, continuity, structure, and discreteness have run persistently through various modes of thought about the world, often on a metaphorical (or metaphysical, in its literal sense) level, but apparently always compelling attention from the working scientist as well as from the historian and philosopher.[14]

---

10 *Ibid.*, 186.

11 *Ibid.*, 192.

12 *Ibid.*, 198. Contrast the analysis of Erich Heller, "Goethe and the Idea of Scientific Truth," *The Disinherited Mind* (New York: Meridian, 1959), in which Goethe appears as opposed to the Romantics as well as to Newton.

13 Gillispie, 199.

14 Indeed, W. T. Jones has argued that analysis at such a meta- or metaphoric level can yield valuable results in cross-cultural and historical research. See *Romantic Syndrome*.

It might be useful to interpret a life philosopher like Bergson as defending a process view of the continuum of human experience against the incursion of a mechanistic or atomistic science. But if it is proper and illuminating to speak of differences between sciences, it is also necessary to see similar divisions within certain disciplines. An example is the difference between mechanistic and field conceptions in physics.

The dualism within the social-process tradition between the group-conflict school and the relational or formal alternative has already been examined. Arthur Bentley comes down on the latter side, but he remained dissatisfied with the static, empty character of Simmel's and Wiese's categories. He needed to create a method of "full process statement" after the example of a science that had absorbed geometry into physics. Within the sphere of physics itself Bentley inclines toward the field theory and the transactional analysis he proposed is comparable to Einstein's search for a pure field theory in its unwillingness to tolerate substantive mechanistic components. In Gillispie's terms, Bentley's preference is consistently for geometry, unity, and the infinity of straight lines rather than for the counting of measurable, separable entities.[15] Bentley may be said to have used physics as an analogy, or even as a source of inspiration, in his development of transactional analysis, but it would be incorrect to call him a natural philosopher who labored to accommodate the new science to a universal cosmology. His completed transactional analysis goes beyond physics in that it anticipates making statements covering the biological-physiological and the social, as well as the physical, realms. From the standpoint of the nature or life philosopher, Alfred North Whitehead has provided perhaps the most complete metaphysical system of modern times, and his version of the process universe will be compared with the "tool" that finally emerges from Bentley's strenuous labors.

In his 1931 article Bentley argued that mathematical terms can perform various functions. They may be "things"—for example,

---

[15] Gillispie, 95. Insofar as the Appendix to *The Process of Government* proposed such "counting" procedures as legislative roll-call analysis, it misrepresented Bentley's position.

natural numbers or line segments; they may be "relations," as in the case of "odd," "even," and "prime"; they may be "operations," such as "plus" and "times." The function performed by any one term at any particular time is dependent upon its place in a system. Relations as illustrated above might appear in another system as things and in yet another as operations. Analysis of the system is a precondition to determination of the use to which a term is being put. That this situation exists in mathematics, our most rigorous discipline, he argued, should be instructive to sociologists. The most basic lesson to be learned is the avoidance of premature formalization, a reluctance to assign a final or fixed place to any term. How, we might ask, is a group to be imagined? As thing, as relation among things, or as operation? Recourse to the "factual" is not much help, since the "what is" just as "thing" must be determined by the system of which it is a part. The concept of space is the vehicle Bentley chose to demonstrate this point.

We may, he argued, discern at least five distinct senses of the word "space": the "vulgar" or personal experience of space; "mathematical" space; "physical" space (mathematical space applied to and used by speech); "social" space; and "sociological" space.[16] Vulgar space is the familiar common-sense world: three-dimensional, Euclidean, based on or at least congruent with Newtonian space. There are various vulgar spaces—those of animals and insects, for example—just as there are many possible mathematical spaces. By social space Bentley intended "those discretenesses and continuities, those separations and distributions and purely social mensurations, which are found among men outspread in societies."[17] Sociological spaces are "theoretical constructions which, with respect to social spaces, hold a position comparable to that of mathematical spaces with respect to physical spaces."[18] Though Bentley does not use this illustration, the measures of social class which combine such variables as educational level and quality of living-

[16] Bentley, "Sociology and Mathematics," 62.
[17] *Ibid.*
[18] *Ibid.*

room carpets to determine social "distance" might be appropriate examples.

Vulgar space is the most natural to us, and, Bentley conceded, it might prove most useful to sociology in the long run. Its great difficulty is its inability to provide an adequate frame for a description of activity. The individual man existing at the moment in Euclidean space represents a form of discreteness which may or may not be important. The question is whether vulgar space can accommodate descriptions of situations in which the discreteness is of a different order. Bentley proposed this example: "If we take two nations with rival commercial interests as the discreteness, we have still the continuities beneath offered by the specifically human social industrial organization of the present era."[19] He concluded that it was as futile to seek an a priori determination of which form of space would ultimately prove most useful for scientific purposes as to ask which conception was "real." Both judgments need to be made in individual cases, dependent upon our purposes.

Although Bentley urged caution in making a definite, final commitment to one space form, there is no doubt that his interest lay in creating forms of statement in social space and social time. The latter dimension is not explored in his 1931 article, but Bentley suggested that an analysis of social time would proceed much as that of space had proceeded. Conceptualization in social space would result in this sort of statement: "We have this society before us in the form of men and their activities and all that those activities involve. This includes the knowledge factors that are in the men and in their activities and their society. It also includes the factual references or implications, and the realisms and externalizations of their knowledge."[20] Rather than "inspecting a factual world with a knowledge factor floating in it," this approach "inspects a living procedure of knowledge-experience-contact, with the stress for knowledge not on its exactness but on its indicative-

[19] Bentley, "Sociology and Mathematics," 80.
[20] *Ibid.*, 78.

ness." This would present the investigator with one great system for research, unbroken by such dualisms as an inner-outer dichotomy.

Here is a final example of how a social theory set in vulgar space might be restated, or at least reinterpreted, in a more sophisticated form: "Sociologies using basic human desires or instincts, or in a more elementary form depending on temperaments, take these factors for dimensions; they do not call them dimensions because they take them realistically, concretely, as forces or agents; but for us, seeing such materials as abstractions, and crude preliminary abstractions at that, they have the dimensional meaning."[21] We would take a "dimension" such as cruelty, study it in its "social manifestations," that is, as people inflicting pain on other people in various contexts including the mental, in order to "establish spatial and temporal transitions in amount of intensity" which could be considered a kind of "social coordinate." Bentley suggested that other dimensions such as "religious intensity" and "industrial organization" would themselves yield new coordinates, and coordinates could be brought together to form a "configuration." This formulation ignores many difficulties, such as how we would identify and measure "pain," and how, on what level, and with what common denominators the coordinates could be joined. This line of reasoning presents an analogue to the field theory of physics. The "older" sociologies mistook dimensions for agents or forces; in seeking to establish causal chains, they committed the sin of reification. Process, or, as I shall come increasingly to call it, "transactional" statement, would forgo the pursuit of causality but extend the surface of inquiry and description along spatial and temporal parameters.

In an article which appeared in 1941, addressed more to psychology than to sociology, Bentley restated the liberation he sought in broader terms. The problem he then saw was this: "The established attitude of the psychologist came to be that his facts were 'in' the Newtonian universe but not technically 'of' it. This

---

21 *Ibid.*, 94.

attitude allotted the behavioral facts locations in the world but not such locations as Cartesian co-ordinates could establish. The locations were quasi-locations, asserting the presence, not definitely, 'in' or 'at' an organism."[22] The solution was to state the behavioral event—boy-planning-college—so as to include the full range of organism and environment within the duration of, say, the period between entry into high school and entry into college. "Duration" was as extended a predicate of "behavior" as "event." Behavioral duration, Bentley argued, had a "much fuller and richer factuality than the 'instant' that any clock records, or than any series of such instances." No adding of instants could represent that factuality, and no false dilemma must be allowed to obscure the fact. "Achilles does in fact catch the tortoise. Behavior does, in fact, what for clocks is impossible; it spans the duration. Organic-boy-living is thus durationally much more complex than infinitely ticking clocks, or for that matter than the infinitely extended parallels in three dimensions."[23] Bentley concluded by indicating some measure of agreement with Gestalt psychologies and with Kurt Lewin and J. F. Brown's use of topological space; but, like Einstein, he was dissatisfied with the residue of "quasi-mechanistic" particles or "forces" in their theories.[24]

We are now approaching an understanding of the basic ideas of transactional analysis of process, and we have a foundation for examining *Behavior Knowledge Fact* and *Knowing and the Known*. Before that examination is begun, however, an uneasiness about the logic of Bentley's proposed analysis should be made explicit, especially as it relates to the underpinning of rational thought, the

---

[22] Bentley, "The Factual Space and Time of Behavior," *Journal of Philosophy*, No. 18 (August, 1941); reprinted in *Inquiry*, ed. Sidney Ratner, 215.

[23] *Ibid.*, 217–18.

[24] *Ibid.*, 219–20. Other scholars have felt the currents of convergence suggested in this chapter and explicitly recognized by Bentley. See the stimulating article by Hubert Bonner, "Field Theory and Sociology," *Sociology and Social Research*, XXXIII (January–February, 1949). "In keeping with developments in relativity physics, organismic biology, and configurational psychology, I shall call this science of society 'field theoretical sociology'" (171). Compare also the rather offhand but suggestive study by Kenneth Boulding, *The Image* (Ann Arbor: University of Michigan Press, 1961).

law of identity. Even if one unreservedly applauds Bentley's criticism of mechanism and causality, his ruthless exorcism of things, and his determination to extend the scope of observation in behavioral space-time, there remains a question about how our thought can master this new world. There is a value problem involved as well. In defense of what might be viewed as a deprecation in some sense of the "individual," Bentley wrote:

> Let no quibble of skepticism be raised over this questioning of the individual. Should we find reason for holding that he does not exist in the sense indicated, there will in that fact be no derogation from the reality of what does exist. On the contrary, there will be increased recognition of reality. For the individual can be banished only by showing a plus of existence, not by alleging a minus. If the individual falls it will be because the real life of men, when it is widely enough investigated, proves too rich for him, not because it proves too poverty-stricken.[25]

The argument should be familiar to us by now, and it is a forthright, though perhaps unsatisfying, reply to those who fear possible moral or ethical consequences of this "displacement" of the individual. But the problem in logic is not so easily dealt with, since Bentley's entire work constitutes a refutation of Dilthey's confident belief that the social, unlike the physical, sciences had their basic unit given in experience. To read Bentley as having replaced the individual by the group is a gross simplification. Moreover, his critique of the particle universe seemed to doom all attempts to find what Howard Becker called an Archimedean point.

The question that begins to emerge from these considerations is, how can we apply the principle of identity in behavioral space-time? Presented in such stark form, the problem appears deceptively simple. If it can be formulated so directly, why did Bentley not recognize and discuss it immediately, or somewhere in his early

---

25 Bentley, "Knowledge and Society," 4. It is well to keep in mind Bentley's doctoral dissertation, much of which appeared as "The Units of Investigation in the Social Sciences," *Annals of the American Academy*, V (May, 1895). His fascination with the subject remained, even while his opinions about it underwent drastic revision.

works? Not until 1935, in *Behavior Knowledge Fact,* did he appear to identify Aristotle as an obstacle. In distinguishing "two great types of linguistic behavior," Bentley finds:

> The first appears where a man affixes a certain word to a certain fact which he regards as assured—to a "fact" which at least ranks to him as certain enough for his needs in so far as he has become aware of them. The second appears where man finds it necessary to erect a great construction of consistent language, and to strive desperately for its ever greater consistency, in order to have richer and wider control of "fact."[26]

In more precise terms:

> The one pole is represented by the Aristotelian canon of identity; the other, by full consistency in mathematics. The strong existential *is,* binding a "word" to a "fact," appears at the former pole. The fully clarified "1 + 1 = 2" appears at the latter pole. In the former case the "existence" is assigned to the fact, and certified to by the word. In the latter case, so far as "existence" enters at all, it is an existence that has its full locus *within* the consistency of the expression and its system of expansion.[27]

Bentley seems now to have concluded that, if the behavioral event "boy-planning-college" has burst the conceptual confines of the Newtonian universe, it has also transcended the capabilities of Aristotelian or traditional logic. It is probable that Bentley was led gradually into this challenge by the development of his own thought. In 1908 the implications of process or transactional analysis were not entirely clear to him, but, when he became convinced that traditional logic was incompatible with it, he identified and attacked the obstacle with characteristic energy and disregard for authority, even that of "the philosopher."

[26] Bentley, *Behavior Knowledge Fact* (Bloomington, Ind.: Principia, 1935), 23.

[27] *Ibid.* Bentley added that "in applying the name 'Aristotelian' the reference must be to run, not to Aristotle's own philosophical system but instead to that linguistic logical construction which has been dominant from medieval times down even into the present age, and which is everywhere labelled by his name." Compare Bentley's remarks on the "Aristotelian Effect" and his "The Case of Definition," in Dewey and Bentley, *Knowing and the Known.*

Bentley's enemy is again unwarranted discreteness. He does attempt to find room in the process universe for discontinuity, but the thrust of his critical thought is nearly always against those who have drawn boundaries arbitrarily, made definitions too rigidly, and "frozen" their categories prematurely. Bentley expected to treat logic and epistemology as knowledge and behavior factors within transactional analysis, not as foundation stones of inquiry.[28]

Nine years intervened between the publication of Bentley's survey of sociology in *Relativity in Man and Society* and the appearance of *Behavior Knowledge Fact*. The latter volume can properly be viewed as an attempt to present the kind of observational framework that the concluding sections of the former had proclaimed necessary. Perhaps the first remark to be made about *Behavior Knowledge Fact* is that its subject matter is much more psychological than sociological. This statement requires immediate qualification; Bentley himself would have been very reluctant to accept—indeed, he would have argued vigorously against—such a distinction. Yet he narrowed the range of his inquiry to study situations between two or among only a few persons rather than situations such as political parties or mass movements. Perhaps the best way to put the matter is to say that *Behavior Knowledge Fact* studies and describes smaller units of sociation, closer to the scale of analysis we have come to expect of contemporary social psychology or psychology proper.

Bentley begins with a survey of the field of psychology, displaying, as usual, his acquaintanceship with the current literature. Various psychologies are examined in terms of their adequacy as expressions and conceptualizations of human behavior; for Bentley this meant how well they provided "observational coherence" in transcending segmentation. He examined these psychologies, these "construction forms," for their "traits," primarily their space and time forms and their segments or units of investigation. Underlying Bentley's classification of construction forms there is a dichotomy

28 Thus in Bentley's "Vagueness in Logic," in *Knowing and the Known*, there is the beginning of an insistence upon the need for a theory of behavior which could incorporate logic as activity.

between two types of systems. The first accepts a dualistic universe in that it postulates a factual situation prior to experiment or investigation. In the second category are psychologies which "proceed *as if*, in the outcome, the specific identification of positive psychological facts with definite psychological names will be the type of 'knowledge' they attain"; these are, nevertheless, somewhat removed from the "heavy stress upon factuality, running often to dogmatic extremes," of the first kind.[29]

Bentley proceeded upon the assumption that everything about these psychological systems ("traits") was to be studied as behavior. In this sense, when he discussed the "two types of linguistic tools," one of which refers to a physical world, the second of which speaks of the mental realm, he was standing "off" from the psychologies as subject matter; that is, he did not imagine himself as accepting or committed to or "within" any system. Thus, Bentley's conclusion that the psychologist fails to bring the two languages into a "common functional organization" says nothing about ontological reality but treats the "linguistic behavior" purely phenomenologically. It is from this same perspective that Bentley speaks of the relations between the mind and physical languages as they denote "sectors" such as "immateriality," "apprehensionality," "isolationality," and the "environmental."[30]

We are now in a position to modify the remark made earlier that the canons of Aristotle's logic, metaphysics, and science were not acceptable to Bentley as "foundation stones of inquiry." They were fundamental to most psychological systems viewed as phenomena, but not as axioms to be accepted as a priori necessary to all thought or science. Their most damning flaw was their assumption that "fact" could be "known" and represented for all time in all contexts by fixed linguistic devices. Instead, "in appraising 'fact,' we must take into account its involvement in procedures called 'knowing' and 'being known.' "[31] In other words, "from within any one single department of inquiry, 'fact' can neither be determined

---

[29] Bentley, *Behavior Knowledge Fact*, 25. See the table, p. 19.
[30] *Ibid.*, 28–31.
[31] *Ibid.*, 135.

certainly nor appraised; above all, no single generation can hope to establish it safely for all time under whatever manner of expression happens to be most characteristic of its own age."[32]

The first group of psychologists Bentley considered were the "behaviorists," particularly John B. Watson.[33] Their use of the word "behavior" is precisely what Bentley meant by "movement space," in which "the specific observable movements are taken as if capable of definite severance, each from the others around, and from before and after."[34] Their temporal form is successional. These behaviors or movement spaces may be described as "events," but their durations are incidental, even external conditions instead of being "necessary components of the primary observation." Watson was interested in the observable "psychological," which he called "reaction," as temporal successor to "a separately observable non-psychological fact, the 'stimulus,'" and in "the observable reaction, under the name of 'behavior,' presented as a gross-body-movement segment of movement space."[35] This Watsonian universe was much too fragmented for Bentley, who compared it to an attempt to solve a jigsaw puzzle by arranging the pieces in one corner of the whole. This criticism might have been anticipated, but Bentley makes a second point which ought to be considered by those who have dismissed him as a "crude" behaviorist. Watson, he argued, betrayed his own criterion of observability by his introduction of words like "implicit" which permitted the reintroduction of the old mentalisms of mind language. Bentley's criticism is not that Watson should have held at all costs to the observability criterion; it is, rather, that he should have recognized that he was transcending it and not insisted that his "gross-body-movements" construction form had been retained intact. Moreover, Bentley did not believe that Watson's observability criterion was adequate. The following passage was addressed to both Watson and Margaret

[32] *Ibid.* This is the kind of remark that has led some commentators to associate Bentley with the sociology of knowledge.

[33] Compare "A Sociological Critique of Behaviorism" and "Situational versus Psychological Theories of Behavior," in *Inquiry*, ed. Sidney Ratner.

[34] Bentley, *Behavior Knowledge Fact*, 53.

[35] *Ibid.*, 54.

Washburn: "Again, for both of them it may be said with respect to their language-thought constructions that 'language,' taken in the form of 'movements' of an 'organism'—stripped, that is, of all implications of thought and meanings—is no more 'language' than 'thought' is 'observable thought,' if stripped of all its linguistic or other physical form."[36]

A second school represented by R. S. Woodworth and Knight Dunlap employed "activity" as "their basic envisionment of the phenomena of inquiry" in place of the orthodox behaviorists' segmented movements. Bentley called these psychologies of "action spaces." Focus upon activity had the advantage of preserving "durations," and a number of activities could be taken as "the facts" and then "clotted" to make durational wholes.[37] This procedure, Bentley argued, had the advantage of avoiding the substances, subjects, and things of the old mind language, but it was subject to a dangerous fallacy: "It makes the individual take the form of 'activity' and nothing more, and then turns around and makes that 'activity' an individual and allots him causal status."[38] A further difficulty with Woodworth's construction forms was his conception of the hierarchy of the social sciences, especially the place of the individual, who was conceived as

> lying between the subject matter of physiology on the one hand, and "the doings of the people," i.e., the "sociological," on the other hand. In this asserted intermediate position, psychology is to "keep its eyes fixed" on this individual as activity. In effect what Woodworth requires of us is that we permit, or compel, ourselves to "see" this active individual as detached or detachable both from the physical organism and from society at one and the same time.[39]

As a methodological device for some specific purposes, this might be admissible, but Woodworth's use of the distinction as serving to mark off the boundaries of this science from that one is illegitimate. We might, Bentley continued, study psychology as a branch

36 *Ibid.*, 58. See also footnote 33 above.
37 *Ibid.*, 66.
38 *Ibid.*, 68.
39 *Ibid.*

of physiology or sociology, but we cannot insert an individual activity between those perspectives. Woodworth's procedure made the "seeing" of blue identical to the physiological process; thus he ended with a formulation that perceiving is activity, and the activity does the perceiving.[40]

Action-space psychology did, however, represent a form of progress in that it encouraged the substitution of verbs and adverbs for nouns and adjectives. John Dewey and Madison Bentley carried this development to a point which Arthur Bentley felt merited classification as "Mind-Language Reconstructions." Of special importance here are Dewey's construction forms, to which Arthur Bentley gave the name "transactional." By this designation he meant that Dewey saw organism and environment as a unity, separable only by analysis and selective abstraction; the interaction between the two constituted a transaction. For Dewey, "structures lie in 'the recurrent modes of interaction taking place between what we term organism, on one side, and, environment on the other.' "[41] Selective abstraction permitted Dewey to identify that "quality" of behavior called "experiencing," which can be considered as "in" the individual only in the sense that he serves as a "locus of observation."[42] This activity or process of experiencing of the human organism is specifically psychological.

Dewey's notion of structure as "recurrent modes" is reminiscent of some sociological theories discussed in previous chapters, and it should not surprise us to find that Bentley reacted to Dewey in much the same way as he had to the sociologists. Specifically, he contended that Dewey had not gone far enough. Transactional experiencing became the acts and attitudes of a person, and behavior, "a developing temporal continuum marked off into specific act situations."[43] The abstraction of organism from environment, and of acts from the total experience, constituted "breaks" in Dewey's system. The break occurred between his

---

[40] Bentley, *Behavior Knowledge Fact*, 70.
[41] *Ibid.*, 76–77.
[42] *Ibid.*, 79.
[43] *Ibid.*, 80.

vision of what psychology's subject matter was and his narrower specification of the science itself. Illustrations of this discontinuity could be expressed in a number of familiar dichotomies: stimulus-response, part-whole, process-content, structure-function, and abstract-concrete. All, or almost all, of these pairs are at least as applicable to sociological concerns as to psychological issues.

The phenomenon of act, continued Bentley, should be process or function, or even structure of the full transaction, but with Dewey it was transformed into a "part" or "content" of a personalized response. The following passage has the virtue of bringing Bentley's criticism to the level of example; if, he argued, his own "act" of writing a paragraph were analyzed, certain segments of transaction might be singled out.

> But such a part so inspected will not be an instance of the abstract "experienc*ing*" which Dewey has shown should be psychology's primary concern, nor will it be a "structure" of the full "transaction." It is not "abstract" in any ordinary rendering of that word; it is "concrete" if the word "concrete" means anything at all, which is very doubtful; it is full of "content"; it is a bit of segmentation of "what is happening," viewed as if "within" the boundaries of the "organism" or "person." If we want to study this bit of "what is happening" with any thoroughness at all, we shall have to deal with it elaborately in a frame of wider happenings across thousands of years and thousands of miles—a frame wherein it secures a significance vastly greater than that of "life-career," though perhaps not so currently interesting. As "act," spatially delimited, it may have a certain quasi-anatomical status. It is most certainly neither synonym nor substitute for experienc*ing*.[44]

If this quotation is read with care, it reveals the difficulty of fully comprehending Bentley's demands. He went far along the road with Dewey, as he had with Simmel and Wiese in sociology; he accepted their images of men in society as process, flux, and activity. He broke with them over the proper procedure of "cutting into," or "abstracting from," the process. Dewey came close to an adequate statement, and what Bentley viewed as his shortcomings illustrate

44 *Ibid.*, 81.

Bentley's true extremism. Given that Dewey had a sense of the meaning of transactional situation, given further that he appreciated the task of selective abstraction of parts, he still fell short because he thought it possible to abstract from the actual "concrete" situation. Bentley argued that, if an act, say that of writing, were to be taken out of the situation of "man-writing-book," it had to be restated in broader terms, but not necessarily those of the original situation itself. We might, for example, need to discuss the "writing" in terms of the physiology of the man's hand, and this might require inquiry into his genetic heritage, and so on.

At least two forms of transactional statement are involved here: the original transactional statement of the man-writing-book and then the new transaction, statement of "writing" per se. Unless this second form of statement was made transactional also, the abstraction "writing" would be nothing but lifeless segmentation. Bentley never accepted the idea that analysis or abstraction from process involved dismemberment, fixity, or any such static distortion. It simply meant that another transactional statement was necessary.

A still more advanced psychological construction form Bentley called the "apprehensional space-segment." He considered the work of J. R. Kantor to have thoroughly integrated object and organism in a temporal (though not spatial) construction. Kantor called his procedure "interactional," which Bentley refined to "inter*actional*" as opposed to "*inter*actional." The reason Bentley gave for this modification is important: "If it were read as '*inter*actional,' the stress would seem to be upon the end-points of behaviors, which is exactly what he does not intend."[45] Kantor's inter*actional*, like Dewey's experien*cing*, was an approximate but insufficient form of transactional statement. Again, as in many previous instances, Bentley was insisting that *all* was process, not only concourse flowing between points, but the points themselves.

In a summary evaluation of the state of psychological construction, Bentley stressed the progress which had been made toward the

45 *Ibid.,* 91.

elimination of the four "issues" or dichotomies of the "old mind-language": organism-object, mind-body, organism-environment, and man-man.[46] The mind-body problem he believed to have lost its importance, but only Kantor had begun work on an adequate construction of organism-object. The man-man dichotomy remained, but Bentley found widespread contemporary discontent with constructions in this sector. Organism-environment, perhaps the most profound of the polarities, in part because it undercut the others, was as yet insufficiently conceptualized, despite the beginnings made by Dewey and Kantor. Bentley viewed this last dichotomy as of such importance that solutions in the other areas could not be reached until it was conquered. In fact, the rest of *Behavior Knowledge Fact* was an effort to overcome that dichotomy.

In the chapter entitled " 'Isonality': Language and Fact," Bentley firmly identified the problem which his improved linguistic construction was to solve by the word "isonality," or "isolationality." Arguing in a manner similar to that of his analysis of "vulgar" space, Bentley contended that to generalize from the personal knowledge that "I perceive individuals" to the statement that "other people perceive individuals" was to become involved in the Aristotelian "naming procedure" criticized earlier, and thus to build isonality into the structure of language via the mind-object dichotomy. Replacement of presentations like "soul," "mind," etc., by "person" or "activity" was an advance, in that the latter might be given a biologically individuated locus; but even so, such a formulation might be insufficient for psychological purposes. Though it may be true that we receive our materials in primarily individual terms, this does not mean that our perception must dictate our linguistic or analytic frames. Physics, for example, retained a notion of matter, though it was used in a highly sophisticated conceptual form.

A satisfactory linguistic construction of transaction must extend "across the full range of knowledge," which for Bentley included not only the realm of "science" but the realms of "Experience,

[46] *Ibid.*, 102. See also table, p. 100.

Existence, and Value."[47] For this reason he rejected George B. Titchener's *Systematic Psychology: Prolegomena* (1929), which, despite its merit in suggesting a functional distinction among the branches of science, refused to extend this construction beyond what its author called "scientific facts."[48] All knowledge is "social," but the social itself must be framed within the wider body of knowledge, including that of the physical, vital, and psychological. These realms do not stand in hierarchical relationship to one another in such a way that we could speak of one as "epiphenomenal" vis-à-vis one more "basic"; rather, to borrow Talcott Parsons's term, they "interpenetrate."

> Neither "social" nor "psychological" can hope to secure permanent formulation except under clarified offsetting with the other; alike they involve participations in, and presentations of, the "outer" world, the "physical," which itself reaches up into and through them, and which "in knowledge," may in the end dominate them.[49]

"Fact" implicates "experience," and "knowledge" implicates "language." As a preliminary statement Bentley suggested the following: "If experience can be taken as personal fact; if facts in general are taken as the scattered 'stimuli' of experience; if knowledge is the wide social embodiment of experience—so Language is the wide social formulation and embodiment of fact and knowledge."[50]

These four terms or "phases," if placed in the "tellurian-sidereal cosmos," need to be expanded "inwards" and "outwards," "backwards" and "forwards." We must "run our construction far backwards from the few thousand years of history which we have used as a base for its consideration" and interpret our constructions "phasally" and "functionally."[51]

---

47 *Ibid.*, 113.

48 *Ibid.*, 124. Another difficulty for those who have regarded Bentley as a "positivist" concerned to keep "science" untainted by "value" must be his contention that Titchener's use of terms like "subject matter," "point of view," "observation," and even "logic" involved him in the realm of value.

49 Bentley, *Behavior Knowledge Fact*, 134.

50 *Ibid.*, 150.

51 *Ibid.*, 180–81.

If, for example, we pause at the description "sensing," we must read it, not as some capacity assignable mechanistically (via the mind language) to a limited bit of "matter" (or "mind") or to a special area of space, but as a functional phenomenon in which "race" and "environment" come functionally into account along with "individual," and without radically disjunctive oppositions between any of these terms.[52]

A series of terms such as "sensing," "speaking," "thinking" should not be "cut apart," separated onto different levels of time of evolution. Rather, "we shall endeavor to learn what beginnings of 'thinking' there may be in 'sensing' and what extensions of 'sensing' there may be in 'thinking.' "[53] As a conclusive analogy, Bentley suggests that the difficulty which physicists encountered in finding a light ray participant both in the realm of the observed and in that of the observing (i.e., "fact" and "knowing") should warn us against placing undulation and perception in separate, alien worlds.

This summary of the primary dimensions, the four phases with which Bentley's transactional analysis begins (fact, experience, knowledge, language), has been somewhat abstract, but as such it has abridged the intricacies and subtleties of Bentley's own exposition. It is understandable that, when he concluded this general section, he felt impelled to encourage weary readers:

I can deeply sympathize with anyone who objects to being tossed into such a floating cosmology. Much as I have stressed its substantiality, I can hardly expect everyone to feel it. The firm land of "matter" or even of "sense" or "self" is pleasanter, if only it stands firm. To anyone whose tasks can be performed on such ground, I have not the slightest thought of bringing disturbance. But for many of us tasks are pressing, in the course of which our finest spots of conventional departure themselves dissolve in function. When they have so dissolved, there is no hope of finding refuge in some chance island of "fact" which may appear. The continents go, and the islands. The pang may be like that felt by a confirmed landsman at his first venture on the ocean, but the ocean in time

52 *Ibid.*, 181.
53 *Ibid.*

becomes familiar and secure. Or, if I may change the figure, the fledgling will vastly prefer his firm nest to falling with untried wings. But the parent sciences are pushing; the nest, even, is disintegrating; and there is air for flight, even though it is not so vividly felt and seen as the sticks and straws of the nest.[54]

I have said that Bentley intended "encouragement," but it may as well have been consolation—even consolation tinged with contempt—for the "confirmed landsman" and the "fledgling" who would not brave the process universe in the name of science. Nor was Bentley entirely frank in his disavowal of any intention to bring disturbance. Of course he wanted to disturb, but he had, since 1908, learned enough about his Heraclitean world to recognize that not everyone could dwell there. For his was the tough-minded course; better to know the limits of coherence than rest content with our incoherence.[55] To the more tender-minded or faint-hearted, Bentley could have echoed the words of the policeman in Kafka's parable, "Give it up."

FURTHER RECONSTRUCTION

Through his transactional-process analysis, Bentley explored some preliminary constructs of simple situations and the form of state-

---

[54] Bentley, *Behavior Knowledge Fact*, 183. In his article "Causality and Time in Political Process: A Speculation," Norman Jacobson pointed to the striking similarity of Bentley's imagery to that in a passage from Nietzsche, *American Political Science Review*, LVIII (March, 1964).

[55] There are certain interesting psychological or personality parallels between Bentley and David Hume, who, when his youthful analyses brought him to the limits of speculation, abandoned philosophy for the "conventions" of history. The dismissal of Hume as "purely negative" recalls the revulsion Bentley's destructive genius occasions among those social scientists who have troubled to understand him. History's case against the essentially critical thinker has been well made by John Stuart Mill: "Hume, the prince of dilettanti, from whose writings one will hardly learn that there is such a thing as truth, far less that it is attainable; but only that the pro and con of everything may be argued with infinite ingenuity, and furnishes a fine intellectual exercise." J. S. Mill, "Bentham," *Essays on Politics and Culture* (New York: Doubleday, 1962), 89. David Braybrooke has pointed out to me that Mill's remarks ignored the "constructive" Hume of his ethical writings. In a similar vein, many of Bentley's critics neglected his efforts at reconstruction.

ment in which they were to be described. He began by trying to characterize (not "define") the social as a field of inquiry. Facts can be known only through human senses, he argued; this meant that every social fact had to be "physical" in the sense that the discipline of physics includes space and time (extensions and durations). Thus, the "full setting and embodiment of the 'social' must be physical."[56] At the same time it must be vital, in that vital processes are exhibited in it and the techniques of the biological sciences are applicable to it. Provisionally, psychology may be associated with individual phenomena, and the social may refer to those characteristics of behavioral phenomena not satisfactorily treated by the former, essentially as a residual category. If we so conceive these two "fields," they cannot be reduced to statement in terms of biology or physics.[57] (Use of the word "provisionally" raises a question of how much Bentley is compromising his earlier critique. This will be considered more fully in the concluding chapter.)

In this sense Bentley certainly maintained the "autonomy" of the social sciences, or more properly the social realm, but this does not place him in the ranks of those contemporary political scientists who bend their ingenuity toward distinguishing a priori the realms of "the political" or "the social." Bentley's distinctions were preliminary and would be maintained only so long as science found itself unable to treat certain phases or aspects of human experience within a unified construction form. On the other hand, Bentley must be vindicated of the charge of "crude reductionism," of believing that social or political matters could be conceptualized and understood in terms of a "physics."

He explicitly rejected the form of the question, "Is there a social?" and suggested that it be rephrased in some such manner as this:

Can we, in the specific case of the "social," select, under verifiable observation, definite presentations which, by the broadest tests of

[56] Bentley, *Behavior Knowledge Fact*, 190.
[57] *Ibid.*, 193–94.

present-day technique and construction, are separable from those other presentations which are dealt with by the techniques and constructions of the physical and biological sciences? And if we do select such presentations, can they maintain themselves in scientific work in correlation with other presentations established through specialized psychological investigation and set forth in terms of the "individual" as separate from the "social"?[58]

There must be no mistake about this. Bentley's requirement that behavioral (social and psychological) facts be "visible" (or "audible," "tactile," etc.) does not mean that they are only observable activity, as some readers have interpreted him. Visibility was necessary but not sufficient. Of course, "observation" itself required analysis in terms in which it was considered as activity as well as in terms of the "what" of observation, but this has been covered more generally above. The point is the provisional nature of the "behavioral fact"; its persistence as a category depended not upon a determination of its existential, ontological "reality," but entirely upon the need within a unified science for residual categories.[59]

How, we may now ask, would this criterion of "visibility" or "observability" be applied in transactional analysis of the behavioral realm? The example Bentley offers is a relatively simple one: a conversational situation between two men. What, in the most rigorous sense, can we say we "observe" of this situation? The sound is not visually perceived, although the framework of men talking, men listening, men gesturing, is. Events such as speaking and hearing have no materiality, but they do have extensions and durations within a field. What is required is the widest possible observation of that field. Exactly at this point Bentley found a subtle danger capable of undoing all the careful preparations he had made thus

---

58 *Ibid.*, 195.

59 This, by extension, would be the case with all other sciences except the most "advanced." If, for example, a way should be found to treat the phenomena of biology in terms of a future physics, the former would simply disappear as a phase or category before the extension of the concepts, constructions, of the latter. This makes nonsense of the claim that one science is ontologically more "basic" than another, as is sometimes urged of the psychology-sociology relationship.

far. The temptation he warned of was the notion of man as "actor," in which man/actor would be isolated and the rest of the situation made "abstract," as environment or history.[60] It is perhaps justifiable to anticipate my later argument to the extent of pointing out that Bentley would have rejected the work of Talcott Parsons and the "General Theory of Action" seminar for what he would have considered the reintroduction of isonality.

In the conversational situation just described, concentration on the "speaking-heard" as event yields a factuality which is technically different from specifically physical and vital facts and is yet visible, capable of scientific observation and extension. Bentley called this event, the speaking-heard, the *Dicaud*.[61] The "thing" that the Dicaud is "about"—the referent of the speaking-heard—he called the *Dicaudane*. Bentley noted the similarity of the Latin roots of "fact" and "act" and contended that each "reported" on something done. "Only in the recent outcome have the senses of 'a doing' or 'a thing done' been stripped away from 'fact,' while the senses of 'reality,' 'actuality,' and 'accomplished fact' have become in counterpart obsolete for 'act.' "[62] Fact, he continued, had come to stand forth "on its own," while act, meaning "deed," required an intelligent "actor": "The 'act' requires an 'actor,' but it also requires its own differentiation of 'actor' from 'act.' In this setting 'speech' as an 'act' receives dictionary classification in a separate compartment from 'speech' as a factual reference in terms of the 'individual' or his 'capacity,' and from 'speech' as 'socially-spread' fact."[63] Thus

---

60 Bentley, *Behavior Knowledge Fact*, 208–9.

61 *Ibid.*, 232.

62 *Ibid.*, 239. I have referred earlier to the notion, found in Wittgenstein, of language as a shaper or determinant of thought. The same idea has been argued from an anthropological basis, notably the "Whorfian Hypothesis," which holds in part that "linguistic patterns themselves determine what the individual perceives in this world and how he thinks about it." F. Fearing, "An Examination of the Conceptions of Benjamin Whorf in the Light of Theories of Perception and Cognition," *Language in Culture, American Anthropologist* 56, Memoir No. 79, ed. H. Holjer (1954); quoted in Ludwig von Bertalanffy, "An Essay on the Relativity of Categories," *Philosophy of Science*, XXII (October, 1955), 243.

63 Bentley, *Behavior Knowledge Fact*, 239.

the speaking-heard is regarded as act, and researchers proceed to insert "between the organic activity and the wider factual presentation a duplicative phenomenon, the 'actor.' "[64] This breaks up the frame of observability; conversely, under an extended observation which is fully durational, the actor fades either into the organism (activity) or into the wider social fact of language.

The Dicaud could be examined from a variety of perspectives and for a number of purposes. A narrower approach than the one Bentley favored is the "behaviorist" approach, which does not attempt to deal with the dimensions of "meaning" and "communication." Such specialized investigations within the field of the Dicaud Bentley compared to histology, as distinguished from physiology; it could deal with "certain tissues of speech" but not with the living process.[65] The general classification of "men seen in communication" would be a specialized observation which ignores the "what" communication is "about." Bentley called this the *Communact*, of which he considered the Dicaud a subclass.[66] As a parallel to the Dicaud he suggested *Scriptilect* for writing-reading activities and *Gest* for communication by gestures.

A more inclusive situation, in which the references, meanings, and objectives of communication, in addition to the Communact, come under investigation, Bentley called the *Communicane*. It denoted the full situation, the description of which Bentley thought beyond the capacity of his contemporary social science. In part, this was due to the complexity of the Communicane's space and time dimensions. While the Communact, "behavioral" in the broad sense, could make use of the Newtonian frame, at least for initial formulations, the Communicane, he insisted, required new constructions. Bentley's use of "behavioral" is somewhat specialized:

Behavior is that specifically separate field of scientific inquiry, set

---

64 *Ibid.*, 241.

65 *Ibid.*, 246.

66 *Ibid.*, 251. He continued, "In this terminology the suffix ane will indicate behaviors inclusive behaviorally of the 'referent' in some one of its many forms, while the terminal consonants *d* or *t*, suggestive of imperfection or suspense, will be used for the partial or aspectual observations."

over against the physical and vital, within which both "social" and "psychological" research must be carried on. It is that great type of activity which cannot be held within a physical description and technique, nor within a vital, but which requires a directly psychological and social form of research, with whatever better descriptions and techniques we may secure to replace the two very imperfect words "psychological" and "social."[67]

This designated area, irreducible to physics or biology, required persistent exploratory research and freedom in the formulation of hypotheses. Bentley sharply differentiated "behavioral" from "behaviorist" insofar as the latter term indicated a restricted area of inquiry and an already established construction form and method.

Reviewing Bentley's progress to this point, we have: (1) the Communicane, representing "full behavioral observation," and its subclasses of Dicaudane, Scriptilectane, Gestane, etc.; (2) the Communact or specialized observation of men in communication, with its subclasses of Dicaud, Scriptilect, Gest, etc.[68] But Communact, or description in its terms, does not include specification of the "what" of communication, its referent. A third set of terms was apparently necessary, and these had to be framed in such a way that they could be stated as Communicane. (Bentley clearly could not "add" referent terms to Communact, for this would be to restore the very dualism he has labored to escape.) This brings Bentley very close to the central difficulty of transactional analysis.

He has suggested a vocabulary with which to distinguish phases of the act of communication from the full situation. When he tried to conceptualize the referent of communication, he again encountered an old enemy, the object, the "thing," the bounded entity, which transactional analysis had promised to eliminate as a block to the course of inquiry. He explicitly recognized this. "We face here a critical issue, not merely in terminology, but in the whole manner of exposition, for the further results of our investigation. We may, if we wish, decide that our 'background' of observation is now sufficiently clear so that we can henceforth display our phenomena—our 'fig-

---

67 *Ibid.*, 262.
68 *Ibid.*; see diagram, p. 265.

ures,' our 'objects'—positively and without qualification."[69] If, that is, we are satisfied that all the prior and painstaking analysis and reconstruction has sufficed to conceptualize a "background" from which an "object" may now be separated, and if we can rest content with the reintroduction of the bounded thing or entity without fear of creating new artificial divisions, then there is no reason to feel that more than an additional set of terms is necessary. But if we believe, with Bentley, that transactional analysis has just begun to restructure its conceptions of background and cannot afford to accept fixities, entities, or any boundaries as fact, then the problem of conceptualizing the referent of the communication situation becomes quite difficult. After all, does not the very idea of a referent of conversation require that the latter be separated, marked off from the naming remark itself—and further, that it be somehow identifiable in its own milieu? Bentley put the issue this way: "We are now at a point where the two great opposed attitudes towards the materials of investigation, the disjunctive and the functional, will begin to show their sharpest conflicts. We must continue to exercise the greatest caution against looseness in the application of words."[70]

This is all very well, but the matter is before us in urgent form. Can process or transactional analysis create linguistic and conceptual frameworks for even the simple conversational situation without introducing Aristotelian designations and fixed entities? Bentley tried to accomplish this task by treating the "object" as "phasal" or, in more familiar terms, "functional" to the situation observed. To understand precisely how he expected this to advance him, we need to look at his conceptualization of perception. Perception, he argued, must be treated on a level parallel to that of communication, and he suggested the term *Perceptane* to indicate "any specific instance of the observable behavior of *an*-organism-in-environment." The term *Personan* would designate the behavioral participation of this separated organism as it was phasal to either the Perceptane or the Communicane. If the individual organism

---

[69] Bentley, *Behavior Knowledge Fact*, 266–67.
[70] *Ibid.*, 267. He refers, of course, to the Aristotelian and the "scientific" attitudes.

were phasal to the former, Bentley called it *P-Personan,* and if to the latter, *C-Personan.*[71]

Objectan was the name given to the reference, considered as behavioral, of either Perceptane (P-Objectan) or Communicane (C-Objectan). Perceptane and Communicane had thus been brought onto the same level, as direct observation of subject matter. Personan and Objectan are "phases of specialized inquiry with respect to Communicane and Perceptane, separately or together."[72] "Specialized inquiry" is the key phrase in Bentley's treatment of the object. This is made clear in the final set of terms to be considered here: *Objectane, Personane, Perceptan, Communican.* These terms stress inquiry into object and person. "Objectane and Personane present 'object' and 'person' as the dominant observations of basic phenomena which are to be the primary subject-matters of inquiry. Communican and Perceptan then name the communicational and perceptional processes as dependent presentations of analysis."[73] Words such as "stress," "selection," "provisional," and "hypothesis" were the constant reminders Bentley addressed to an audience that might be tempted to establish an object as distinct object beyond conceptualization as environment.

Communicane and Perceptane were repeatedly presented as observations of the full situation within which various experimental segmentations might be constructed. Transactional analysis was to deal with the problem of "object" not by refusing to make any segmentation whatever, but by creating a vocabulary which expressed categories and concepts of relative stresses and emphases. This meant, despite Bentley's repeated dismissal of the term, a holistic bias in that the provisionally segmented Objectane must never be considered without reference to some system. This was what he meant by the phrase, "always to take objects and organisms together in moving systems."[74] But if all that Bentley had done was to insist upon conceptualizations in which "part" would be related

---

[71] *Ibid.,* 267–68.
[72] *Ibid.,* 268.
[73] *Ibid.,* 269.
[74] *Ibid.,* 283.

to "whole," he would have said nothing even remotely new. The distinctive step he took was to link this notion of system with a denial of any fixed boundary or structure to the part-whole relationship. That is, a part isolated for certain purposes from its environment might well blend back into the system (environment not to be stressed) for other purposes. The same part, object, or Objectane might, for other purposes, receive stress in another system or, under still different circumstances, might itself constitute a Communicane embracing its own parts.

The liberation from restrictive formulation afforded by process analysis is finally a very fragile thing in that it rests ultimately upon the willingness and ability of the investigator to regard his segmentations as tentative and hypothetical. Once he forgets this, he slips back into Aristotelian usage and the universe of basic separation.

It must seem at this point that the painstaking creation of a new vocabulary was not needed to establish a cautionary principle. However, some of the best minds of the twentieth century have regarded the analysis and reconstruction of language as indispensable to the clarification of thought. A more important defense of Bentley may be made on epistemological grounds. This rests upon Bentley's conception of the relation between knowledge and fact or, as he and John Dewey were later to put it, between knowing and the known.

THE COSMOLOGY OF TRANSACTION

The general postulate of "scientific uniformity" could, Bentley argued, be formulated in two ways; and the two statements could be contrasted

> according as they do or do not take into account the communicative behavioral phases of the world-presentations they set forth. One of these we may call the postulate of *uniformity of nature*; the other, that of *uniformity of knowledge*. The first presents "nature" as so thoroughly and uniquely "known" that it is before

us in transcendence of the limiting conditions of its "being known"; the second retains this limiting condition in its statement.[75]

Bentley formulated both postulates precisely. First, the postulate of the uniformity of nature:

> The physical world, as extrapolated from the knowledge of it, is the basic presentation of science. Physically located "within" this world and as "part" of it are living organisms, themselves of ultimately physical constitution. Physically and vitally located "within" the range of living organisms—and, more particularly, "within" certain "higher" organisms of that range—are neurological-psychological processes, themselves of ultimately physical and vital constitution.[76]

Then, the postulate of the uniformity of knowledge:

> Knowledge of the physical must be taken as basic knowledge, and as applicable, so far as its descriptions and techniques extend, to *all* the vital and to *all* the behavioral; and with full freedom for the unlimited extension of its specialized techniques, so far as it can achieve satisfaction through its own success. Knowledge of both physical and vital must be taken as applicable, so far as their descriptions and techniques extend, to *all* the behavioral, and with full freedom for unlimited extension across the behavioral field. All of this knowledge, all of these descriptions and techniques, exhibit involvement in communicative behaviors in the sense that neither as Fact, nor as Knowledge, nor as Experience, nor as Language, can any "part" of it be basically, radically, fundamentally, absolutely, severed from the other "parts," so far as either our present powers or definite outlooks suffice to indicate.[77]

Bentley thought that the differences between these formulations turned on their treatments of the part-whole and within-without dichotomies. According to the first postulate, physical nature is "reported upon" by certain "parts" of itself. This idea had worked out reasonably well with regard to the natural sciences because its users seem to have had "adequate structural comprehension of such dis-

[75] *Ibid.*, 275.
[76] *Ibid.*, 275–76.
[77] *Ibid.*, 276.

tinctions." The postulate of the uniformity of knowledge does not contain any adequate notion of them.[78] Psychology and sociology are in a situation represented by the latter; thus, they require an "analytic and functional" statement. If we tried to apply the postulate of the uniformity of nature to the social disciplines, we would find that "it involves the position that the C-Objectan, or whatever that term 'really' indicates, lies outside of behavior and behavioral knowledge."[79] The principle of the uniformity of knowledge contains the "limiting condition" that the "what is known" is, at our present stage of knowledge if not in principle, inseparable from the "knowing" of it. This condition of knowledge in the social and psychological realms underlies the necessity for tentative, hypothetical procedures in the sciences which investigate them. The two postulates do not seem to me formally incompatible as stated. They do, however, as Bentley's language suggests, endorse quite different working attitudes toward scientific inquiry—attitudes which in practice might prove incompatible.

Bentley's conviction that knowledge must be regarded as "behavior" because of its intimate connection to knowing has sometimes been regarded as evidence that he accepted the "sociology of knowledge." A recent article insists that on the basis of the fact that "meaning" was to Bentley a "social event": "The transactional approach yields this cosmic view. This involves an extreme form of what has come to be called the sociology of knowledge, a view which reduces ideas to factual responses of interests to the environment. Bentley embraced the sociology of knowledge in *The Process of Government*."[80] Bentley did regard behavior in the broad sense of all activity as an aspect of interest; and any particular interest had, of course, a relation to other interests within society. If this is what is meant by "sociology of knowledge," then the argument must be accepted. But that term has a more precise application in the literature of social science; it denotes the works of its best-known

[78] *Ibid.*, 276–77.

[79] *Ibid.*, 277.

[80] Myron Q. Hale, "The Cosmology of Arthur F. Bentley," *American Political Science Review*, LIV (December, 1960), 958.

exponent, Karl Mannheim.[81] While scholars can no doubt find propositions to which both Bentley and Mannheim would assent, the differences between the two are more revealing. The "transactional approach" is both much more and much less than the sociology of knowledge. Though Bentley admitted Mannheim's fundamental point, that "knowledge" is decisively conditioned by adoption of a perspective, the adoption itself being conditioned by the social milieu of the investigator, he then proceeded to create a tool which could convey the investigator beyond linguistic and cultural limitations. Mannheim's effort was devoted to uncovering the unexpressed presuppositions underlying certain periods and types of thought and to establishing what might be called a metalogical theory of thought. It was largely a historical enterprise. Bentley casually conceded that thought was an aspect or phase of behavior—more, that science did advance and make its former "truths" obsolete—but his vision of transactional analysis left little room for any preconceptions to mediate between perception and the observable. Indeed, the whole thrust of Bentley's effort was to eliminate all verbal and conceptual obstacles to direct observation of behavior, and, while he made the prudent reservation that another generation might achieve an unanticipated breakthrough on some unspecifiable scientific front, he clearly intended to ground his science in the unassailable bedrock of the observable.

The fact that Bentley had earlier endorsed "interest" as a means toward conceptualizing what man in society does, and that his mature formulations of transactional analysis emphasize the hypothetical nature of a "truth," does not suffice to include him in the camp of the sociology of knowledge. Moreover, a reading of his postulate of the uniformity of knowledge indicates that by extending the boundaries of inquiry in the social realm he hoped to transcend any partial or limited perspective. The passage describing the uniformity of knowledge might even be seen as Bentley's vision of human experience as process. If it is contended that "truth" or "thought" depends, in both Bentley's and Mannheim's formula-

81 *Ideology and Utopia.* See also Werner Stark, *The Sociology of Knowledge* (Glencoe, Ill.: Free Press, 1958), and the works of Max Scheler.

tions, upon perspective, then it is also true that for Bentley this was a concession blithely made and for Mannheim it was the basis of a science. Mannheim chose to press "backward" toward the preconditions of the choice, while Bentley preferred to march forward toward a broader and more reliable conceptualization.[82]

But if Bentley sought less to peform an "unmasking" function than did sociology of knowledge, he attempted much more through his determination to put knowledge into a behavioral framework and yet preserve its integrity and consistency. In the essay, "The Terminological Problem," written in collaboration with John Dewey, Bentley spoke of the need to treat the two factual aspects of "event" and "designation" as equally "in" a cosmos: "Designation is the naming through which Event appears in our Knowing as Fact."[83] Designation and the designated are not ultimately separable but constitute one event in behavioral space-time. Designation is itself event. Bentley saw no need to make a name, designation, or logic

[82] The text interpretation rejects Hale's argument from sociology-of-knowledge grounds, including his interpretation of Bentley as consenting to a test of truth between critics and defenders of the status quo based upon "a practical contest of power." This is plainly an extension of Hale's preoccupation with ideology beyond any sympathetic chord in Bentley. In fact, Bentley's position is much closer to that of Ludwig Bertalanffy: "The categories of knowledge, of every-day knowledge as well as of scientific knowledge, which in the last resort is only a refinement of the former, depend, first, on biological factors; second, on cultural facts; third, notwithstanding this all-too-human entanglement, absolute knowledge, emancipated from human limitations, is possible in a certain sense" (247).

Still, Hale merits applause for his willingness to read beyond *The Process of Government* and his consequent ability to avoid some of the cruder positions taken by other critics. For example, R. E. Dowling, writing in the same symposium, feels no discomfort in classifying Bentley, Catlin, and Hobbes as men who have fallen victim to "the centuries-old attempt to appropriate the success of dynamics or mechanics to politics." Dowling continues to explain that "the reduction of phenomena to the primary qualities of matter and motion" was the chimera bewitching these men. "Just as Newtonian physicists speak of material bodies and particles, and the forces they exert upon each other, so we must confine ourselves to the description of the motions of atomic political bodies and the forces they reflect upon each other" (944). This caricature of Bentley's position might be explained by the fact that Dowling's article contains, in addition to *The Process of Government*, one reference to *Relativity in Man and Society*. "Pressure Group Theory: Its Methodological Range," *American Political Science Review*, LIV (December, 1960).

[83] Dewey and Bentley, *Knowing and the Known*, 61.

stand outside of event, behavior, or cosmos. "We shall regard these naming-knowings directly as a form of knowings. Take this statement literally as it is written. It means we do not regard namings as primarily instrumental or specifically ancillary to something else called knowings (or knowledge) except as any behavior may enter as ancillary to any other."[84]

Bentley freely admitted that this was a circular procedure, but he thought it could not be avoided. "We observe world-being-known-to-man-in-it; we report the observation; we proceed to inquire into it, circularity or no circularity. This is all there is to it. And the circularity is not merely round the circle in one direction: the course is both ways round at once in full mutual function."[85] In technical psychological language Bentley expressed the idea this way: "To describe the full situation of the Communicane as behavior is precisely the same as to say that the phenomena present themselves to us in behavioral space time."[86] To be able to make a statement in behavioral space-time is to conduct a transactional analysis of the process of human experience as it appears in the postulate of the uniformity of knowledge. We might paraphrase Bentley's often-quoted remark about groups in this way: "When the Communicanes are stated, everything is stated."

Further elaboration of Bentley's systematic theory is not necessary. His books themselves present that much more fully than a hasty summary could hope to. There is, however, another set of terms which illustrate the final stage of Bentley's effort. They relate to what we have here identified as the central problem of process analysis, namely, conceptualization of the object or Objectane as dominant observation. Bentley wrote increasingly about "tech-

84 *Ibid.*, 58–59.

85 *Ibid.*, 63. Thus, "explanation" in the mechanical sense is not even to be attempted. Hale's criticism of Bentley's identification of "activity" and "interest," which concludes that this usage "deprives the word interest of any explanatory value, and banishes the economic substructure from the system" (Hale, 959), misses the point. More incisive is Charles Hagen's remark that "interest is a posteriori not a priori, and it is consistent with the observed behavior and not contrary to it." "The Group in Political Science," in *Life, Language, Law,* ed. Taylor, 117.

86 Bentley, *Behavior Knowledge Fact,* 281.

niques of isolation," and, although he remained insistent upon flexibility and the investigator's freedom of choice in hypothesis, he became more concerned with the "cutting into" stage as a source of error. In *Knowing and the Known* he suggested that events might be differentiated "with respect to a certain range of plasticity that is comparable in a general way to the physical differentiations of gaseous, liquid and solid."[87] Bentley did not admit, at this point, the existence of qualitative differentiations among events, but he did seek to establish what might be called quantitative rankings. The terms "Situation," "Occurrence," and "Object" were suggested as preliminary benchmarks along what appeared to be a scale of isolationality. "Situation" denoted the full subject matter, environment not detachable from object. "Occurrence" was defined as "event designated as in process under transitions such as are most readily identifiable in everyday human-size contacts."[88] "Object" was a bit less plastic, "event in its more stabilized forms," but never, of course, firmly fixed in language or implanted in our minds as "fact." The key definition is that of "Occurrence," since it is here that a criterion for distinguishing events, an index of plasticity, must emerge. Not surprisingly, Bentley is vague. The test is framed in the phrase, "everyday human-size contacts." A few pages earlier Bentley had provided a somewhat more operational criterion: "When an event is of the type that is readily observable in transition within the ordinary spans of human discrimination of temporal and spatial changes, we shall call it occurrence."[89] Provisionally, then, we are referred back to our vulgar, common-sense notions of space and time.

We have now gone about as far as Bentley can take us. His final suggestion looks toward change that is humanly perceivable as a means of identifying an object, but we are left to speculate about how something undergoing change can be detected in the first place. Once the difficulty is put in this form, a wider perspective opens before us and several lines of convergence may be seen. The Her-

[87] *Ibid.*, 63–64.
[88] *Ibid.*, 73.
[89] *Ibid.*, 70.

aclitean challenge to ordered thought, and the compromise worked out between it and the alternative of Parmenides, have already been discussed. And the dimensions of that conflict in a brief and general way have been indicated by a quotation from Alfred North Whitehead, who sought to accommodate both permanence and change within a natural philosophy. His speculative thought provides us with a link between this classical debate and the crisis of the object in Bentley's process analysis.

The brilliant series of Lowell Lectures delivered by Whitehead in 1925 and published as *Science and the Modern World* contains an extensive historical discussion of what he liked to call the philosophy of organism. As with most such systems, it went through various stages and modifications; its most profound formulation is contained in *Process and Reality*, published in 1929. In some of its aspects, Whitehead's notion of process both reflects the classical dilemma and constitutes a parallel to Bentley's vision. Whitehead's fascination with identity and change found expression in passages such as these:

> Things are separated by space, and are separated by time: but they are also together in space, and together in time, even if they be not contemporaneous. I will call these characters the *separative* and the *prehensive* characters of space time.[90]

> The general principle, underlying these special cases, is that the erroneous notions of process devoid of individualities, and of individualities devoid of process, can never be adjusted to each other. If you start with either of these falsehoods, you must dismiss the other as meaningless.[91]

Of the two visions of experience, Whitehead, at one time at least, seemed to find the process version more challenging or problematical, if not more fundamental. "Without doubt, if we are to go back to that ultimate, integral experience, unwarped by the sophistications of theory, that experience whose elucidation is the final aim

[90] Alfred North Whitehead, *Science and the Modern World* (New York: Macmillan, 1958), 65.

[91] Alfred North Whitehead, *Modes of Thought* (New York: Macmillan, 1958), 132.

of philosophy, the flux of things is one ultimate generalization around which we must weave our philosophical system."[92] What is perceived is the passage of nature; Whitehead meant that this "process" was a given fact of nature which demanded expression but could have no "explanation."

One critic of Whitehead's thought has seized upon this point as the premise of an interesting analysis.

> In his acceptance of process as simply given and inexplicable, as sheer flux, and in his position that all that can be done is speculatively to demonstrate it and express its relation to other factors presented in sense awareness, Whitehead has failed to come to grips with the fundamental problem. The latter is precisely the *explanation of process*, the discovery of structure within process and in terms of process.[93]

Whitehead rejected the attempt to capture nature in an instant, without acknowledging its passage; we must, he insisted, include the duration which can accommodate process. This, of course, required a conception of space consistent with the temporal form. Harry Kohlsaat Wells's formulation of the problem presented by acceptance of this position could stand as a summary of Bentley's difficulty.

> Sense awareness delivers durations as an essential characteristic of nature. But durations are not atomic entities. They retain within themselves the passage of nature. Further, the relation between durations blurs distinctions. They overlap and contain one another. There are no sharp lines of demarcation so that it is impossible to say of a duration that it is here and now, and in this, not that. Instead of being able to define a duration as just what it is, it must be seen as in transition and as part of larger durations, and as having smaller durations as parts of it.[94]

Experience yields a continuum, and thought requires demarcations;

92 Whitehead, *Process and Reality*, 317.

93 Harry Kohlsaat Wells, *Process and Unreality* (New York: King's Crown, 1950), 15–16.

94 *Ibid.*, 20–21. Whitehead rejected Aristotle's subject-predicate logic as the basis for the misleading subject-object dichotomy (*Science and the Modern World*, 152).

what is to become of the laws of identity and contradiction? We are back to Heraclitus and Parmenides, but the Aristotelian compromise no longer seems acceptable, since it purports to have ontological as well as logical validity.

Anaximenes and Heraclitus, and Hegel many centuries later, explained process in terms of the struggle among opposing forces which was resolved in the form of qualitative change. Aristotle had recognized contradiction or change to the extent of distinguishing between actual and potential characteristics and assigning the troublesome matters of flux to the latter category. Plato had made the law of identity require the principle of noncontradiction (or non-opposition), thus banishing qualitative change from the world of forms.[95] "Mechanical" change would not have presented anything like the Heraclitean problem, for the internal, "qualitative" nature of the object would not have to be regarded as unstable. Whitehead did undertake to extend the phenomenon of flux to the internal nature of the object, but he could not leave the matter there. In *Process and Reality* he distinguished two kinds of "fluency": "One kind is the concrescence which, in Locke's language, 'is the real internal constitution of a particular existent.' The other kind is the transition from particular existent to particular existent."[96] More specifically:

> One kind is the fluency inherent in the particular existent. This kind I have called "concrescence." The other kind is the fluency whereby the perishing of the process, on the completion of the particular existent, constitutes that existent as an original element in the constitutions of other particular existents elicited by repetitions of process. This kind I have called "transition."[97]

Whitehead continued to explain that concrescence was a name for the process in which the "universe of many things" acquires unity in the subordination of the multiplicity to the one. The "thing," then, *is* the concrescence; we may not speak of the "thing" and the

---

95 See Wells, Chap. 6, "Traditional Method," and contrast Northrop.
96 Whitehead, *Process and Reality*, 320.
97 *Ibid.*

concrescence. The analogue to Bentley's discussion of interest, activity, and group immediately comes to mind, and it is certainly clear that Bentley, too, pressed the notion of flux (or "fluency") beyond "transition" into "concrescence."

It is beyond the province of this book to inquire fully into Whitehead's method of removing himself from the eternal flux, except to point out the teleology apparent in the notion of concrescence. Whitehead also proposed what he called the "method of extensive abstraction," an operation in which the quantitative continuum of events is stripped away until its "intrinsic character"—what he called the "object"—is discovered.[98] Wells's critique points out that Whitehead, in *Process and Reality*, altered Heraclitus's phrase, "all things flow," to the "flux of things," thus de-emphasizing internal contradiction. If, Wells contended, Whitehead had read Hegel instead of his English disciples, he would have realized that a new method was necessary to deal with his duality, a method which Hegel had begun to construct. In a sympathetic account, Wells argued that Hegel's idea of internal contradiction had been largely misunderstood; Hegel intended to maintain that the principle of identity was complex, not simple. Thus the negation is not a nullity but results in a higher unity of the history of an entity and its "what-is-to-be."[99] Had Whitehead read Hegel directly, instead of expositions of his system, he would have found inspiration in the logic and realized that "to have identifiable and separate things does not require that there be unchanging eternal entities."

Whitehead, unlike Bentley, refused to accept the position of many modern philosophers that the laws of thought govern logic (though not necessarily a single logic) but have no force in the ontological realm. Wells suggested P. W. Bridgman's formulation of the principle of identity as a case in point. "From the point of view of operations, the meaning of identity is determined by the operations by which we make the judgment that this object is the *same*

---

98 See Wells, Chap. 3, for the contention that Whitehead is finally unable to reconcile his original dualism and that the reintroduction of "object" through "extensive abstraction" was simply wasted effort.

99 *Ibid.*, Chap. 7.

as that one of my past experience."[100] But, Bridgman continued, "this involves the possession by the object of certain characteristics —it must be a discrete thing separated from its surroundings by physical discontinuities which persist. The concept of identifiability applies, therefore, only to certain classes of physical objects."[101] Bridgman thought that if we were in fact dependent upon the law of identity on those levels on which it could not be given an operational meaning—for example, some situations in microphysics— we might confront an impassable barrier to knowledge. This, of course, was precisely the wall Bentley thought he had encountered.

Peter Strawson's recent and interesting essay offers another example of the problem. It poses the question of how we can recognize the recurrence of a process name such as "battle" without somewhere referring to things if we must also account for the continuity of space and time of the entities themselves. He rejects the suggestion that a category of four-dimensional "process things" might offer a conceptual solution. The category of material bodies, he argues, "alone supplies enduring occupiers of space possessing sufficiently stable relations to meet, and hence to create, the needs with which the use of such a framework confronts us." Strawson concludes:

> We do in fact distinguish between a thing and its history, or the phases of its history; we cannot appropriately speak of one in the ways appropriate to the other; and we do not speak of either in ways appropriate to the category of process-things. Granted the distinction we do draw, there is, as we have already seen, a general identifiability-dependence of processes which things undergo upon the things which undergo them, and not vice versa. This is partly,

[100] P. W. Bridgman, *The Logic of Modern Physics* (New York: Macmillan, 1960), 92.

[101] *Ibid.* In his "Physicists and Fairies," in *Inquiry*, ed. Sidney Ratner (originally published in 1938), Bentley had some kind words for Bridgman's early book, but he found his *Nature of Physical Theory*, which appeared in 1936, nine years after *The Logic of Modern Physics*, a migration toward conceptual obscurity. Of course, as we have seen in the analysis of *Behavior Knowledge Fact*, Bentley was aware of difficulties in conducting firm operational research in the behavioral sector, an awareness which grew to the proportions of a major concern in *Knowing and the Known*.

though not only, because, granted the distinction, it is the things themselves, and not the processes they undergo, which are the primary *occupiers* of space, the possessors not only of spatial position, but of spatial *dimensions*. If one tried to give the spatial dimensions of such a process, say a death or a battle, one could only trace the outline of the dying man or indicate the extent of the ground the battle was fought over.[102]

There is no need to repeat what Bentley would have replied to an argument grounded upon the way in which, in fact, we customarily use words, even an argument as sophisticated and analytic as Strawson's. That argument, however, is crucial to Bentley's entire enterprise. He proposed to surmount a wall that Bridgman saw as a barrier to operations, that Strawson found in our linguistic representation of space and time, and that Wells identified as the lack of a fully worked-out method to accommodate internal contradiction.

Bentley and Whitehead must probably be placed on opposite sides in the dispute over the applicability of reason to nature, but there remains a number of interesting affinities and parallels in their ideas of process. Whitehead was ultimately forced to introduce some notion of "object" (intrinsic characteristic) in order to save the permanence polarity of his cosmos, just as Bentley strove to define "more plastic" segments of the process in order to put his tool to work at all. They faced in common the difficulty of finding viable analytic units, but both were unwilling to accept any easy alternatives. They shared the perception that a process universe was somehow an incomplete world. For Whitehead this idea was involved with freedom: "Process is the way by which the universe escapes from the exclusions of inconsistency"; and, "by means of process, the universe escapes from the limitations of the finite. Process is the immanence of the infinite in the finite; whereby all bounds are burst, and all inconsistencies dissolved."[103] For Bentley the universe was open, because knowledge was inextricably behavior in the world.

Another similarity between Whitehead and Bentley was their

102 Peter Strawson, *Individuals* (Garden City, N.Y.: Doubleday, 1963), 48.
103 Whitehead, *Modes of Thought*, 75.

common preoccupation with developments in the physical and vital sciences; this is especially apparent in Whitehead's *Science and the Modern World*, but Bentley was certainly not a novice in those areas. Both men thought that a process must be seen as consisting "of" its parts, but also that the parts must be "functionally" related to the larger dimensions of the process as a whole. Both accepted the premise that knowledge was "in" the world of behavior and not floating freely outside. Bentley the skeptic and critic was more overtly hostile to the idea of "explanation," but Whitehead, too, viewed the task of science (though not of all abstract thought) as description. Perhaps as a consequence of their shared interest in twentieth-century science, they found the Newtonian universe outmoded and restrictive. The following quotation illustrates a final parallel.

> The whole understanding of the world consists in the analysis of process in terms of the identities and diversities of the individuals involved. The peculiarities of the individuals are reflected in the peculiarities of the common process which is their interconnection. We can start our investigation from either end; namely, we can understand the process and thence consider the characterization of the individuals; or we can characterize the individuals and conceive them as formative of the relevant process. In truth, the distinction is only one of emphasis.[104]

This was Whitehead speaking in 1938 and, except for the absence of warnings against taking his words "fixidly" or "too concretely," it could have been Arthur Bentley writing in 1908.

> Such interest groups are of no different material than the "individuals" of a society. They are activity; so are the individuals. It is solely a question of the standpoint from which we look at the activity to define it. The individual stated for himself, and invested with an extra-social unity of his own, is a fiction. But every bit of the activity, which is all we actually know of him, can be stated either on the one side as individual, or on the other side as social group activity.[105]

104 *Ibid.*, 135.
105 Bentley, *Process of Government*, 215.

But Bentley's transactionalism must be distinguished from the general convergence just detailed. In *Science and the Modern World* Whitehead referred to William James's essay "Does Consciousness Exist" (1904), in which James had replaced the Cartesian self or entity with consciousness as a function. Whitehead thought that this challenge mirrored the objection of twentieth-century science to the seventeenth-century concept of "matter," and there is surely a case to be made for that belief. He saw the challenge as victorious against Descartes's notion of independently existing substances with simple locations in temporal durations, but he was not eager to embrace either alternative in toto. Instead, Whitehead read James narrowly as criticizing a "stuff" or substance idea, such as Spinoza's, and contented himself with the equivocal remark that a function was, after all, not nothing, and that therefore it was "something"—in that sense, an "entity."[106]

This was not a very heroic, though perhaps a thoroughly understandable, posture. Bentley, however, could not be satisfied with such caution; for him, the Jamesian challenge had to be squarely met, and in 1943 (after a series of James Centenary papers had been presented at a meeting of the Conference of Methods in Philosophy and the Sciences in November, 1941), he published "The Jamesian Datum."[107] Much of this essay was devoted to correcting what Bentley took to be misrepresentations and misunderstandings of James. In particular, he felt that commentators had seized upon parts of James's work but had not treated it as a life's—hence, evolving—work. James's psychology began with monism, moved through dualism, and ended in pluralism; he belonged to a post-Darwinian era, by which Bentley meant simply the idea of an evolving universe, including organisms and man's activity. As early as 1884, James had "overcome" his atomism with what Bentley called "a brilliant figure of speech about the flow, current, flux, or stream of consciousness."[108] The analogy was especially praiseworthy for its sense of

---

106 Whitehead, *Science and the Modern World*, 144.

107 Bentley, *Journal of Psychology*, XVI (July, 1943), reprinted in *Inquiry*, ed. Sidney Ratner.

108 Bentley, "Jamesian Datum," 241. Bentley noted that the subjectivism of the

continuity and the absence of segmentation. In 1890, in *Principles of Psychology*, James advanced to a conceptualization of activity as stream and referred to "the passing thought that seems to be the thinker," and still later he asserted that "we need no knower other than the 'passing thought.' "[109] The "datum" was "experience," "indivisible fact," "the process in full sweep." Bentley gave generous credit to James for this conception of the datum (the "raw materials," in an earlier phrase), but he preferred John Dewey's "free broad account in historic-geographic setting" to James's "static snapshot of the stream."[110]

The Jamesian datum is passage and process, not substance. The world is movement. Whitehead was reluctant to give himself over to this universe of flux; the philosopher is always wary of abandoning the power of thought, even if the alternative is a tool created by a very philosophically minded social scientist. Whitehead's prudence had impressive historical antecedents. Aristotle tells us of one Cratylus, a disciple of Heraclitus and instructor of the young Plato, who determined that the universal flux prohibited any truthful statement whatever and confined his communicative life to wagging a finger.[111] R. G. Collingwood has remarked that, to a young man who had known the "varied and vigorous intellectual life of Socrates," Cratylus "must have appeared as a man who had committed intellectual suicide because he had got hold of the stick by the wrong end and had not the strength of will to let go."[112] Cratylus, Collingwood continued, was obsessed by the world of nature as we perceive it, and in searching for a modern parallel Collingwood makes this startling, but in our context perfectly reasonable, analogy: "Obsession by the perceptible, one sees, had led him where it led William James. The world had melted into a 'buzzing, blooming confusion.' What Plato carried away from his training under

phrase "stream of consciousness" might be overcome by translation into John Dewey's "course of experience."

109 *Ibid.*, 246.

110 *Ibid.*, 261.

111 Aristotle, *Metaphysics*, 987a, 1010a.

112 R. G. Collingwood, *The Idea of Nature* (New York: Oxford University Press, 1960), 66.

Cratylus was quite clearly the solid experimental knowledge that when you allow yourself to be obsessed by the perceptible that is what happens to you."[113]

Solid footing goes, said Collingwood; continents and islands go, said Bentley and Nietzsche. Certainly *Behavior Knowledge Fact* and *Knowing and the Known* may be read as chronicles of a lost mariner, a man who has thrown the compass of reason over the side as so much excess ballast. As we have seen, Bentley came to focus on progressively narrower situations as his technical vocabulary and conceptual categories grew increasingly intricate and unwieldy, until language itself seemed in need of fundamental reconstruction. Indeed, one might say with some justification that Bentley's series of publications should have been reversed: *Knowing and the Known* should have appeared before *The Process of Government.* The trouble is that, had Bentley arrived at the point he ultimately reached in *Knowing and the Known,* he probably would never have written *The Process of Government,* or at most he would have written Part One as a critical essay for *Philosophy of Science.*

The complete description that was to be the complete science became more difficult to accomplish, even to envision, and Bentley's attention shifted to epistemology and away from intensive examination of sociology and politics. But it is not so easy for us to dismiss the specter of Cratylus as it may have been for the young Plato. We are an empirical century; most of us accept the fact that empirical science has succeeded brilliantly in giving an account of the world without consulting sovereign reason at every step of the inquiry. In Karl Popper's words, empirical science has dispensed with "methodological essentialism." Even Whitehead, certainly to be counted among the great speculative minds of our century, found the location of a point at which reason might plausibly enter the flux of nature a vexing and arduous problem. It will not do, finally, to dismiss Bentley as a twentieth-century Cratylus, unless we are prepared to do the same with the century itself. Bentley's process analysis does employ "reason," but it applies reason to the creation

[113] *Ibid.*

of the tool by which reality is to be known and described and not directly to reality itself. I am, of course, speaking in the dualistic terms Bentley hoped to banish, for both the tool and reason are, in his sense, "in" the reality, the process.[114] If this final version of the tool was not adequate to the tasks envisioned, Bentley could with justice say that he had persistently stressed the tentative and hypothetical nature of his science, and he always expressed the reservation—even the hope—that his writings would shortly be superseded by the works of more sophisticated generations. In this sense, his process analysis was truly "speculative."

Ironically, it was one of Bentley's severest critics who recognized this when he remarked, "In practice Bentley was the least pragmatic of pragmatists," but that insight was blemished by the accompanying complaint that, in contrast to Lincoln Steffens, Bentley "never" gave examples of "scientific procedure and verification in politics."[115] Of course he never did; he was not a logical positivist, or a scientific empiricist, or a member of any school that can be designated by adherence to a verifiability criterion of meaning. As to "scientific procedure," Bentley said very clearly that science was description, and his transactional analysis was primarily an instrument of observation and a means of description. True, it may have rested upon some sort of "prescientific" personal or private "vision" of the universe, but he constantly urged the incompleteness and provisional nature of this descriptive technique.[116]

The misinterpretation seems to arise from attempting to fit Bentley into pre-established categories and to judge him by criteria of "science" that he did not accept. He considered himself scientific rather than speculative, but his understanding of experience, knowledge, thought, and science was not such as can be rendered

[114] This distinguishes Bentley from the theorists criticized by Reinhard Bendix, "Social Science and the Distrust of Reason," *University of California Publications in Sociology and Social Institutions*, I (1951), especially Chap. 3.

[115] Crick, 124.

[116] See, for example, Michael Polanyi's argument concerning the private, fiduciary element in thought and knowledge, *The Study of Man* (Chicago: University of Chicago Press, 1958), and the more detailed presentation in *Personal Knowledge* (Chicago: University of Chicago Press, 1958).

by the mechanical application of general categories.[117] The question of interest here is less, as Bernard Crick would have it, "does Bentley's tool satisfy a criterion of science of my choosing?" than "did Bentley's tool accomplish what *he* demanded of it?" This, of course, does not preclude further argument about the adequacy of Bentley's conception of "science."

In the alternative cosmologies of continuity and discreteness suggested by Gillispie, we must conclude that Bentley's sympathies lay with the Stoics, not with the atomists; with continuum and geometry, the bucket of molasses instead of the pail of sand, and with measurement, not with counting or classification. Within the narrower confines of sociological theory and the process tradition, he preferred Wiese to Small, formal sociology to group-conflict theories. In the end, transactional analysis of the process of sociation paid the penalty of theories of continuity, the heritage of Heraclitus. Bentley gradually gave up energy, conflict, and the "active" aspect of activity for wider, more comprehensive statement, but, when he had achieved a measure of the latter, he could not reintroduce discreteness or object. He could stipulate that various perspectives were permissible, to be selected for purposes of the investigator, but he could not get the sense of solidity and constraint, of "structure," to come alive. Neither the "habit background," nor frequency of occurrence (for how could one recognize "recurrence"? as Strawson might have asked), nor "plasticity" could serve to introduce qualitative distinctions when they had been ruled out by the most fundamental postulations of the idea of process.

This judgment applies essentially to the success which transactional analysis enjoyed in the "behavioral" sectors, particularly

---

117 The same critic accused Bentley of a "naive view of physics"; seized upon a comment in *The Process of Government*, "my epistemological point of view is admittedly naive, as naive, I hope, as the point of view of the physical sciences"; and concluded somewhat ambiguously that "a naive man could scarcely make much of the methodological literature of modern physics." Crick, 126n. On the preceding page, he further defined the naive view of physics as "the analogy of interacting force and friction as applied to pressure groups, with human interests regarded as mechanical forces in society." Compare the remarks about Dowling's critique above.

the social. Perhaps transactional analysis was and is more viable in the physical and vital fields, but this measure of achievement would not have pleased Bentley, for he worked as a social scientist despite strong interest in and considerable knowledge of many other disciplines. Certainly he thought that, if transactional analysis had validity as a scientific technique in one field, it would have it in all. Arthur Bentley hoped that the transactional analysis of a process reality was capable of transcending dualism; he hoped to abolish boundedness and entities by dissolving all in a qualitatively uniform passage of activity which would be analyzable from a number of qualitatively equal perspectives.[118]

In this attempt he was not successful.

[118] Again, I have used a dualistic construction which might, as a suggestive phrase only, be altered to read: "transactional analysis is process with the stress on knowing; process is a transaction with the stress on the known."

V

Process and System

> The difficulties of communication with other workers
> form the most serious obstacle. Indeed I know not a
> single specialized word in the indicated regions of in-
> quiry upon which I can safely rely to convey to a hearer
> just what I say it stands for to me in the present
> undertaking.
> —Arthur F. Bentley

> "Do you still hear nothing?" the prophet went on.
> "Does not the sound of rushing and roaring arise from
> the depths?" Zarathustra was again silent and listened:
> then he heard a long, protracted cry, which the abysses
> threw from one to another, for none of them wanted
> to retain it, so evil did it sound.
> —Frederich Nietzsche

TENSIONS

AMERICAN POLITICAL SCIENCE AND SOCIOLOGY have accepted and
stressed secondary strains in Arthur Bentley's social thought. Political science has welcomed the notion of group analysis, but there
is almost no discussion in the literature of process per se. The situation in sociology has been somewhat more complex. Bentley's notion was one of a number of conceptions of process in that field,
but his was distinctive because it sought to transcend the dualism
of activity-relation that had developed during the first three decades
of the twentieth century. The central importance of Bentley is that
the evolution of his thought presents a microcosm of the larger
dualism which is as yet unresolved by social science theory.

Perception of this situation has been obscured by the transfer of
attention from the more philosophical level of process discussion
to the more empirical plane of group theory. The debate about the
adequacy of the group concept for political analysis has been tangential to my concern here and is primarily a means of illuminating
a more central issue. Nevertheless, the discussion of group theory

has often resulted in judgments which characterize the whole of Bentley's contribution, or at the very least include the idea of process in an indiscriminate evaluation. In some instances this means that conclusions have been drawn at a philosophical level from premises located on the empirical plane.

For example, a recent essay asserts that Bentley's "cosmology" implies a science of politics which "ended in a science of control within a closed system."[1] Transactional analysis of group conflict, it concludes, cannot accommodate alteration in the parameters of the system. Transactional theory is contrasted to that of the "socialist sector of the world," which assertedly seeks to replace the rule of conflict with the principle of cooperation. I have commented earlier on the interpretation of Bentley as an exponent of the sociology of knowledge, and the conclusion that Bentley accepted some sort of closed system is something of a corollary. My own examination of transactional analysis leads to the opposite conclusion. Ludwig von Bertalanffy, a founder of general systems theory, has remarked that "in philosophy . . . the trend toward 'transactional' as opposed to 'self-actional' and 'interactional' viewpoints closely corresponds to the open-system model (Bentley)."[2]

Although I believe the interpretation of Bentley as a "closed-system" theorist to be fundamentally mistaken, the opposition it suggests between socialism and equilibrium analysis is interesting and important. The concept of process was largely ignored by American political scientists in favor of group theory; American sociologists, however, although they did not follow the direction of Bentley's later theory, did find significance in the idea of process. Process has functioned on somewhat different levels than has "group"; it has served as a more microscopic concept, in the sense of a process of interaction "within" the group, and as a more general milieu in which the group itself "functions." In terms of American political science it is the latter, more general use that has been historically dominant, though quite recent interest in psychology may be altering that judgment.

[1] Hale, 961.
[2] Bertalanffy, "General System Theory," in *Life, Language, Law*, ed. Taylor, 64.

Political scientists found Bentley's group concept a liberation from a barren formalism and a welcome exhortation to dirty their hands in empirical research, but, when they became concerned with the lack of a framework with which to order the mass of accumulated empirical data, they turned to their theoretically more sophisticated cousins in sociology and anthropology. The theoretical framework which they found and adopted can be given various names, but for the time being I will designate it as "equilibrium theory." This theory or outlook is today the dominant heir of the idea of process, but its contemporary form is not at all what Bentley's transactional analysis sought. Indeed, it would be inimical to Bentley in several important respects. Not only are the forms of equilibrium theory in political science and sociology hostile to Bentley's idea of process, but they are inadequate to their task as he conceived it. Bentley's developed process analysis represented his refusal to accept the compromise and dualism which are the characteristics of contemporary equilibrium theory.

The most influential single school of equilibrium theory has certainly been that represented by Talcott Parsons, Robert Merton, and Marion Levy, variously called "functionalism" and "structural-functional analysis."[3] An indication of the pervasiveness of this type of theory is given by the comment of the anonymous sociologist quoted by Theodore Caplow and Reece J. McGee: "In that generation, the Davis-Merton generation, everyone is Parsonian."[4]

The roots of functionalism are deep, extending most immediately into the soil of social anthropology in which the most prominent names are probably A. R. Radcliffe-Brown and Bronislaw Malinowski.[5] Parsons himself has recently begun to apply his con-

[3] Among the most important statements are: Talcott Parsons, *The Social System* (Glencoe, Ill.: Free Press, 1951); Parsons and Edward Shils, *Toward a General Theory of Action* (Cambridge, Mass.: Harvard University Press, 1959); Merton; and Levy.

[4] Theodore Caplow and Reece J. McGee, *The Academic Marketplace* (New York: Science Editions, 1961), 90.

[5] Radcliffe-Brown, "On the Concept of Function in Social Science," *American Anthropologist*, n.s., XXXVII (July–September, 1935); Radcliffe-Brown, *A Natural Science of Society* (Glencoe, Ill.: Free Press, 1957); Radcliffe-Brown, *The Andaman Islanders* (Glencoe, Ill.: Free Press, 1948); Malinowski, "The Functional Analysis of Culture," *A Scientific Theory of Culture* (New York: Oxford University Press,

ceptual apparatus to specifically political matters, but political scientists themselves have made the most important attempts to bring such constructs to bear on empirical research.[6] Gabriel Almond is among the most prominent advocates of a functionalist approach to politics; his introduction to the widely used textbook which he edited jointly with James Coleman, *The Politics of the Developing Areas*, makes explicit reference to its use of the Weber-Parsons schema.[7] A few years earlier Almond had described the terms of his method of analysis as having "emerged out of the Weber-Parsons tradition in social theory."[8] David Easton has suggested a similar approach to comparative analysis.[9] Morton Kaplan's *System and Process in International Relations* leans heavily upon concepts of structure and equilibrium,[10] but perhaps the most consistently functionalist view of comparative social science theory was taken by the authors of "The Functional Prerequisites of a Society."[11]

Much of the impetus toward adoption of a functionalist or similar

1960). See Merton for an excellent summary of the origins and development of functionalism; Parsons, "Durkheim's Contribution to the Theory of Integration of Social Systems," and Albert Pierce, "Durkheim and Functionalism," in *Emile Durkheim: 1858–1917*, ed. Kurt Wolff (Columbus: Ohio State University Press, 1960).

6 See, in particular, two essays by Parsons, "Some Highlights of the General Theory in Action," in *Approaches to the Study of Politics*, ed. Roland Young (Evanston, Ill.: Northwestern University Press, 1958), and " 'Voting' and the Equilibrium of the American Political System," in *American Voting Behavior*, ed. Eugene Burdick and Arthur Brodbeck (Glencoe, Ill.: Free Press, 1959). It is interesting to compare Parsons's prose in these essays with his analysis of the radical right in which the categories of the theory of action do not appear, in "Social Strains in America," *The Radical Right*, ed. Daniel Bell (Garden City, N.Y.: Doubleday, 1963). Parsons seems to me to write much more significantly about politics when he is free of the necessity of fitting his materials into systematic categories.

7 (Princeton: Princeton University Press, 1960). See also his "Interest Groups and the Political Process," *Comparative Politics*, ed. Roy C. Macridis and Bernard Brown (Homewood, Ill.: Dorsey, 1961).

8 Gabriel Almond, "Comparative Political Systems," in Eulau et al., 34.

9 Easton, "The Analysis of Political Systems," in Macridis and Brown.

10 (New York: Wiley, 1957). "Process," however, is simply taken as a basic term and not analyzed.

11 D. F. Aberle, A. K. Cohen, A. K. Davis, M. J. Levy, and F. X. Sutton, in Macridis and Brown. See also Levy's "Some Aspects of the 'Structural-Functional' Analysis and Political Science" in *Approaches*, ed. Young.

form of equilibrium has stemmed from dissatisfaction with the country-by-country approach to comparative politics. This traditional method of study was condemned by a recent Northwestern University conference as essentially "noncomparative," "descriptive," "parochial," "static," and "monographic."[12] An improved science would presumably provide the investigator with categories which could isolate variables, for example, "elites," from total political systems and enable him to compare them on some as yet undeveloped scale. The functionalist approach has been attractive in this area, in part because of its "neutral" (i.e., not parochial to Western political experience) terms, and in part because it promised a framework capable of sustaining a "general" theory of politics. Functional theory has thus far been applied more vigorously and with greater success to the developing areas (those we formerly called the "underdeveloped" areas) than to the more sophisticated systems of the West. This would be expected, if we accept the argument of some of functionalism's critics, who maintain that it cannot be successfully applied to complex systems. Functionalists, of course, do not agree. Merton has analyzed the American political machine in functional terms,[13] and Almond certainly believes his framework is applicable to the United States.

The men I have been discussing thus far are more or less sophisticated exponents of functionalism; they have consciously adopted it, are familiar with the basic texts, and have made some changes in the theory to accommodate their particular interests. They are to be distinguished from "group theorists" such as Earl Latham and David Truman, for, even though they employ the group unit on occasion, it does not play a major analytic role in their constructions. Almond, for example, prefers the Parsonian concept of role as the basic unit of the political system. "The advantage of the concept of role as compared with such terms as *institutions, organizations,* or *groups* is that it is a more inclusive, and more open

12 Roy C. Macridis, *The Study of Comparative Government* (Garden City, N.Y.: Doubleday, 1955).
13 Merton, 71–82.

concept."[14] There are important differences between the "schools" that must not be minimized, but there is also an important similarity.

The functionalists, perhaps because they have more consciously adopted a system, are relatively sophisticated and aware of their methodology. The tradition of group study was conspicuously less sophisticated until the early 1950s. Since then group theorists have begun to feel the need for a more general theory of groups in society. David Easton has documented the birth and evolution of American political scientists' determination to build "factual inventories."[15] A number of factors, intellectual and social, converged in the immediate post–Civil War period to turn attention away from speculative theory toward the accumulation of monographic studies describing "the way in which people act politically together with the determinants of this activity."[16] We are now familiar with the difficulties of this simple empiricism. Without a general orienting theory the monographs lacked comparability and were not, as a consequence, cumulative. In the absence of agreement on units of analysis and parameters of the field, it proved difficult to make any statements about the political realm as a whole. For students of interest groups the notion of equilibrium, in a more or less articulated form, lay ready at hand. Bentley had mentioned equilibrium in *The Process of Government*, but in a loose, almost analogical way. Interest groups, through their exercise of "pressure," press upon each other and upon the "government," producing a certain "adjustment." Bentley spoke most directly about equilibrium when he discussed his conceptualization of the formal instruments of political society, "government" and "law."[17]

Beyond this highly impressionistic statement, equilibrium theory as employed by the group theorists becomes diffuse and entangled

[14] Almond, "Comparative Political Systems," 35.
[15] Easton, *Political System*, especially Chaps. 2 and 3.
[16] *Ibid.*, 66.
[17] See Bentley, *Process of Government*, Chaps. X and XI, especially pp. 260 and 274.

187

with a number of other ideas. For example, it is sometimes maintained that the formal apparatus of government (in the narrow sense of the term "government") is an essentially passive agent, simply recording or "ratifying" the victory of one coalition over another. Earl Latham, on the other hand, argues that the legislature is not an "inert cash register" nor a "mindless balance pointing and marking the weight and distribution of power among the contending groups."[18] When equilibrium is viewed from this perspective, it becomes closely involved with the problem of the public interest, as Glendon Schubert's essay demonstrates.[19] The question is this: Are the formal agencies of government nothing more than Latham's inert register on which periodic gains and losses are "rung up," or do political rulers themselves introduce demands and policies apart from, perhaps in conflict with, those of dominant coalitions? The convergence of the two concepts occurs through inquiry into the origin of the imperatives that constitute public policy. Both empirical or descriptive and normative questions then arise.

Another convergence of more direct interest here is that of equilibrium theory and functional theory. This comes about through the mutual adoption of the notion of "systems" which are analyzed in terms of "input" demands and "outputs," or public policy. Easton offered this simple diagram, which illustrates the basic characteristics of "input-output analysis":

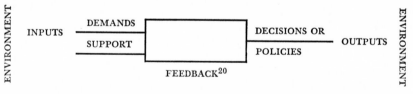

Gabriel Almond's work represents this convergence between a modified functionalism and a form of input-output equilibrium

[18] Latham, "The Group Basis of Politics," 391.

[19] Schubert, *The Public Interest* (Glencoe, Ill.: Free Press, 1960), especially Chap. 4.

[20] Macridis and Brown, 83. A more detailed discussion will be found in Easton, *A Systems Analysis of Political Life* (New York: Wiley, 1965).

theory.[21] The key point of convergence between some forms of equilibrium theory and functionalism is the notion of system. Easton has correctly stressed its importance. "The equilibrium idea implies that the interrelated parts tend to cohere. This is the fundamental meaning of system."[22] System plays a dual role for Easton; it purports to be both a substantive vision of political action and an orienting construct for the understanding of politics. System, he contended, was intimately connected to both equilibrium and process. "Process," considered as a patterned interaction over time, goes on within a "system"; "equilibrium" is a judgment of "fact" about the state of both process and system. As a tool, system was an orienting principle, and as a substantive vision it was the "relatedness" of the interaction process, the *Sinnzusammenhang* of the German idealists.

When group theorists or, more properly, group researchers felt the need to talk about "societies of interacting groups," system was a natural concept to adopt, but their stress continued to be placed upon the components—the unit groups.[23] In contrast, more functionally oriented political scientists have inclined toward the system aspect of equilibrium. Almond's preference for the "role" concept is an example, for, while a study of group conflict may very well conclude with a generalized statement about "readjustments" or "realignments" of the system's equilibrium, a theory which makes role its fundamental unit cannot begin without reference to that of which a role is a "function." This is not to say that a role may not be, or become, dysfunctional. It is simply that, unlike the term "group," role requires some sense of purpose or wider relatedness.

[21] See also Avery Leiserson, *Administrative Regulation* (Chicago: University of Chicago Press, 1942), and Schubert, 186.

[22] Easton, *Political System*, 291. Almond and Coleman list the attributes of a system as "comprehensiveness," "interdependence," and the "existence of boundaries" (7). Morton Kaplan's definition is more elaborate, if not more informative: "A system of action is a set of variables so related, in contradistinction to its environment, that describable behavioral regularities characterize the internal relationships of the variables to each other and the external relationships of the set of individual variables to combinations of external variables" (4). For a critical view of Easton's use of these ideas, see my "Self, System and Significance."

[23] See, for example, Truman, *Governmental Process*, Chap. 2.

We need to understand it as a role in something. The idea of system, the "general theory," is more involved, more integrated in the conduct of research. This, of course, is precisely the goal sought by many empirical theorists. Talcott Parsons's 1949 presidential address to the American Sociological Society commented on the lack of integration of theory and research:

> But *probably the most crucial factor* has been precisely this lack of an adequate *working* theoretical tradition which is bred into the "bones" of empirical researchers themselves so that "instinctively" the problems they work on, the hypotheses they frame and test, are such that the results, positive or negative, will have *significance* for a sufficiently generalized and integrated body of knowledge so that the mutual implications of many empirical studies will *play directly into each other.*[24]

Easton's contention that if equilibrium is to serve as a general theory it must reduce the qualitative stuff of politics to quantitative units and the complaints about the "essentially non-comparative" nature of traditional study of comparative politics voiced by Macridis are variants of the demand that monographs "play directly into each other."[25]

[24] Parsons, *Essays*, 350. The address was given during the preparation of *Toward a General Theory of Action*, which extends this theme; see especially Part I. In the same address, Parsons used an analogy that strikingly illustrates his distance from Bentley: "In the early stages these 'islands' of theoretical implication may be scattered far apart on the sea of fact and so vaguely and generally seen that only relatively broad empirical statements are directly relevant to them. . . . But with refinement of general theoretical analysis, and the accumulation of empirical evidence directly relevant to it, the islands get closer together, and their topography bcomes more sharply defined. It becomes more and more difficult and unnecessary to navigate in the uncharted waters of unanalyzed fact without bumping into or at least orienting to several of them" (353–54).

For Bentley, the islands and continents disappear; for Parsons, they multiply and converge.

[25] Compare Easton's conception of the nature of a theoretical system: "It consists, first, of a set of concepts corresponding to the important political variables and second, of statements about the relations among these concepts. Systematic theory corresponds at the level of thought to the concrete empirical political system of daily life" (*Political System*, 98). See also Robert Merton's essays, "The Bearing of Sociological Theory on Empirical Research" and "The Bearing of Empirical Research on Sociological Theory," in *Social Theory*.

Here again is the familiar dichotomy or dualism. The group theorists who found their way to a vague statement of equilibrium remain in the Gumplowicz-Ratzenhofer tradition, while the functionalists incline toward the more formalist, relational sociology of Weber and Simmel. Almond seemed on the verge of recognizing this tension when he wrote:

> The term *system* satisfies the need for an inclusive concept which covers all of the patterned actions relevant to the making of political decisions. Most political scientists use the term *political process* for these purposes. The difficulty with the term *process* is that it means any pattern of action through time. In contrast to process the concept of system implies a *totality* of relevant units, an interdependence between the interactions of units, and a certain stability in the interaction of these units (perhaps best described as a changing equilibrium).[26]

Almond's belief that the difficulty with process is its reference to "any pattern of action through time" is certainly correct, in perhaps a more profound sense than he knew. This is what Easton meant by the need for orienting concepts to isolate certain variables from the flux, a procedure which entailed a certain artificiality.

> This artificiality is imposed upon political scientists by the need for simplification of their data. Since everything is related to everything else, the task of pursuing the determinants of any given relation would be so vast and ramifying that it would defy any tools of investigation available either to the social or physical sciences.[27]

Parsons speaks continually of "boundaries" and their "maintenance."[28] An "economy," for example, is defined in terms of its functional imperatives, the institutional patterns in the larger society especially relevant to regulation of economic activity, and the "adaptive exigencies" of the general society.[29] Parsons's essay, written in 1958, contains an input-output chart which suggests com-

---

[26] Almond, "Comparative Political Systems," 34–35.
[27] Easton, *Political System*, 97.
[28] "General Theory in Action," 296–99.
[29] *Ibid.*, 296.

parisons between the economy and the polity, but the 1951 edition of *Toward a General Theory of Action* had reservations about this relationship. The concluding "Note" to "A General Statement" suggests that political science, unlike economics, has been unable to orient itself around a few fundamental variables, and

> if the empirical focus of political science is to remain on the phenomena of government, it will not as a discipline be able to attain a sharpness of theoretical focus comparable to that of economics. It is more likely to draw from a much wider range of the components of the general theory of action and to find its distinctiveness in the way it combines these components in relation to its special empirical interests, rather than in the technical elaboration of a narrow and sharply focused segment of the theory of action, as is the case with economics.[30]

I do not know whether Parsons has changed his mind about the futures of political science and economics, but in the 1958 paper, and in a recent address, he seems to have decided that power can serve as a conceptual unit in political science, parallel in some way to value in economics. If such a unit could be made operational (and neither Parsons nor anyone else has yet managed this), then Easton's demand for quantitative units in general equilibrium theory might be close to satisfaction. We do not now have such a unit in political science, nor do we have anything like a consensus upon the closely related problem of the "scope of the field" (the boundaries of the political system).

Before turning to a comparison of Bentley's process analysis with various forms of equilibrium theory, we should return for a moment to Almond's juxtaposition of system and process. Almond may have suggested more than he intended, but he is not the only contemporary political scientist to recognize an uncomfortable tension. Richard Snyder, perhaps the foremost exponent of the "decision-making" procedure in political analysis, has offered a tentative distinction between "static" and "dynamic" modes:

> Relatively speaking, dynamic analysis is *process* analysis. By process

[30] Parsons and Shils, 29.

is meant here, briefly, *time* plus *change*—change in relationships and conditions. Process analysis concerns a *sequence of events,* i.e., behavioral events. In general, static analysis is a snapshot at one point in time. One basic difference between the two types is in the way (or ways) the time factor is handled. An important brand of static analysis (namely structural-functional analysis) can yield information on the nature of change between two periods in time and on the conditions under which change took place but not on the reasons for change or how it actually unfolded.[31]

Snyder thought that descriptive studies of formal institutions, what he called "head counting" (voting or opinion research?), and equilibrium analysis were other examples of static method. It is difficult to specify what social scientists mean by "equilibrium," beyond the level of an umbrella concept as I use it here. It is not helpful to hold that a system is at equilibrium at any point in time, provided only that a population has not been physically devastated. It seems equally implausible to specify an equilibrium deemed somehow "proper" to a particular society, and in any event we do not even know the parameters in which to think about such a question. Some sociologists and political scientists follow Parsons and speak of a "moving equilibrium"—presumably a dynamic adjustment of demands and satisfactions. Parsons himself goes further and specifies "equilibrating tendencies" at work in societal subsystems. If the concept is used in such a fashion, one in which "system" is so emphatically subordinated to "tendencies," it should not be considered static, but in that case it has virtually become Bentley's process.

The most interesting part of Snyder's account is the division he made within process or dynamic analysis itself.

In turn, there are two kinds of process analysis: *interaction* and *decision-making.* So far as I can see, there are only two ways of scientifically studying process in the sense employed here: the making and executing of decisions and the patterns of interaction between individuals, states, organizations, groups, jurisdictions, and so on. Interaction analysis does not and cannot yield answers to

[31] "A Decision-Making Approach," in *Approaches,* ed. Young, 10–11.

"why" questions. Thus interactions can be described and measured but the explanation of the patterns—why they evolved as they did—must rest on decision-making analysis.[32]

Let us for the moment lay aside functionalism and equilibrium theory (although in doing so we must not forget that the Easton-Almond conception links process and equilibrium), and look only at Snyder's two kinds of process analysis. There is striking similarity between the "patterns of interaction" and Wiese's action *patterns*, Giddings's form patterns, Eubank's analytic process, and Hayes's relationships; and between "decision-making" analyses and Wiese's *action* patterns, Giddings's action patterns, Eubank's evolutionary process, and Hayes's activities. Snyder's distinction suggests some form of description-explanation dichotomy and is reminiscent of the Wiese-Becker position that processes result in relations.

Snyder's consignment of functionalism and equilibrium to the static category is based on their presumed inability to accommodate a time dimension, or history. Although he does not for that reason reject them, other critics of functionalism have done so. Lewis Coser wrote:

> A persistent theme runs through almost all of the writings of Talcott Parsons: concern with those elements in social structures that assure their maintenance. Although interest in the process of social change is occasionally present in Parsons, such concern is distinctly marginal. It may be said that all of Parsons' work, beginning with *The Structure of Social Action*, is an extended commentary on the Hobbesian question: How is social order possible?[33]

Coser links this concern for order to a systemic bias which appears in Parsons's view of conflict and dysfunction as strain and sickness.[34] This results in an ideological commitment to existing structures, which Coser believes extends to the work of George Lundberg,

[32] *Ibid.*, 11.

[33] Coser, *Functions of Social Conflict*, 21.

[34] *Ibid.*, 22–23. Compare Coser's remarks about Parsons's medical analogies with Renford Bambrough's article, "Plato's Political Analogies," *Philosophy, Politics and Society*, ed. Peter Laslett (New York: Macmillan, 1956).

Lloyd Warner, Elton Mayo and F. J. Roethlisberger, and Kurt Lewin.

Ralf Dahrendorf is another contemporary who has been disturbed by the treatment of change and process in much of sociological theory. He credits Parsons with a realization of the need to conceptualize change and process, but he argues that the attempt to build dynamic or variable elements into a structure necessarily subordinates "function." Dahrendorf's conclusion merits quotation at length.

> Parts of a structure have a function in relation to this structure as a whole. In this sense the category is certainly important. However, it is not "all-important": it is rather the first requisite of a dynamic analysis of structure to find variables which are not subordinated to the category of structure (and are in this sense "within the system") but which operate as forces or factors changing the structure. That Parsons, and with him many other recent "theorists," have overlooked this fact may be due to a more or less deliberate identification of organic and social structures or "systems." For this is the most difficult problem of the analysis of structural change: by contrast to organic structures, the "dynamically variable elements" which influence the construction of social structures do not necessarily originate outside the "system" but may be generated by the structure itself. There are, in other words, within social structures certain elements or forces which are at the same time their constituent parts (and therefore "function" within them) and impulses operating toward their supersedence and change.[35]

The suggestion of a dialectic method is unmistakable. In the more philosophical terms of an earlier discussion, we might say Dahrendorf is reminding us that identity is complex, not simple. Processes, for Parsons, need not imply change—that is, they may be processes of maintenance—and he is thus led to a formulation not unlike Whitehead's:

> According to Parsons, we must distinguish between two types

---

[35] Ralf Dahrendorf, *Class and Class Conflict in Industrial Societies* (Stanford: Stanford University Press, 1959), 123. Chap. IV contains a more generalized discussion of the problem of change; it is among the best in the literature.

of change: change that goes on within the system and changes of the system. Changes within the system are termed as "processes," centering about the notion of equilibrium and system maintenance. These processes are concerned with the motivation of members or socialization, and deviance or its control: namely, processes of social control.[36]

Dahrendorf is more sympathetic to functionalism (in his terms, the stress is laid on the "structural" component of the theory) than is Coser, in that he considers a theory of structure a preliminary step toward conceptualization of structural change. Barrington Moore, in two essays highly critical of contemporary trends in social theory, has put the case for historical theory in sharp opposition to systematic theory. In comparing the "strategies" of nineteenth-century sociology to those of current theory, Moore lists these differences:

> First of all, the critical spirit has all but disappeared. Second, modern sociology, and perhaps to a lesser extent also modern political science, economics, and psychology are ahistorical. Third, modern social science tends to be abstract and formal. In research, social science today displays considerable technical virtuosity. But this virtuosity has been gained at the expense of content. Modern sociology has less to say about society than it did fifty years ago.[37]

He contends that a tradition of "abstract formalism" is apparent in Max Weber's later work, and that this trend was also carried forward by Simmel and Wiese. The second point, that social science has abandoned the temporal dimension, is linked to a conception of events as isolated atoms which may be "aggregated" in statistical operations. This, Moore argues, ignores the continuity of history.

The "abstract and formal" character of contemporary theory, its "substanceless" nature, stems from precisely the desire for "true" comparability found in Roy Macridis's criticism of comparative political science. This occurs because the generalized categories cannot accommodate the richness of the material they are to order,

[36] William C. Mitchell, *Sociological Analysis and Politics: The Theories of Talcott Parsons* (Englewood Cliffs, N.J.: Prentice-Hall, 1967), 148.

[37] Moore, "Strategy in Social Science," in *Political Power*, 123.

and hence they must be framed in the most general terms at the most abstract level.[38] The result is a "formalist deductive tradition in search of laws" because of its disregard for what the German schools called the *Einmaligkeit* of social situations. The static bias enters at this point. "Closely related to the preceding difficulties are those derived from the importation of equilibrium theory into social science, which may also produce a static bias. In equilibrium theory the key assumption is that any social system tends toward a state of rest in which the conflicts and strains among its component parts are reduced to a minimum."[39] Moore's complaint here is that the shift described by Earle Eubank, from evolutionary to analytic versions of process analysis (with Park and Burgess's adoption of Simmel's forms), occurred at all. The loss of a sense of the material, and of its connectedness, is the result. It is difficult to know to what extent Snyder's version of decision-making study could meet the objections raised by Coser, Dahrendorf, and Moore. Snyder's division between process and static analysis seems overelaborate in that his "interaction patterns," the second mode of process analysis, do not seem to possess much "dynamism" insofar as, by his admission, they do not answer causal questions. Indeed, the sociologists examined in this book have inclined toward viewing the patterned aspect of interaction as static and thus have placed it within what Snyder defined as static analysis—namely, functionalism and equilibrium theory. (This is not, of course, to say that interaction patterns cannot change: into some other pattern, or no pattern at all.) For purposes of simplicity, we can proceed with the two categories of process theory and static or equilibrium theory. In this context, we would be dealing only with decision-making as Snyder's dynamic alternative. His desire to incorporate time, the "why" factor of explanation, would earn him the applause of formalism's critics, but his use of the Parsonian frame—"actor (or actors), goals, means, and situation"—would probably fall under Moore's indictment as "abstract formalism." Still, Snyder seems clearer about these issues

---

[38] This critique is applied more specifically in "The New Scholasticism and the Study of Politics," in *ibid.*

[39] "Strategy in Social Science," 137.

than are most of his colleagues who use or imagine they use equilibrium theory.

There is a final criticism of function and equilibrium concepts that should be mentioned—namely, that they contain an implicit conservative bias. This is expressed in Moore's regret at the demise of the "critical spirit." Taken in context with formalism (lack of substance) and lack of interest in history, it means that contemporary social scientists have abandoned their role as social critics and have written to celebrate the status quo. Alvin Gouldner has made an analogous argument in which he divides sociologists into those who conceive it as a "profession" (and value neutral) and those who imagine themselves and their colleagues as a "learned society" with all the critical responsibilities of the intellectual toward improving his world.[40] There appears to be a tendency on the part of the former toward systematic study, and of the latter toward a more Marxian orientation.[41] In political science, Henry Kariel has voiced a similar criticism of what he considers a retreat from criticism and an endorsement of naked power politics.

To know America is to know it as a community within which those who care will struggle fraternally for public power. To have knowledge of America's political process is coincidentally to have knowl-

[40] "Anti-Minotaur: The Myth of a Value Free Sociology," *Sociology on Trial*, ed. Maurice Stein and Arthur Vidich (Englewood Cliffs, N.J.: Prentice-Hall, 1963).

[41] A related but by no means identical division within sociology should be mentioned, though it is tangential to our interest here. It is represented by the work of C. Wright Mills, especially his criticism of the lack of social awareness and relevancy in contemporary sociology, and by those persons identified with the "end of ideology," as presented by Daniel Bell in the volume of that name. The latter group is associated with the Congress for Cultural Freedom, publishers of the British monthly *Encounter*, and includes: S. M. Lipset—see "A Personal Postscript," *Political Man* (Garden City, N.Y.: Doubleday, 1960)—Edward Shils, and Raymond Aron. To my knowledge, the phrase "end of ideology" was originated by Shils in 1955.

Mills's position has been espoused by the younger sociologists (notably Maurice Stein), intellectuals of the "New Left," and the magazine *Studies on the Left*. The issue is clearly joined in Mills's "The New Left," in his *Power, Politics and People* (New York: Oxford University Press, 1964); and in the essay by Stephen Rousseas and James Farganis in Irving Horowitz (ed.), *The New Sociology: Essays in Social Science and Social Theory in Honor of C. Wright Mills* (New York: Oxford University Press, 1964). One has the feeling that the full impact of Mills's influence is yet to be felt.

edge of America's substantive goals as well. What had once been dealt with by an inexact political philosophy concerned with eliciting, juxtaposing, and sifting common opinions—a philosophy aspiring to discriminate between right and wrong conduct—is to become an amoral, natural science of human behavior.[42]

Kariel also finds that the new goal of social research is "to identify the social structure and determine what is functional in it," and to "restore upset balances, resolve conflicts, heal sore spots, facilitate assimilation, and, most important, remove the innumerable blocks to understanding."[43] He approves Robert Nisbet's conclusion that "the social group has replaced the individual as the key concept in a great deal of social science writing, and it is almost as apt to observe that social *order* has replaced social change as the key problem."[44] Nisbet specifically identified functionalism as part of the "conservative revolt." Much of Kariel's criticism of American political science affirms Bernard Crick's indictment in *The American Science of Politics*.[45] Myron Hale's juxtaposition of a conservative functionalism built on a closed system and a comparatively "open" socialism emphasizing "cooperation" might also be included. One could further expand the list of indictments by adding Herbert Storing's volume, which is hostile to virtually the entire empirical movement in political science.[46] The dissenters are numerous and vocal, though scarcely in agreement on the proper therapy.

In reply, Robert Merton has forcefully argued that functionalism need not bear a conservative bias, and one can certainly sympathize with the impatience of Talcott Parsons and his allies, who have become a bit shrill in answering so persistent and sometimes uninformed a charge. Despite this reaction, I am inclined to side with the critics on this point and to concur with Moore's remark that

42 Kariel, 133.

43 *Ibid.*, 116.

44 Nisbet, *The Quest for Community* (New York: Oxford University Press, 1953), 28.

45 See above, pp. 11n. and 85.

46 Herbert Storing (ed.), *Essays on the Scientific Study of Politics* (New York: Holt, Rinehart and Winston, 1962).

"the bias is in the air more than in the print."[47] Functionalists would be right to feel dissatisfied with so casual a judgment, but I will note—less in the hope of proving the point than to indicate that the feeling in the air has some substantiality—Merton's argument that functionalism can escape an alliance with the status quo if it denies the "postulate of indispensability," that is, if it holds that there are functional equivalents, alternatives, or substitutes for some particular *existential* institution or cultural form.[48] Functionalism, he concludes, does not need to maintain that any given arrangement of concrete parts is inviolate. This seems reasonable, but it has a corollary that is somewhat disturbing. Merton's application of the theory in his stimulating discussion of the American political machine stresses the unanticipated consequences which followed its demise, and he warns of the needs left unfulfilled by the formal instrumentalities of the political and constitutional systems. His conclusion is striking: "To seek social change, without due recognition of the manifest and latent functions performed by the social organization undergoing change, is to indulge in social ritual rather than social engineering . . . in the deliberate enactment of social change, they [manifest and latent functions] can be ignored only at the price of considerably heightening the risk of failure."[49] The ideas of latent and multiple functions are the crux of this passage, but the hook in the argument is the question, "what constitutes 'due recognition'?" The problem is that often we simply cannot know the infinite ramifications of an action before it is taken, nor can we entirely ignore the specter of the self-fulfilling prophecy. We may well be cautious about inducing change, but the admonition to look beyond and at the "underside" of all proposed actions sounds very much like Edmund Burke.[50] Ironically, because Merton rejects the postulate of indispensability but retains the notion of infinite interconnection, he must postpone action

---

[47] Moore, "Strategy in Social Science," 137.

[48] Merton, "Manifest and Latent Functions," 37 and 32–35.

[49] *Ibid.*, 81.

[50] Compare also Karl Popper's argument for "piecemeal" social engineering in *The Poverty of Historicism.*

presumably until he has exhaustively examined the possibilities and complexities, and when that task is completed the system will have changed. Is this not the classical conservative dilemma?

ALTERNATIVES

Bentley's transactional analysis was intended as a different kind of procedure, and there are important lines of divergence in historical perspective. It will be convenient to return to Easton's remarks on Bentley and equilibrium, but first a quotation from Nathan Hakman seems relevant:

> The fact of the matter is that any model which involves some sort of equilibrium-disequilibrium analysis is incompatible with the other philosophical postulates in the transactional schema. The transactional schema requires freedom from the acceptance of any given relationship established before inquiry begins. Equilibrium analysis, however, is usually conducted within the framework of a set of postulations which posit a determined system as a point of departure.[51]

As Easton points out, Bentley talked about balance, adjustment, and equilibrating tendencies that went on among the lower-lying groups in society. And Bentley did not provide much of a suggestion about the nature of politics, preferring to speak casually about "narrow," "broad," and "intermediate" senses of the word "government."[52] He thought that political groups, more "highly differentiated" and thus presumably more visible, were more accessible to study than those operating at "deeper" social levels.[53] But precisely because he spoke of tendencies toward equilibrium, and because he declined to set any limits or definite boundaries to "the political," the notion of system is inappropriate to *The Process of Government.*

Bentley's writing in that volume is deceptive on this point, as it was on the subject of the group as an analytic unit. He consistently yielded to the temptation to suggest examples of the kind of analysis

---

51 Hakman, 42.
52 Bentley, *Process of Government*, 260–63.
53 *Ibid.*, 209.

he had in mind, always adding that the actual work cited was preliminary or in need of changes here and there, but with the optimistic implication that some people were on the right track. An early example was the appendix to *The Process of Government,* which Bentley included as a modest attempt on his own part to get at the raw material of politics. It describes his early studies of municipal elections and roll-call analyses of the Illinois legislature and the Chicago city council. The trouble with this lies not in the crudity of the measures but in the fact that Bentley's vision of adequate social theory required a tool that had not yet been created, and these preliminary examples hopelessly compromised the demands and hopes of the text. The appendices to *Relativity in Man and Society* abound with additional examples. It would seem to a casual reader that a massive convergence toward Bentley's recommendations was well under way in the social and the physical sciences. One example must suffice. Bentley warmly endorsed Wiese's work as quite close to what he had in mind, but he then proceeded to suggest a "minor" improvement—abolition of the distinction between personal-instinctual and social-external realms —which would have completely transformed the formal nature of Wiese's sociology. Becker's complaint that Bentley's work lacked an "Archimedean point" indicates either a more profound understanding of Wiese or less interest in effecting a theoretical revolution.

One wonders why Bentley, otherwise so analytically discriminating, should consistently mislead his readers by offering incomplete and partial illustrations of his vision, when they could only weaken the "confirmed landsman's" resolve to leave the islands and the continents altogether. I think there were three reasons. First, the very depth of his criticism combined with his vision to produce a deep hiatus between existing social theory and the minimum requirements of adequacy. Bentley may have felt the need to offer examples, even partial and incomplete ones, as guidelines to those who must do research in the absence of refined tools. Second, he did, in fact, have a conviction of a vast theoretical convergence, and in the face of the revolutions in twentieth-century science the divergent and contradictory currents appeared trivial and temporary. Finally, and this is particularly applicable to the 1908 appendix, Bentley simply did not foresee the divergence between a developed transactional analysis and the examples of empirical study he had offered.

Easton noted Bentley's disinclination to apply "his equilibrium framework to the details of political research," and his conclusion that American political scientists have not pressed beyond this point to inquire into the need for a general conceptual framework seems correct.[54] What Easton does not mention is that the process analysis which emerged from the later Bentley was not in harmony with the idea of a bounded system. We have already seen how the units of political analysis dissolve in transaction and the apparently insurmountable difficulty of reintroducing entities or object-in-environment. Ironically, it is Easton himself who has argued for the intimate connection between analytic units and the idea of system, and for the necessity that these units be quantitative. Bentley's difficulties arose because a rigorously quantitative description precluded the segmentation requisite to system. On this point Kariel has been one of the more perceptive commentators.

> There is always an impinging environment. The specific organization, it becomes evident, must be seen in a progressively broader context. For those few whose vision penetrates all boundaries, there is finally nothing but an undifferentiated whole, the wonderful unity of nineteenth century German idealism and romanticism. The plurality of previously esteemed parts fades entirely. No valid theory can reveal their distinctiveness, and it becomes unnecessary to consider the possibility of conflict between them.[55]

German thought was not quite so unified as this passage suggests, and the attempt to distinguish parts is not so much unnecessary as impossible, but Kariel's central point—the disappearance of distinctions into the "all togetherness of everything"—is perceptive and important. Easton insisted upon the indispensability of orienting concepts because the task of tracing undifferentiated interrela-

[54] Easton, *Political System*, 271.
[55] Kariel, 126.

tions "would defy any tools of investigation available either to the social or physical sciences";[56] what he does not seem to recognize was that Bentley's radical statement of "full description" was offered as a substitute for such tools.

Bentley's process analysis was thoroughly inductive; its mistrust of ghosts, originally those of the spirit or the soul, was no more willing to entertain concepts of actor, goals, or function (in the technical sense). A strong contemporary argument is that order or meaning is always imposed on the facts by application of analytic categories and that, "therefore, it is better to make these categories and hypotheses as explicit and logically watertight as possible at the outset of the inquiry, in order to force the data to yield a clear-cut decision in respect to the tenability of the theory."[57] Bentley did not accept this. The constant thrust of transactional analysis, and in particular of Bentley's writings, was toward tentative formulation, freedom and scope in hypothesis formulation, and the provisional nature of knowledge or, more properly, "knowing."[58] This is the truth in Bernard Crick's complaint that Bentley did not say much about how to be scientific, and it is one reason that *The Process of Government* is more often encountered in political-parties courses than in political-theory bibliographies.

There is the further question of whether, after uncountable transactional studies, Bentley would have entertained the idea of synthesizing the results into a system. I cannot offer a final answer, but, if he would have conceded the possibility, it would lie so far in the future and be created out of such radically new materials that we could not now envision its nature. Certainly he believed that his mission, and probably that of several succeeding generations, was and would be the sharpening of the tool. Bentley did talk about "function" and the constant need to relate one factor or event to

[56] Easton, *Political System*, 97.

[57] Moore, "The New Scholasticism," 97.

[58] Instructive in this regard is John Dewey's instrumental logic, which takes its departure from a problem, an irritation in experience. See F. S. C. Northrop, *The Logic of the Sciences and the Humanities* (New York: Meridian, 1959), especially Chaps. I–III, and Justus Buchler, *The Concept of Method* (New York: Columbia University Press, 1961), Chaps. X and XI.

others but the relations were relative to the inquiry which was always to be provisional and "open." The "process-content" distinction was of course a matter of stress and selection, and Bentley explicitly tells us it is not analogous to "form-content," or "process-product," or "function-structure."[59]

Relativity in Man and Society represented a crucial phase in Bentley's relation to the mainstream of American sociology and political science. "Formalism," in the sense of the descriptive study of institutions, had been successfully challenged, and the question had become, "what units of investigation can the new social science discover or create?" Group theorists had an answer, but, though many of them presented the idea of group as a concept, a "construct," their empirical work was usually done with existential, organized, "concrete" groups. The landmark studies invariably cited have described the Anti-Saloon League, the American Medical Association, the Farm Bureau Federation, and so on. In brief, these studies expanded the boundaries of the field beyond the specifically governmental sphere (Latham's groups possessing "officiality"), but they continued to work with actual social collectivities. In Dilthey's terms, they found the units of their science given in experience, even though these were now plurals instead of individuals. A more thoroughgoing attempt to restructure social science accepted historical and experiential flux but determined to construct a body of knowledge by abstract and formal categories. In one sense this second alternative can be traced to Max Weber's ideal-typical constructs. Parsons's theory of action would then appear as a lineal descendant (though individual action can take place in both their conceptions). Nathan Rotenstreich takes this view and concludes that Parsons's advance beyond Weber lay in his ability to conceptualize a social framework within which individual action takes place.[60]

59 Bentley, *Behavior Knowledge Fact*, 361.

60 Rotenstreich, 179. Mention should be made of contradictory interpretations of the Weber-Parsons relationship. Peter Blau contends that Parsons has exaggerated Weber's concern with structure, organization, and rationality. "[Weber] did not view social structure as a functionally unified *Gestalt* but as a complex pattern governed by opposing forces and hence in continued flux." "Critical Remarks

Bentley did not reject the study of formal groups, though he thought it insufficient. But, although he moves steadily toward the second alternative, toward the continuum, he refused to accept the introduction into the flux of the abstract categories of the functionalists. Bentley's revolution emancipated social science from bondage to formal institutions and their historical development, but political scientists betrayed his revolutionary agenda by reintroducing concrete entities discovered in the "social" sphere outside the traditional scope of political institutions. The functionalists betrayed him on opposite grounds; they established their units by systematically emptying their categories of precisely the content, the activity, that for Bentley was the sum of experience and of science. The idea of system is simply a further extension or "progression" of both betrayals.

Neither group theory's rather foggy notion of homeostasis nor the more rigorous efforts of functionalism, both branches of what I have loosely characterized as "equilibrium" theory, are compatible with Bentley's vision of full transactional analysis and the process universe. Bentley's efforts fell short of success in crucial regards. These are disheartening conclusions, because we have been concerned with mainstream theories; and, if the post-Bentleyan world has not been able to solve major theoretical difficulties, must we return to 1908 and try to get around Bentley's damaging criticism? This is not a reasonable expectation. The empirical revolution, including Bentley's contribution, has been too successful in discrediting its predecessors to imagine that a full-scale reopening of debate could win much support. The issue which emerges seems to be this: Is there a way to accept Bentley's critical position, and his vision of a process universe, without adopting the categories, the boundaries, and the system of the equilibrium idea?

Another and perhaps better formulation would be this: Can Bentley's destructive genius provide the basis of a new social science? There seem to be, at present, two possible paths which hold promise of retaining the idea of process without betraying it. The first of

on Weber's Theory of Authority," *American Political Science Review*, LVII (1963), 306. Blau prefers Reinhard Bendix's stress on the Hegelian elements in Weber's theory.

these rests upon the possibility of distinguishing between the ideas of "field" and "system." Dorothy Emmet's interesting book *Function, Purpose and Powers* (which is as yet insufficiently recognized by social scientists) makes the distinction on the basis of the relative "openness" of the two concepts.[61] Her analysis draws primarily upon social anthropologists, notably Meyer Fortes, E. E. Evans-Pritchard, and Radcliffe-Brown, although she is also aware of the work of Kurt Lewin. Fortes, inspired by Whitehead's natural philosophy, sought to define and express relationships without establishing a total system which could descriptively embrace the "society" and also serve as a universal framework of investigation.

> Pointing out that no *total* description of a society is in fact possible, he says that if a society is to be analyzed at all, it must be with reference to certain selected interests or institutional complexes. How people group themselves vis-à-vis others in these will yield a certain structure of social relations which can be called a "field."[62]

The "field," so understood, might serve as a mediating concept between the idea of society as simply an "aggregate," a "heap," and that of society as a total, structured system. As Miss Emmet remarks: "The appeal of the 'field' analogy lies in the fact that it suggests a range of interaction within a region which can be taken as wider or narrower according to the relations selected. It also allows us to think of a society as exhibiting a number of overlapping fields."[63] S. F. Nadel has presented a carefully constructed theory of social structure built upon various degrees of role abstractions, but he was wary of the pitfalls of reification and the difficulties of accounting for change in equilibrium theories. In answer to Raymond Firth's critique of the static bias of "structure" theories, Nadel argued:

[61] (London: St. Martin's, 1958), especially Chap. II.

[62] *Ibid.*, 32. This demand that a system framework be capable not only of describing a total society, but of serving as the ultimate orientation of political research, is well illustrated by David Easton's recent volumes: see *A Framework for Political Analysis* (Englewood Cliffs, N.J.: Prentice-Hall, 1965), and *A Systems Analysis of Political Life.*

[63] Emmet, 35n.

When we analyze social structure (the positions of actors relative to one another, the "network" of their relationships), we do use language suggestive of, and suitable for, static states, *as if* the positions were fixed and timeless, and the relationships simply continuous. But let us be clear that this is only "as-if" language. For we cannot but define social positions in terms of behavior sequences, which consume time and happen on a time scale; relationships cannot but be abstracted from successive, repetitive actions . . . which we collect together in such class concepts as subordination, reciprocity, respect, loyalty, rivalry, and the like. Time "enters" in all of these. If our descriptive categories do not refer to the time factor more explicitly, we yet imply it, much as we may say of two seaports that "they *are* linked by boat," meaning, of course, that boats move between them more or less regularly.[64]

Nadel carries the argument further than the field-system distinction, but in his terms it certainly seems possible to conceive of "constellations" of relationships which are constructed for purposes of particular investigations and do not pretend to embrace an entire social system. This kind of concept would satisfy Bentley's demand for flexibility; it would not incur the onus of postulating "boundaries" or the other difficulties of a total system approach. On the other hand, the very freedom of postulation achieved by the field idea militates against a demand for cumulative research. It is doubtful that Bentley would have approved Nadel's use of "role"as the basic unit, nor would he have approved the use of introspective means toward the specification and determination of role. Before "field" can be considered a genuine alternative to the equilibrium or system idea, we would have to know much more about its possibilities than we know today. Kurt Lewin's use of the idea seems more illustrative than theoretical, and to my knowledge there is no developed field theory in political science.[65] It is questionable to what

64 Nadel, *The Theory of Social Structure* (London: Cohen and West, 1957), 128. For Firth's argument see his *Elements of Social Organization* (London: Watts, 1951), 39–40. Nadel's analysis is, of course, opposed to Richard Snyder's contention that decision-making is dynamic while equilibrium and structural theory is not. See especially Chap. VI.

65 I am indebted to my former colleague Raymond Tanter for suggesting that a possible exception to this judgment is the field theory of international politics de-

degree "field" can serve as more than an analogical and illustrative instrument. There have been suggestions about field construction which border on the second alternative to contemporary theories of equilibrium: the idea of complementarity.

Miss Emmet's suggestion that the flexibility of the field construct permits the investigator to choose the focus as well as the subject matter of his study is the first step toward complementarity. Hubert Bonner takes a large second step when he distinguishes between "typological" and "dynamic" constructs in field theory; the former is the general science of spatial relations especially suited to part-whole analyses, and the latter is the general science of the motion of bodies, a science better able to depict social mobility. Typological concepts would include space, boundary, region, and barrier. Dynamic constructs might be field, vector, and fluidity. The central point is that the two do not share a universe of discourse, nor can the concepts be interchanged.[66] Bentley himself came close to the complementarity idea when he explained that "the distinction between 'process' and 'that which is processed' is one of selective observation; and our phenomena are functional as much in the one phase of selection as in the other."[67] "Habit," he added, must not be distinguished sharply from "process," and it certainly must not be viewed as a "product" or an "outcome" of process.[68] This distinguishes Bentley from those sociologists who have considered patterns to be "congealed" activity. Earle Eubank and Kimball Young expressed the complementarity idea, but they did not distinguish it from constructs in which both process and structure inhabit the same universe.

In a complementarity theory we may view the social universe as

veloped by Quincy Wright, *The Study of International Relations* (New York: Appleton-Century-Crofts, 1955), and its extension in the "attribute" and "behavioral" space dichotomy. See an unpublished paper by R. J. Rummel, "A Field Theory of Social Action with Application to Political Conflict within Nations," prepared for the Airlie Conference, Warrenton, Virginia, June 17–18, 1965, of the Special Operations Research Office, Project "Camelot."

[66] Bonner, 172–73.
[67] Bentley, *Behavior Knowledge Fact*, 361.
[68] *Ibid.*, 359.

process or as structure, dynamically or statically, but we cannot see both simultaneously. C. A. O. van Nieuwenhuijze's brilliant book *Society as Process* is to my knowledge the only effort to confront the problems of complementarity theory in social science. He presents the inadequacy of contemporary treatments of change in these words: "Whatever one could say about the logical relationship between 'change' and 'structure,' to expect that this conception of change, as a shift from one structure into another, could be an efficient tool of the intellect is little short of a miracle of imaginative power."[69] If, instead of concerning ourselves with the dualism of permanence and change as an existential problem and with attempting to find a logical link between the two categories, we focus on the logical link itself, we can make complementarity a sensible concept.[70]

> If, then, complementarity is chosen as the starting point of reasoning, one obtains a prospect of promising results in regard to the relationship between what is stable and what is not. They would feature as two ways of approaching reality, with a complementarity relationship between them: mutually exclusive in the strict logical sense, yet not effectively contradictory on account of the existential circumstance that man cannot conceive of reality in terms of stability and in terms of instability at once.[71]

Nieuwenhuijze uses some terms in a rather specialized manner that cannot be fully indicated here, but his remarks about Marion Levy's work are readily translatable.

> The structural approach should bring out static, formal, structural aspects of reality; it should center around such terms as equilibrium, in an attempt to postulate or vindicate the legitimacy of its inherent one-sidedness. The "process-wise" approach should be functional-analytic; it threatens to be confounded with the former. The temptation for either of them is to pass for the one encom-

---

69 (The Hague: Martinus-Nijhoff, 1962), 54. A stimulating book which treats complementarity ideas from a psychoanalytic orientation is George Devereux, *From Anxiety to Method in Behavioral Science* (The Hague: Mouton, 1967).

70 Nieuwenhuijze, 46–48.

71 *Ibid.*, 48.

passing approach to reality,—which neither of them can be. Between them, again, a complementarity relationship obtains. When applying one, one cannot hold on to the other.[72]

These brief remarks about field and complementarity concepts can only indicate alternative paths for contemporary social and political theory. I have been most concerned to show that equilibrium, functional, and system concepts are not compatible with Bentley's idea of process analysis. Nieuwenhuijze, too, finds a tension between process and system, and he concludes that current systematic theories do not adequately conceptualize change and permanence.[73] The case is made very convincingly. But, although both field and complementarity theory seem compatible with transactional analysis, Bentley himself probably preferred the former. Some formulations of field theory introduce complementarity at one point or another (though this would not appear to be necessary to all versions), but it is difficult to associate Bentley with the complementarity idea.[74]

Transactional analysis was to be the complete description of a process universe, and by "process" universe Bentley did mean to speak ontologically. The world was, in fact, in process, and the descriptive tool had to be shaped accordingly. He insisted upon the freedom of the investigator, but that freedom which permitted various stresses did not imply the constraint of having to choose between the perspectives of change or permanence. The reconstruction of thought patterns which required rejection of at least what he considered the ontological implications of Aristotelian logic was part of the effort. It was, however, to be a process logic to fit a process universe. Nieuwenhuijze devotes a section of his book to a criticism of what he calls the "Platonic-Aristotelian" framework of thought, and it is probable that the dissatisfaction with our basic patterns of

---

[72] *Ibid.*, 160n.

[73] *Ibid.*, Chap. II. I might add that Nieuwenhuijze also finds a bias toward the permanence category in much structural-functional theory (55).

[74] I have benefited considerably from conversations with Norman Jacobson about complementarity notions in Bentley's work. The text represents, of course, my own interpretation.

thought transcends particular social theories.[75] Bentley's process theory needed new descriptive categories, but it did not need a complementarity principle to mediate between structural and process viewpoints; if geometry could be translated into a new physics, the persistent dualism we have encountered in so many contexts would simply disappear.

These are some of the major mid-century conceptualizations of society and its science. While they are heirs or extensions of the process idea, they are also at odds with that idea, at least as it was developed by Arthur Bentley. Equilibrium theories have not met Bentley's standards of descriptive statement; indeed, they have departed from his recommendations by introducing conceptual elements (ghosts) at an early—and for him, a premature—stage of inquiry. A second, closely related tension arises from the drive toward holism and closure which is characteristic of some varieties of social-systems theory. Third, and perhaps most basic of all, the contemporary theories examined here have not resolved the tension between the demands of ordered social thought and the dynamic nature of its subject matter. Finally, I have tried to suggest two avenues of escape from the apparent dilemmas encountered in this way of formulating social theory.

[75] Nieuwenhuijze, Chap. III. "We need another pattern of thought to do jobs we cannot satisfactorily perform in our inherited one" (121–22).

VI

The Legacy Today

It is not possible to write a viable history of social theory today without creating a new intellectual genre— a genre which will be one part history, one part sociology, one part criticism, the whole encased in a membranous boundary permitting the mutual access of facts to values and of technical analysis to cultural interests.
—Alvin Gouldner

We rehearse for various roles all our lives, and for various patterns of behavior. We rehearse our national, our local, and our personal styles. These things we rehearse so that we may participate in a predictable world of social and environmental interaction. But we also must rehearse the power to perceive the failure, the necessary failure, of all these patterns of behavior.
—Morse Peckham

THE MINIMUM PROGRAM IN POLITICAL RESEARCH

IT HAS NOW BEEN some sixty years since Arthur Bentley made his initial contribution to political science, and since 1908 some of the major research in the field has fallen within the roughly drawn contours of his tradition. This literature can be inscribed within the three areas of group theory, systems theory, and transactional analysis. In addition, the adequacy of Bentley's epistemological and philosophical recommendations must be considered in the light of contemporary writings in linguistic philosophy. Finally, I will offer a speculation about the idea of process in relation to some traditional assumptions of Western political thought. Before discussing the literature, however, it may be helpful to introduce an important distinction.

An ambiguity in Bentley's presentation of process analysis has already been noted. While counseling adoption of provisional and tentative formulation, he persistently warned that "full" or adequate statement in transactional terms had not yet been achieved. Even when applauding the works of certain psychologists, he insisted upon their primitive or pioneering nature and stressed the distance that still had to be traveled before the mature formulation could even be glimpsed. This tension is often a focus of Bentley's critics who urge that Part Two of *The Process of Government* reintroduces precisely those elements presumably banished by the earlier argument.[1] Some scholars have reacted in a hostile manner to this ambiguity and seem to charge Bentley with incompetence if not conscious dishonesty, but there is a more generous, and in view of his later works a more persuasive, interpretation. That reading would suggest that Bentley's revolutionary vision contained both "minimum" and "maximum" programs, and that, although he did not always distinguish the proposals clearly (initially because he did not fully understand the radical demands of the maximum program), that failure cannot reasonably be attributed to bad faith.[2] Bentley's almost monotonous admonition to hold formulations "provisionally" and his often frustrating warning that any particular exposition must be viewed as partial may testify to a perverse conviction, but not to deceit. It is more just and more illuminating to imagine that Bentley's writings were attempts to develop a mode of observation and statement capable of sustaining the fully transactional science of the maximum program, but that in those attempts he drew upon his contemporary literature for undeveloped, proximate illustration (the minimum program). The confusion of the programs is often irritating, but, in the context of Bentley's insistence on the provisional nature of his statement and the progression of thought apparent in his life's work, it is thoroughly understandable. After all, he had not only to persuade social scientists of the futility of their present course; he also had to win them to a vision which he could not yet articulate except by primitive example.

It is hardly surprising, under these circumstances, that the mini-

---

[1] Leo Weinstein, "The Group Approach: Arthur F. Bentley," in Storing.

[2] David Braybrooke has elaborated this distinction in an unpublished manuscript, "Bentley's Transactional Thesis" (April, 1967). He refers to a strong version of transactional analysis which itself has several variations.

mum program should gain the early attention and allegiance of political scientists and that the more difficult and problematic outlines of the full statement remain shadowy. It was not only that political researchers already knew how to study groups and that they were anxious to extend their efforts to the unmapped sphere of nongovernmental political behavior. They could read Part One of *The Process of Government* as a welcome liberation from the formalism of constitutional law and institutional description, endorse its attack on prevailing modes of explanation, and then proceed to apply their instruments directly to the raw material of behavior with its locus in the individual.[3] What they forgot, of course, was that Bentley's maximum program would no more tolerate the idea that phenomenal individuals could be examined and then aggregated as a group than it would the postulation of a group mind.

Group theorists proceeded to implement Bentley's minimum program, and, although the high tide of their school seems now to have passed, the observation remains valid. David Truman's revival of group orientations was much less reductionistic and much more open to employment of conceptual and nonobservable elements as categories of explanation and description. In 1960 Vernon Van Dyke anticipated Weinstein's conclusion that Bentley had been unable to rid his statement either of ideas or of individuals and endorsed the more moderate post-Truman revision.[4] Oran Young echoes this acceptance of the minimum program: "Although Bentley's original criticism of 'simple psychologism' was largely valid, new and considerably improved methods of dealing with such intangible factors are now available."[5] Since Professor Young does not document this cheerful assurance, it is difficult to determine the

[3] See David Truman, "The Implications of Political Behavior Research," *Social Science Research Council Items*, V, No. 4 (December, 1951), for a mid-century statement of this position.

[4] Vernon Van Dyke, *Political Science: A Philosophical Analysis* (Stanford: Stanford University Press, 1960), 148. Van Dyke's account, however, is much more sympathetic than Weinstein's.

[5] Young, *Systems of Political Science* (Englewood Cliffs, N.J.: Prentice-Hall, 1968), 91.

degree of confidence it should afford us. If he means simply that social scientists have recently developed more and more complicated instruments for the investigation of ideas, motives, and other mind stuff than they could previously deploy, he is probably right, at least in a quantitative sense, but this response ignores the fact that Bentley's most important critique rests upon philosophical grounds and must be encountered at that level. To say that we are now capable of making a greater number of more sophisticated errors is hardly reassuring, no matter how "sensible" or intuitively necessary they may appear. In the most recent comprehensive review of the group-theory literature, Harmon Zeigler lauds Truman's willingness to adopt neo-Freudian psychology, notably the work of Karen Horney and Harry Stack Sullivan, and proclaims this product superior to both Bentley's group-as-activity and orthodox Freudian individualism.[6]

Zeigler supports his judgment by a quotation from George Herbert Mead's *Mind, Self, and Society*, a somewhat puzzling choice since Truman does not, to my knowledge, refer to Mead, while Bentley was much preoccupied with that literature and the problems it considers central. Apparently Zeigler is concerned to rescue "refined" group theory from the charge that it inadequately conceptualizes the role of individuals; that indictment may run against Bentley, he seems to say, but not against his more sophisticated progeny.[7] It seems to me that Zeigler's priorities are reversed. His position is all the more difficult to understand since he had just

[6] Zeigler, *Interest Groups in American Society* (Englewood Cliffs, N.J.: Prentice-Hall, 1964), 15.

[7] Mead's seminal contributions are, of course, ill served by so fragmentary a presentation. A sympathetic introductory commentary is Herbert Blumer, "Sociological Implications of the Thought of George Herbert Mead," in Blumer, *Symbolic Interactionism: Perspective and Method* (Englewood Cliffs, N.J.: Prentice-Hall, 1969). Zeigler intends to enlist Mead as an ally against those radical behaviorists who would deny the self as entity, preferring to conceive it as a locus or intersection of forces. Had he looked in another direction, toward, for example, phenomenology or existentialism, he might have discovered some doubt that Mead had sufficiently guaranteed the intensional dimension of self against the responsive mechanism of socialization. See Gibson Winter's critique of Mead, *Elements for a Social Ethic* (New York: Macmillan, 1968).

offered one of the more perceptive capsule commentaries on *The Process of Government* and correctly observed that the issue of psychological attributes versus group norms is intimately connected to the status accorded introspection and mental states as explanatory factors. To recognize this dimension of the problem would seem to require at least the admission of serious philosophical differences —differences that could scarcely be resolved by later assertions such as: "a person never gives himself entirely to any group with which he identifies" (and is *that*, incidentally, true?), "there is no individual attitude which is exclusively determined by any single group," and, one attributed to Alfred de Grazia, "Are they [non-group attitudes] not in the last analysis a personal, private and, in an absolute sense, unique combination of his group roles?"[8]

Adoption of the more sensible or less fantastic posture of Bentley's minimum program had significant consequences for political research. First, it enabled scholars to assume a rather conventional or common-sense framework of observation and discourse; there was no need to follow Bentley into the morass of epistemology and logic which their dominant image of scientific activity held in considerable suspicion in any case. Their predominant role conceptions urged that they be engaged in doing operations, not in asking what such activity might mean.[9] Even Arnold Brecht, in a book which is remarkably abstract by contemporary professional standards, dismissed the maximum program of Dewey and Bentley as a more or less pious hope; thus he concurred in the judgment of his empirically oriented colleagues (though Brecht must be recognized as one of the few political scientists who has examined Bentley's collaboration with Dewey).[10]

---

8 Zeigler, 16.

9 For an astute discussion of this issue, see Hugh Petrie, "A Dogma of Operationism," in Petrie, "The Logical Effects of Theory on Observational Categories and Methodology in Verbal Learning Theory," *Office of Education Report*, Contract No. 0-8-080023-3669 (010), 1969.

10 Brecht, *Political Theory* (Princeton: Princeton University Press, 1959). "In all fairness I feel it must be said that concentration on the transactional as distinct from interactional (causal) aspects of events in social life is as yet a vague program rather than an achievement" (513).

The direction of post-1950 group analysis is indicated by the structure of Truman's study.[11] It begins in a Madisonian vein with a discussion of the "alleged mischiefs of faction" and proceeds to an examination of the origins and orientation of political groups and a review of findings regarding leadership, tactics, influence, and dynamics of group activity. The focus of *The Governmental Process* is empirical in several respects. Truman is concerned with second-order problems, i.e., he takes philosophical questions of group identity and social dynamics for granted by citing research in which these issues are no longer problematic. To write, for example, of an "inevitable gravitation toward government" is to assume that some satisfactory account of government has been given. The very fact that Truman's concluding chapter can concern itself with "group politics and representative democracy" suggests that the major problem lies not with the epistemological or ontological status of groups or government as entities, but with an eighteenth-century constitutionalist framework whose questions were the institutional and normative ones of political theorists. That this is the case is demonstrated by most criticisms of group theory written by political scientists; they wonder whether group theory truly accounts for legislative behavior, whether judges truly follow the election returns, or whether group analysis must sacrifice an idea of the public interest. These are, no doubt, important questions, but they lie in a different realm of discourse from those which Arthur Bentley raised, questions which Bentley thought logically prior to eighteenth-century concerns. Sidney Verba's recent work demonstrates that group theorists have not abandoned their preoccupation with second-order questions. There are no references to Bentley, to process, or to transaction in his index; instead he summarizes the considerable literature of small-group experimentation, with leadership a central concern. To understand the processes of government, one must look beyond its formal structure. Realizing this, political scientists have studied nongovernmental organizations—parties, pressure groups, and the like—as well as the

[11] Truman, *Governmental Process.*

impact of the individual personality on political affairs. But a significant level lies between that of the organization and that of the individual personality—the level of the face-to-face group. These groups—families, committees, juries, informal discussion groups, face-to-face groups of all sorts—are basic units of the political system.[12] Significantly, Bentley's dissatisfaction with available tools of description moved him toward psychology and the philosophical dimensions of naming procedures. Verba, apparently satisfied with those aspects of observation, sees the frontiers as extension of inquiry to experimental situations. This is not, of course, to suggest that experimental literature has nothing to teach political scientists; it is simply to say that inquiry of this sort does not reach those issues of basic construction so important to Bentley.

There is at least one exception to this general trend of group theory.[13] Mancur Olson does not share Bentley's broad methodological concerns, but he has, nevertheless, contributed a critique that goes to the heart of their political application, the nexus of group, activity, and interest. Olson levels a charge of inconsistency against such "analytical pluralists" as Truman and Earl Latham (distinguished from "ethical" pluralists such as Figgis and Cole). "They have assumed that, if a group had some reason or incentive to organize to further its interest, the rational individuals in that group would also have a reason or an incentive to support an organization working in their mutual interest. But this is logically fallacious, at least for large, latent groups, with economic interests."[14] Olson develops his argument by drawing a limited analogy between market and organizational behavior. He points out that

[12] Sidney Verba, *Small Groups and Political Behavior* (Princeton: Princeton University Press, 1961), 17.

[13] Mancur Olson, Jr., *The Logic of Collective Action* (New York: Schocken, 1968). Olson acclaims *The Process of Government* as "probably one of the most influential in American social science" and recognizes it as "partly an attack on certain methodological errors that had troubled the study of politics." Yet, he concludes, it is "mostly a discussion of the dominant role that pressure groups play in economic and political life" (119). While this observation may be correct if made of *The Process of Government* itself, the judgment must be reversed if applied to the corpus of Bentley's work.

[14] Olson, 127.

among firms within an industry there may be a common interest in maintaining a given market price, but individual producers have particular and opposed interests in capturing as much of that market as they can. If an inelastic demand curve is assumed, the decision of individual firms to increase production can result only in a reduction of industry-wide price levels, a violation of common interest.

> When the number of firms involved is large, no one will notice the effect on price if one firm increases its output, and so no one will change his plans because of it. Similarly, in a large organization, the loss of one dues payer will not noticeably increase the burden of any other one dues payer, and so a rational person would not believe that if he were to withdraw from an organization he would drive others to do so.[15]

Situations in which the common or collective goods are "public" present especially difficult problems, since individuals who do not contribute toward their achievement or maintenance can be denied access to their benefits only with great difficulty (for example, implementation of an extreme sanction such as Hobbes's willingness to declare a man an outlaw).

> A lobbying organization, or indeed a labor union or any other organization, working in the interest of a large group of firms, or workers in some industry, would get no assistance from the rational, self-interested individuals in that industry. This would be true even if everyone in the industry were absolutely convinced that the proposed program was in their interest. . . .[16]

Olson's argument, at least that part of it related above, is formal rather than empirical or experimental, and it applies to rational behavior in large, peak, or secondary associations. He admits that primary-group behaviors may be very different, in part because

---

[15] *Ibid.*, 12. This argument has implications for interest theories of politics far broader than group analysis. The tradition deriving from Thomas Hobbes is a prime example. For a consideration of individual rationality and the public good, see my "The Web and the Tree: Metaphors of Reason and Value," *Midwest Journal of Political Science*, XIII (August, 1969).

[16] Olson, 11.

individuals can be subjected to more intense and varied controls. In terms of its contentions and its methodology, Olson's study should be read in conjunction with a book like Verba's. For the more limited purposes of this essay, the major importance of Olson's contentions is that they should force contemporary group theorists to offer a more adequate conceptualization of their analytical primitives. Olson is particularly effective if he is read as raising questions about how the stabilizing and equilibrating tendencies of the larger political system can be explained. What, for example, becomes of Truman's comfortable defense of "democracy" as group competition if the analytical identification of group and interest is severed and their connection becomes historically contingent? This analysis is somewhat less damaging to Bentley if only because of his rather early abandonment of the group-interest-activity framework. Olson's point unquestionably strikes deep at the formulation presented in *The Process of Government*, but Bentley soon afterward gave up conventional political discourse; Olson's argument reaches his later work in only a limited, though important, way. This critique has implications at both the micro and the macro levels; it raises problems concerning the adequacy of explanatory frameworks and conceptualization at the system level.

Oran Young's four-point critique of group theory contains both arguments in embryo. First, he asserts, group theory tends to reify groups; second, "interest" and its relation to "group" are never rendered unambiguously; third, group theory is anti-individual and reductionistic; and finally, it is subsystem-oriented and tends to treat inclusive properties as residues of analysis.[17] Zeigler's discussion notes a number of attempts to respond to these and related criticisms. George E. G. Catlin's emphasis on power as the focus of political analysis stresses rational control rather than the conflict pattern of Bentley and Truman. Harold Lasswell's many contributions include an attention to the function of political symbols and the distribution of political values. The latter area has been developed most recently by Murray Edelman. Robert MacIver has

17 Oran Young, Chap. VI.

always been somewhat unhappy with the peripheral position group theorists have accorded the concept of a public interest, and he has sought to restore it to more central concern. Merle Fainsod, among others, has lamented the proclivity of group theorists to ignore the institutional matrix of activity, or to relegate it to a "habit background."[18] Many of these traditions stem from intellectual roots quite different from those of group theory and are not of direct concern here, but the fourth of Young's criticisms, that analytical pluralists cannot or do not operate on the systemic level, is. This point is implicit in the more traditional complaint of Fainsod, that the shaping and restraining function of institutional matrices receives insufficient attention.

We might approach the point another way by asking how an essay on government and politics (Truman's) or a review of the group literature (Zeigler's) is organized. What divisions are made? How are case studies clustered together? How does the author know his task is finished? Both Zeigler and Truman proceed in similar fashion; each arranges his literature to fit the formal constitutional system of separation of powers, and each proceeds to enrich these categories with such broadly functional additions as business, labor, and agrarian interests.[19] Weinstein's assessment of the early

---

[18] Zeigler, 17–27. Some representative works include: George E. G. Catlin, *A Study of the Principles of Politics* (London: George Allen and Unwin, 1930); Alfred de Grazia, "Interest Group Theory in Political Research," *Annals of the American Academy of Political and Social Science* (September, 1958); Harold Lasswell, *Politics: Who Gets What, When, How?* (New York: McGraw-Hill, 1936); Harold Lasswell and Abraham Kaplan, *Power and Society* (New Haven: Yale University Press, 1950); Murray Edelman, *The Symbolic Uses of Politics* (Urbana: University of Illinois Press, 1964); Robert MacIver, *The Web of Government* (New York: Macmillan, 1948); Schubert; Merle Fainsod, "Some Reflections on the Nature of the Regulatory Process," in *Public Policy*, ed. Carl J. Friedrich and Edward S. Mason (Cambridge, Mass.: Harvard University Press, 1940); Samuel J. Eldersveld, "American Interest Groups: A Survey of Research and Some Implications for Theory and Method," in *Interest Groups on Four Continents*, ed. Henry Ehrman (Pittsburgh: University of Pittsburgh Press, 1958).

[19] These examples are chosen simply for convenience. The same pattern of organization dominates text and monograph literature of this sort. A paradigm case is V. O. Key's influential text, *Politics, Parties and Public Opinion* (New York: Thomas Crowell, 1958).

Bentley needs little modification to be applicable to his mid-century disciples.

> Bentley has not presented 'action' or 'strictly empirical' material as the raw material of politics, but has instead taken as his first sample an organized description, based on an unspecified criterion of significance. At the very outset of his enterprise, when he seeks to find a unit of activity to serve as an example, Bentley shows himself and his method to be entirely dependent on what an organ or agency of public opinion says is relevant.[20]

This comment is addressed to Bentley's search for units and recalls the micro-level analysis of earlier chapters of this book; here it appears at the systemic level in the question of how and in what kind of framework group activity or research shall be organized. To opt for the present institutional structure is not only to betray a certain parochialism but to readmit a formalism banished from the level of micro-inquiry. Critics of a group approach have been more vocal about the former, in part because many of them have been beneficiaries of the postwar bonanza of area studies. Confronted with their felt need to develop "genuinely comparative" categories of cross-cultural analysis (a phrase they apparently took to mean "the same" categories), these new theorists indicted pre-1945 studies of comparative government as parochial (limited to western Europe, Britain, and the Commonwealth), "configurative" (not "systematic"), and "formalistic" (arrested at the legal and institutional stage).[21] Their specific areas of innovation have been described by Almond and Powell as the search for a more comprehensive scope, for realism (the study of "actual behavior"), for precision (the quantitative and mathematical models of psychology and economics are cited as illustration), and for ordering concepts such as political culture and socialization.[22]

The role of innovator can certainly be, perhaps must necessarily be, rather intoxicating. Still, it is somewhat unsettling that two

[20] Weinstein, 173.

[21] Gabriel Almond and G. Bingham Powell, Jr., *Comparative Politics: The Developmental Approach* (Boston and Toronto: Little, Brown, 1966), 2–3.

[22] *Ibid.*, 6–8.

scholars could, in the mid-1960s, reflect so little regard for the realism, precision, and comprehensiveness of their predecessors, or that they feel no need to illustrate the superiority of culture and socialization (which, incidentally, are not usually considered discoveries of the mid-twentieth century) to state and constitution as ordering concepts for the discipline. The point here, however, is less what and how well these innovators built than it is what kinds of goals and priorities were in their minds. A few years earlier, Gabriel Almond and Sidney Verba sought to articulate some of these goals through the concept of political culture. It is, they felt, a connecting link between macropolitics and micropolitics; attitudes and motivations are distinguished "as a research approach from 'macropolitics,' or the more traditional concern of the student of politics with the structure and function of political systems, institutions, and agencies, and their effects on public policy."[23] To this point the priorities of comparative-systems theory seem to consist in expanding the scope of the field and in directing research to those areas in which more rigorous or quantitative methodologies are most appropriate. But a few pages later there is an amazing passage:

> ... the social scientist *no longer assumes that the facts of social or political life are known*, or that they are easily accessible through casual observation, introspection, or systematic reading. One questions not merely the interpretation of facts, but in the first instance the facts themselves. Most important, perhaps, the criteria by which one accepts or rejects statements about social life are of a special nature. *The ultimate criterion is the method by which they are gathered.*[24]

It is difficult to decide where to begin in an attempt to understand these lines, let alone to evaluate their claims. Is one to understand that no "facts" about political life have been uncovered prior to the mid-twentieth century, or that no (important) facts have come

[23] Gabriel Almond and Sidney Verba, *The Civic Culture* (Princeton: Princeton University Press, 1963), 32. Two years earlier Verba had discovered the primary group and assigned it a similarly vital intermediary role. See the quotation from the volume above.

[24] *Ibid.*, 43. (My emphasis.)

to light, or that we do not know what "political and social life" is and consequently cannot make the judgment, or instead that social scientists may never assume a fact as evidence which they have not themselves verified? If "systematic reading" of our colleagues' work will avail no more than casual observation, the burden on individual researchers will be heavy indeed. It is not much help to learn that propositions about social life must be judged by criteria of a "special" nature. Are these criteria different from those we apply in natural or biological science, in logic, or in the ordinary conduct of our lives? Surely we must wonder, if the authors intend their last sentence literally, what has become of interpretation and the ordering function of science, whether facts truly speak for themselves, whether a proper methodology can never yield conflicting results, and, finally, if a method is logically and ontologically prior to facts (that is, if it must validate them), how is the method derived and how is it validated?[25]

These questions are of considerable importance, but their pursuit must be the province of another study. Of interest here are the ways in which systems theorists have sought to respond to charges of disciplinary parochialism and inadequate systemic conceptualization, especially as these have been directed against group theory. A first step has apparently been that recommended by Almond and Verba in the passage quoted above.[26] Social scientists are enjoined to adopt a suspension of belief, to scrutinize the assumptions they and their cultures make about the nature and contours of the political and social realms. Something (actual behavior perhaps) is to be observed *sans* categorical preconceptions. Judgments of fact or significance must await creation of a method which will include the

---

[25] The authors later tell us that a proper method must be "systematic and relatively reliable," "amenable to replication," and "public and explicit." These, of course, are phrases which should initiate, not terminate, discourse.

[26] I am here using the term "systems theory" in the broad sense employed in the previous chapter. Many kinds of distinctions can and should be made in appropriate contexts. Almond and Powell, for example, distinguish the intellectual origins of their enterprise from those of David Easton's. Generally, see Oran Young, and Walter Buckley, *Sociology and Modern Systems Theory* (Englewood Cliffs, N.J.: Prentice-Hall, 1967).

new, universalistic categories which alone can sustain them. Almond and Powell use the separation-of-powers principle as an illustration. They note its development over the last three centuries as a "real world" political instrument and as a means of ordering political research, and they then propose the substitution of their categories of rule-making, enforcing, and adjudicating functions, later broadened to a sixfold taxonomy.[27] In this example the parochial and institutional basis of organization employed by Key, Truman, and Zeigler has certainly been transcended, and the theoretical chasm between mid-range and systemic discourse has been bridged, if at this point only by definition. How exactly has this been accomplished, or to put it another way, when reference to concrete institutional frameworks is abandoned, to what principles have the authors applied to permit a reconstruction?

In the case of Almond and his collaborators, the answer seems clearly to be structural-functional requisite analysis (I will not here distinguish between "requisites" and "prerequisites.") One asks either "what is necessary in order that *a* political or social system exist" or the narrower question, "what is necessary for *this* polity to exist in its present form." Some of the logical and normative issues surrounding functional, equilibrium, and systems theories have already been examined. This will not be an extended review of the literature generated by those approaches, but David Easton's recent work further illustrates the point about system-level discourse.[28]

In *A Framework for Political Analysis*, Easton raises the issue of the recognition of social and political systems and distinguishes those which occur naturally from the purely analytic variety.[29] Oran Young has put the distinction somewhat more generally:

[27] Almond and Powell, 14.

[28] Those readers seeking a comprehensive review of the literature will find Walter L. Wallace, "An Overview of Sociological Theory," in *Sociological Theory*, ed. Wallace (Chicago: Aldine, 1969), a useful essay. Wallace is more comprehensive than is Oran Young, though neither finds need for more than passing mention of contemporary Marxist thought.

[29] Easton, *Framework*, 27. See also the more complete statement, *A Systems Analysis*.

"One can take the position that the term system should apply only to elements that are significantly related to each other in the sense that their level of interdependence is high. Here a system would be distinguished from a random aggregation of elements. But this leads to serious problems of operational judgment."[30] A second approach to definition is the "constructivist" view: "The idea here is that the difficulties . . . regarding criteria for the existence of systems are either false problems or else insoluble. The answer therefore is to treat any conglomeration of elements that seems interesting for the purposes of research as a system at least for the preliminary activities of data gathering and initial analysis."[31]

Discouraged by the operational problems of the first view, Easton opts for the "constructivist" position, in his terms, for the analytic character of systems. Our choice, he asserts, "is solely a matter of conceptual convenience."[32] I have elsewhere undertaken an examination of this claim, and of the wider theoretical and aesthetic issues which underlie the ideas of analyzability and convenience, but my interest here is considerably narrower.[33] The point, whether we are discussing Easton, Almond, Karl Deutsch's communications approach, or other contemporary theories of this sort, is that we encounter the attempt to create a means of conducting discourse and making judgments at the systemic level: an effort which finds the boundary problem, or the problem of identity, a central difficulty.[34] It would appear that Bentley's minimum program (including his extreme critique) was accepted in modified form by early group theorists, who were able to de-emphasize system-level discourse by implicitly accepting established institutions as the

---

30 Oran Young, 15.

31 *Ibid.*, 16.

32 Easton, *Framework*, 27.

33 See my "Self, System and Significance." There are, in my view, legitimate grounds to question whether functional and systems theorists have escaped the traditional framework of political science as successfully as their criticism of its shortcomings would suggest. However one may feel on that score, efforts to better understand the origins and nature of the scientific discourse they propose seem not only proper but urgent.

34 For Deutsch in particular, see *Nationalism and Social Communication* (New York: Wiley, 1953) and *The Nerves of Government* (New York: Free Press, 1963).

ordering foundation of theory and discourse. But this foundation proved inadequate to the needs of later comparative theorists, who found reliance upon it both parochial and unsuited to their "scientific" ambitions. In an ironic way, Bentley's problem, the investigation of which took him in the direction of micro-analysis, has emerged today at the macro level.

Before a more philosophical exploration of that issue is begun, however, one other research tradition of the Bentley legacy should receive some attention. The literature explicitly acknowledging itself as transactional is not extensive—certainly not so in political science, nor, according to my limited acquaintance, in psychology.[35] David Danelski's *A Supreme Court Justice Is Appointed* and the ambitious study by Raymond A. Bauer, Ithiel de Sola Pool, and Lewis A. Dexter, *American Business and Public Policy*, are recent and representative illustrations of the genre.[36] These works provide an interesting comparison of transactional analysis at the micro and macro levels; Danelski's effort analyzes a particular event, while Bauer, Pool, and Dexter conducted an extended and extensive research project. It is the expressed purposes and methodology of the authors, rather than their substantive conclusions, which are of interest here.

Danelski presents his orientation in terms which should now be very familiar.

In transactional explanations, events are understood within the situation in which they arise, and are explained in terms of postulated relationships among activities. The phenomena of man perceiving, describing, and otherwise acting in process with his environment are observed in fields of connected activity called *transactions*. The prefix *trans* means that the fields of activity are seen in overview just as they appear in time and space. They are not broken up into their so-called component parts, such as perceiver and thing perceived without taking into account the perceiver.

35 See Hadley Cantril, *The "Why" of Man's Experience* (New York: Macmillan, 1950); William H. Ittelson and Hadley Cantril, *Perception: A Transactional Approach* (Garden City, N.Y.: Doubleday, 1954), and F. P. Kilpatrick (ed.), *Transactional Explorations in Psychology* (New York: New York University Press, 1962).

36 (New York: Random House, 1964) and (New York: Atherton, 1963).

In other words, perception can be understood only within the situation—that is, the transaction—in which it arises. And just as perceivers and perceived cannot be separated in perception, neither can perceiving, describing, nor acting be separated from each other, for all are facets of a single, common process, and ultimately must be understood together in that process.[37]

Despite its length, this passage is a considerable abridgment of an adequate theoretical statement of transactional analysis, but of greater interest is the manner in which Danelski sets about conducting research congruent with this perspective. Precisely what are some concrete elements of a transactional analysis? He proceeds by offering a contextual account of individual responses to Pierce Butler's candidacy and the timing, strategies, and motives of those involved. For example, William Howard Taft's opinion is recognized as part of the explanation for Butler's success. But, he continues, "far more must be taken into account. Indeed the entire transaction—the manifold connected perceptions, descriptions, and other activity of Harding, Daugherty, Taft, Van Devanter, Butler, LaFollette, and scores of others—must be mapped and specified. Only when this is done can an adequate explanation be ventured."[38] Other dimensions of the transaction include conversations, friendships, filial relationships, and "past perceptions impinging on present perceptions." Danelski correctly observes that a basic difficulty of transactional analysis is specifying the connection of events. He chooses the concept of "influence" as an illustration and makes two initial assumptions: first, that x occurred prior to y; second, that, *ceteris paribus*, if x had not occurred, y would not have occurred.

Assuming both requirements are met, an influence relationship is said to be present, but that is not to say that x caused y. There are two reasons for this. 1. X is part of a complex of activities and has no independent status. The same is true of y. Both can be understood only in terms of the transaction of which they are a part, and not simply in terms of each other. 2. Though x may be said to be

[37] Danelski, 146–47.
[38] *Ibid.*, 149–50.

connected with y in the sense that it contributes to y's occurrence, other activities are similarly connected with y.[39]

So far we might imagine that Bentley would be reading Danelski with warm approval, but a considerable ambiguity remains. Danelski's mode of organization seems promising; he proceeds through stages of the event—nomination, campaign, etc. He draws upon historical sources, correspondence, public documents, newspapers, memoirs and autobiographies, and secondary scholarship for data. He is, of course, denied direct or contemporary access to the actors involved, but what else distinguishes his treatment from that of any conventional historian's account? In fact, there is no distinguishing feature. Danelski makes much of two points: first, that the past interpenetrates and conditions the present; second, that the true state of affairs, concerning motivation and action, cannot be adduced from appearance or even from personal statement. The actions of a Taft must be viewed within the context of a life history and a complex political matrix. Misunderstandings, accidents, and unconscious influences all require investigation and careful evaluation. But this is precisely what historiography seminars have urged upon generations of more or less attentive graduate students. No competent historian ignores vestigial but vital elements of the past, nor need he be prisoner of some simplistic notion of causation; if anything, historians are inclined to vitiate brilliant analyses by disclaiming any causal relationships.[40]

It is in no way to disparage Danelski's study to say that he has written a critical history and that he has absorbed the lessons first taught to the West by Thucydides. Further, I suspect that Arthur Bentley would have had words of praise for the book. The fact remains, however, that this research lies within the range of Bentley's minimum program; it is still a man who acts, thinks, and writes,

[39] *Ibid.*, 154.

[40] Social scientists, in contrast, are often less cautious, perhaps because quantitative correlations foster the illusion that facts speak for themselves and somehow the researcher is not responsible for them.

and legislatures, courts, and other institutions stubbornly resist banishment.

The same conclusion is forced on the reader of *American Business and Public Policy*. On the first page the authors raise the problem of scope. The study of trade policy (in this case, the Trade Expansion Act of 1962), they write, requires a transactional framework which can accommodate the actions of domestic industries and trade unions as well as the policies of NATO. "Before such a bill could be enacted into law, American attitudes had to change. That attitude change and its transformation into action is our story."[41] *American Business* is a case study, on however grand a scale, and the authors identify themselves with the group-theory tradition of Stephen Bailey's *Congress Makes a Law* and Fred Riggs's *Pressures on Congress*, but they are also sensitive to a difference which has escaped many of their contemporaries: "The transactional analysis here employed makes the concept of 'power' and 'pressure' in the ordinary political science sense of the terms somewhat more difficult to employ; Arthur F. Bentley himself pointed out to one of us in 1936 that he had long since abandoned these notions as not useful for systematic analysis."[42]

Bauer, Pool, and Dexter were fortunate to have resources which permitted them methodological tools equal to the magnitude of their problem. These included "sample surveys of the heads of American business firms, analysis of historical and contemporary documents, and relatively informal interviews, such as are employed by newspaper reporters."[43] Still, they were apprehensive, and concern about the adequacy of their research design led them to make this un-Bentleyan defense: "Many friendly critics have already protested that focusing on tariffs vastly oversimplifies the problems of foreign-trade policy. This is true, *but without such*

[41] Bauer, Pool, and Dexter, 1.

[42] *Ibid.*, 460. Earlier chapters of this study have reached a similar conclusion arguing from more abstract grounds; see especially the discussion of Gumplowicz and Simmel.

[43] *Ibid.*, 6.

simplification the study would have been impossible."[44] *American Business* compares in technique, spirit, and narrative style to Danelski's book, despite the differences in scope between the two studies. Both are substantially intellectual histories written from historical, survey, and secondary sources. But in spite of its comprehensiveness and reliance on behavioral data, *American Business* does not move beyond Bentley's minimum program, for the authors permit too many "segmentations" to remain. Their defense of simplification is itself a segmentation of what the total description of relevant factors would be; the maximum program would never approve the idea that complex questions could be answered by "adding" partial simplifications. The same point applies to the conclusion reached in the book. How, Bentley might have asked in a critical mood, can you expect to compare, evaluate, or otherwise bring such diverse data bases to "lie down together"? Without observational coherence, the ability to hold data within some qualitatively similar frame, one cannot have comparability or additivity. From the perspective of maximum-program standards, *American Business* fails the crucial test of reconstruction.

Both transactional studies examined here conform to the minimum program for two reasons. First, they endorse Bentley's critical posture and attempt to see and write in a manner congenial to it, that is, free of the ghosts, segmentations, and circularities he exposed; second, both books accept his injunction to seek out the dynamics of politics beyond the confines of institutional settings, in "public opinion" or transnational organization or interests, or wherever inquiry seems promising. In summary, transactional analysis within political science conformed to the general pattern of the discipline: it accepted Bentley's minimum program by adopting his critique of "traditional" political science, but it failed to develop research capabilities satisfactory to the maximum standards.

In this respect, Bentley must always have viewed political researchers as perennial residents of the anteroom of science. For their part, political scientists might have thought Bentley as arcane

---

44 *Ibid.*, 7. (My emphasis.)

and quixotic as the gatekeeper in Kafka's fable who tells the expiring suppliant that the door was his to open all the time. Certainly they are entitled to demand an account of precisely what kind of research will satisfy the standards of the maximum program. This, perhaps unhappily, cannot be done, at least within the universe of discourse and activity that is contemporary social science. It was precisely because he could not transcend the minimum program's form of statement that Bentley abandoned social science for epistemology and logic. The question before us now is whether the demands of his maximum program can be met by a social science, and, derivatively, if it is possible, is it desirable to make the effort? In order to offer at least provisional answers to these questions, we must follow Bentley's course of moving from the literature of social science to more abstract and philosophical discourse.

THE MAXIMUM PROGRAM: A SPECULATION

Even by the standards of the minimum program, Arthur Bentley suspected "person based" accounts of events, certainly if they were made to rest upon some introspective hypothesis, but perhaps even if they were given a behavioral statement. David Braybrooke suggests that individual biographies would be insufficiently general to conform to Bentley's standards of scientific explanation. Person-based biographical propositions might still be saved by "bridge generalizations" of a form linking individual a and individual b, but such statement would remain interactional. The strong statement of transactionalism would seem to insist that person- (or entity-) based propositions must be replaced by process terms in both observation and explanation, but even in this form the thesis is subject to differing interpretation. Bentley may be read as contending: (1) that person-based formulas must be replaced throughout the whole of social science; (2) that the substituted process statements do not presume the truth of any person-based formulation (Braybrooke gives the example of the process term "Reagan's 1966 campaign"—does it presume a true assertion that there is one such person of the name "Reagan"?); (3) alternatively, that, where possible, process terms should supersede personal formulations, though the former may depend more or less heavily upon the truth of the latter.[45] The last interpretation quite clearly presents fewer and less formidable difficulties than the others. It might, for example, permit us to form process statements from descriptions of persons and particulars whose properties would then be attributed to the process. Braybrooke gives the example: "Reagan's campaign was shrewdly paced." In this view, process statements would appear as a kind of reformulation of person or object language.

It is impossible to determine "what Bentley really meant" with respect to questions such as these. It is doubtful that he was very clearly conscious of such subtle distinctions as these, and his works yield evidence in support of each. It is true that his critical, sometimes polemical, writings generally express the stronger versions of the maximum program. This is the Bentley whom behaviorally oriented political scientists celebrate, but standards of theoretical evaluation demand also that we assess the possibility of alternatives. This can best be accomplished by examining transactional analysis in its stronger form.

At a minimum, Bentley must be understood as calling for the replacement of our ordinary common-sense or person-based categories of discourse, and perhaps also those of observation. The question of perception cannot be dealt with directly here, though it will be approached through an examination of discourse.[46] Peter Strawson's comment, that it is of dubious value to posit a person with radically different conceptual and experiential apparatus and then propose to assess the nature and possibility of such an hypothesis, seems sound. If, however, we begin with the forms of our speech and consciousness, it can be profitable to ask what beliefs must be held if a rational

[45] I am indebted to David Braybrooke's manuscript for these basic distinctions. My text abridges much of his supporting argument.

[46] On the role of theory and expectation in perception, see N. R. Hanson, *Patterns of Discovery* (Cambridge: Cambridge University Press, 1961); W. T. Jones, *The Sciences and the Humanities: Conflict and Reconciliation* (Berkeley and Los Angeles: University of California Press, 1965); Paul F. Kress, "On the Role and Formation of Concepts in Political Science," in *An Introduction to the Science of Politics*, ed. Donald Freeman (New York: Free Press, publication forthcoming); and Petrie.

account of their operations is to be given.[47] If we are to escape solipsism, he argues, there must be a common spatio-temporal framework in which we and the objects of our perception reside. Strawson develops his study by inquiring how it is possible to identify particulars ("individuals"), whether bodies, events, or processes, and how we can ever assert that a state or happening is the "same," either in the sense of "this is another manifestation of the identical thing" or in the sense of "something is now happening which is similar (for example in shape) to a previous observation." One method of identification is the "story-relative" mode, in which a particular is identified by describing its unique relationship to previously fixed points in a universe shared by speaker and hearer. But such a procedure appears to admit a certain relativism to description, one which becomes uncomfortable when the full range of particulars and their possible duplications are considered.

> The particulars we refer to are so very diverse. Can we plausibly claim that there is a single system of relations in which each has a place, and which includes whatever particulars are directly locatable? To this question the reply, very general at first, may run as follows. For all particulars in space and time, it is not only plausible to claim, it is necessary to admit, that there is just such a system: the system of spatial and temporal relations, in which every particular is uniquely related to every other.[48]

A common system of this sort is at least theoretically capable of being mapped into spatial coordinates from some selected reference point, and all particulars could then be located by demonstrative (as opposed to story-relative) identification. But how can we be certain that such a common framework is available, or how often?

> Yet it cannot be denied that each of us is, at any moment, in possession of such a framework—a unified framework of knowledge

[47] Strawson considers his effort "descriptive metaphysics" as contrasted to "revisionary metaphysics." "So if metaphysics is the finding of reasons, good, bad, or indifferent, for what we believe on instinct, then this [essay] has been metaphysics" (257).

[48] *Ibid.*, 10.

of particulars, in which we ourselves and usually, our immediate surroundings have their place, and of which each element is uniquely related to every other and hence to ourselves and our surroundings. It cannot be denied that this framework of knowledge supplies a uniquely efficient means of adding identified particulars to our stock. This framework we use for this purpose: not just occasionally and adventitiously, but always and essentially. It is a necessary truth that any new particular of which we learn is somehow identifyingly connected with the framework, even if only through the occasion and method of our learning of it. *Even when the identification is "story-relative", the connexion with the framework remains, through the identity of the story-teller.*[49]

At least two objections might be made at this point. First, it might be urged that to concede the existence of such a framework does not entail the further concession that its significant dimensions are spatio-temporal. Why could not some other primary relationship substitute? (We might construe some of Bentley's criticisms of the common-sense frame in this fashion.) Strawson's rebuttal may be convincing.

> To this it may be replied that the system of spatio-temporal relations has a peculiar comprehensiveness and pervasiveness which qualify it uniquely to serve as the framework within which we can organize our individuating thought about particulars. Every particular either has its place in this system, or is of a kind the members of which cannot in general be identified except by reference to particulars of other kinds which have their place in it; and every particular which has its place in the system has a unique place there. There is no other system of relations between particulars of which all this is true.[50]

A second objection might take a more radical course. We might agree that each individual has a unique point of reference within a framework but argue that this suggests the existence of many

49 *Ibid.*, 12. (My emphasis.)

50 *Ibid.*, 13–14. A somewhat different treatment of these themes of "identificatory definition" can be found in W. Donald Oliver, *Theory of Order* (Yellow Springs, Ohio: Antioch University Press, 1951), especially Chap. IV; despite its differences from Strawson, spatial and temporal position in series remains central to Oliver's argument.

unique frames within persons at any moment rather than a shared universe. "Such philosophers deprive themselves of a public point of reference by making the point of reference private. They are unable to admit that we are in the system because they think that the system is in us; or, rather, that each has his own system within him." Strawson continues to insist that, if we intend to understand the framework within which we do operate, we must accept, at least provisionally, that such common words as "here," "now," "you," and "I" testify to the functional use of a common or shared universe.[51]

This second point is somewhat tangential to Bentley's proposals; he suggested a redefinition of spatio-temporal coordinates rather than their abolition or relegation to subjective states of consciousness. Of direct importance, however, is Strawson's defense of the shared universe which is presumed by the use of conventional language, for if Bentley's maximum ambitions are to be vindicated we must show both the possibility and the advantage of alternative construction forms. The point is made forcefully in Strawson's later argument, in which he attempts to show that, given our scheme of things, "it appears that a central place among particulars must be accorded to material bodies and to persons. These must be the primary particulars."[52] This argument is too extensive and complex to be fully analyzed here; its central contentions will be summarized.

Strawson begins with two questions: why are states of consciousness attributed to anything at all, and why, if they are so attributed, is the reference to the same thing as defined by physical or corporeal attributes? Philosophers as different as Descartes, Hume, and Wittgenstein have questioned the necessity or desirability of such ascrip-

---

[51] Strawson, 19. Professor Nancy Metzel has suggested to me that it might be possible here to argue against Strawson to the effect that his priorities are reversed; that the common spatio-temporal framework must be made to rest on existences which need to be established, located, or described in some other, prior, terms. Such an effort is clearly beyond the scope of this essay; it should, however, carefully consider Strawson's discussion of monads, Chap. IV. A useful collection of essays on the temporal dimension of this issue is Richard M. Gale (ed.), *The Philosophy of Time* (Garden City, N.Y.: Doubleday, 1967).

[52] Strawson, 256.

tion and suggested either that mind has no locus within the physical body or that the existence of states of consciousness does not suffice to imply that a person contains them. Strawson seeks to vindicate both beliefs, in part through analyzing the claim to ownership in the phrase, "I feel a pain."

> For if we think, once more, of the requirements of identifying reference in speech to *particular* states of consciousness, or private experiences, we see that such particulars cannot be thus identifyingly referred to except as the states or experiences *of* some identified *person*. States, or experiences, one might say, *owe* their identity as particulars to the identity of the person whose states or experiences they are.[53]

> The condition of reckoning oneself as a subject of such predicates [states of consciousness] is that one should also reckon others as subjects of such predicates. The condition, in turn, of this being possible, is that one should be able to distinguish from one another, to pick out or identify, different subjects of such predicates, i.e., different individuals of the type concerned. The condition, in turn, of this being possible is that the individuals concerned, including oneself, should be of a certain unique type: of a type, namely, such that to each individual of that type there must be ascribed, or ascribable, *both* states of consciousness *and* corporeal characteristics.[54]

Strawson later contends that there is a "close connection between the idea of an individual in the logical sense, and the idea of existence, of what exists. . . ."[55] This contention, of course, runs directly counter to Bentley's attack on what he thought to be Aristotle's mistaken attribution of an ontological dimension to the law of identity.

There are powerful arguments against the possibility of achieving Bentley's maximum program, insofar as that program sought the replacement of person-based concepts and the elimination of states of consciousness from scientific discourse. Since the latter ar-

53 *Ibid.*, 92–93.
54 *Ibid.*, 100.
55 *Ibid.*, 256.

gument is still a source of considerable dispute within political science, especially as it appears within the context of explanation, a further word should be said about that literature.[56] As noted earlier, Bentley did not directly confront the task of constructing an account of explanation, though his critical writings offer some hint of what direction such an effort might have taken. Some of his formulations, as Braybrooke has noted, could be made congenial to the "hypothetico-deductive" or "covering law" account often associated with the writings of Carl Hempel and Felix Oppenheim.[57] In the spirit of critical appreciation, I will limit myself to an examination of recent challenges to Bentley's radical hostility to mental states as sources of explanation.

Several philosophers might loosely be grouped under the rubric of a "later Wittgenstein" orientation, though there are significant differences in the strength with which their claims are formulated. Peter Winch's study, *The Idea of a Social Science*, is one of the stronger statements of this position. Winch attacks the belief that the model of explanation attributed to natural science is appropriate to social science; that belief holds, in part, that particular behaviors are explained by bringing them within the scope of a general law. Whether explicitly causal or not, so-called "scientific" explanation in social science prefers to classify and aggregate particular events or happenings in the form of law-like statements and to "apply" such generalizations in a deductive manner. This position, which asserts that there is one and only one valid idea of explanation, is sometimes called the "symmetry thesis."[58] After noting John Stuart Mill's insistence on the logical symmetry of natural and social scientific explanation, Winch presents his alternative view.

---

[56] See, for example, John G. Gunnell, "Social Science and Political Reality: The Problem of Explanation," *Social Research*, XXXV (Spring, 1968); and the exchange between Gunnell and James Gregor, *American Political Science Review*, LXIII (December, 1969).

[57] For Hempel's position, see his *Aspects of Scientific Explanation* (New York: Free Press, 1965); see my "Role and Formation of Concepts" for an overview of the major literature in social science.

[58] Maurice Natanson (ed.), *Philosophy of the Social Sciences* (New York: Random House, 1963) contains an extended exchange on the symmetry issue.

It is a necessary consequence of this [Mill's position] that the methodological issues concerning the moral sciences should be seen as *empirical*: an attitude involving a wait-and-see attitude to the question of what can be achieved by the social sciences and, incidentally, ruling the philosopher out of the picture.

But the issue is not an empirical one at all: it is *conceptual*. It is not a question of what empirical research may show to be the case, but of what philosophical analysis reveals about *what it makes sense to say*. I want to show that the notion of a human society involves a scheme of concepts which is logically incompatible with the kinds of explanation offered in the natural sciences.[59]

Having vindicated the pursuits of philosophy, Winch proceeds to entrust its practitioners with the primary role in social analysis. In brief, his argument contends that human activity takes place according to a system of rules, the behavioral manifestations of which are social roles. Arguing from Wittgenstein's metaphor of languages as games, Winch conceives social action as rule-conforming behavior; to give an explanation of action is thus to illuminate the social setting in which such rules are operative. It should be clear that such explanation has no necessity to be general and, indeed, is usually ad hoc.

Philosophers of sympathetic inclination have nonetheless found some of Winch's formulations ambiguous or overly ambitious. A. R. Louch raises two related objections to Winch's conclusions. First, he doubts that general conventions or value patterns can illuminate very much of the spectrum of human activity, and those questions they can resolve may not be very significant. Winch, he fears, reads social actions as a code book. "Most human actions may be governed or guided by conventions, but to discover the rules in most cases involves close description of actions and their contexts."[60] Louch is also concerned that Winch has drawn too rigid a distinction between philosophical, or conceptual, and empirical inquiry. The

---

59 Winch, 72.

60 A. R. Louch, *Explanation and Human Action* (Berkeley and Los Angeles: University of California Press, 1966), 178.

result, he contends, is an attempt to legislate an a priori philosophical analysis (understood as the explication of convention) as the sole legitimate procedure of social science. This is to make sociology "philosophy's foster child" and to eliminate or greatly devalue such empirical procedures as participant observation. Louch's statement is the more carefully detailed, but whether his reservations point to a substantial or rhetorical difference with Winch is unclear.[61] Certainly, for present purposes, their agreements are much more significant. Louch's essay is well rooted in the literature of various social sciences as well as in twentieth-century analytic philosophy, and an attempt to abridge its argument in summary form would be both difficult and imprudent. It is, however, possible to indicate its flavor and some of its conclusions. Wittgenstein's notion of explanation, Louch writes, consists of a family of cases brought together to make something plain to someone; this entails that the natures of the puzzle and of the audience are variable factors.

> The paradigm which I have tried to uncover in various contexts is rooted in the concept of an action itself, viewed as a performance. Performances, in turn, are actions which can only be identified as appropriate, felicitous, or successful. And so the puzzles that occur to us in contemplating conduct seen as performances are, in a broad sense, moral puzzles, requiring the techniques of justification, warrant, or excuse to make them clear. And thus an epistemological query joins with a moral query.[62]

This logical underpinning may soften the reader's shock at Louch's pronouncement that history and sociology are branches of ethics.

In one respect Louch is perhaps even more disturbing than Winch, if Winch is read as recommending philosophical analysis to social scientists as a general method. Not only does Louch reject

---

[61] John Gunnell, writing in a sympathetic vein, minimizes their differences. "Although Winch . . . appears at times to suggest that social knowledge consists of something like empathetic understanding . . . and does tend to suggest that explanation is largely a matter of analyzing the language and symbols of a society and specifying its values, the issues between Winch and Louch are not substantial for Winch never denies that social inquiry includes detailed empirical work both in terms of formulating and justifying explanations." "Explanation," 180.

[62] Louch, 233–34.

the generalizing requirement of the hypothetico-deductive theory of explanation (thus endorsing ad hoc accounts), but he doubts that there should be such a thing as "social science methodology" at all: "I have argued throughout this book against the conception of a general theory of human behavior and consequently against a general method for behavioral science"; and, even more strongly: "There can be no social science, if this means that all the ways we talk about human doings can be deduced from a set of laws or that all our inquiries into human action can be characterized by a common procedure."[63] The important point about these arguments, as John Gunnell has observed of Winch, is that they suggest far more than alternatives to the symmetry position. "But properly to clarify Winch's argument, it must be understood, first, that he is concerned with demonstrating 'the central concepts which belong to our understanding of social life are *incompatible* with the concepts central to the activity of scientific prediction.' "[64]

Gunnell's study must be regarded as a form of the Wittgenstein orientation, as this passage should demonstrate. "When the explanation of an action is required, the cause, in a strict sense, is already known, that is, the agent; what is required is the meaning or the symbols that the action expresses."[65] But in an earlier passage he notes a rather typical confusion of considerable import for our consideration of Bentley's maximum program.

> But, again, to reject Cartesian dualism and the conception of action as a complex event analyzable into physical and mental events and to realize that much of everyday language about mental processes may contain category mistakes involving speaking of mental events as analogous to physical events does not entail the dismissal of mentalistic concepts from our language and our explanations of action or their reduction to statements about observables. The concepts denoting mental episodes refer no more to phantasma or inscrutable private experiences than do the theoretical

[63] *Ibid.*, 233 and 182. Compare the brave new world of methodology envisioned by Almond and Verba as quoted above.

[64] Gunnell, "Explanation," 182. (My emphasis.)

[65] *Ibid.*, 196.

concepts that occur in the explanatory language of the natural sciences.[66]

He then remarks that we require only the concept of a person or agent as a logical primitive—precisely what Strawson had tried to provide. A theoretical formulation of Bentley's mistake should now be possible. His war on Descartes, on "segmentation" generally construed, led him to believe that ordinary language could not serve as the vehicle for scientific analysis of either physical or mental acts. He did not rule out reference to mental phenomena except when cast in the form of interactive or causal factors; thus, unwilling to trust the identity of persons, he sought the way out in transactional statement. One might say that for Bentley the concept of actor or person had to be sacrificed to rid social science of ideas employed as causes (in the mechanistic sense). If Strawson and the others considered above are right, this heroic course was not only unnecessary but impossible, given a faith in the integrity of our conceptual and linguistic systems. Bentley's mistake was to seize upon the explanatory weaknesses of common-sense thought and then find himself forced to repudiate the integrity of human experience itself. Like Cratylus, he got hold of the wrong end of the stick and did not know how to let go.

A brief mention of converging themes is in order. Charles Taylor, in *The Explanation of Behavior*, has also been critical of the covering-law, symmetry thesis of explanation: "Our accounting for behavior by a law governing movement is incompatible with its being brought about by an intention or purpose concerned, and therefore with its being action in the usual sense of the word."[67] Actions, he insists, must be independent of antecedents. "It is a peculiarity of an action that its having a given direction or being an action of a certain kind is a fact which holds it independently of the antecedent conditions which give rise to it. We first identify the action and then search for the conditions which brought it about."[68]

---

66 *Ibid.*, 192.

67 (London: Routledge and Kegan Paul, 1964), 44.

68 *Ibid.*, 45. Part I of this volume is especially relevant to Bentley's critique of feelings and sentiments as causes.

Richard Taylor, writing in a more Aristotelian tradition, has argued strongly for the concepts of purpose and teleology as essential to explanation of human action. He sets out several criteria for the concept of action, important among them those of *agency* and *activity*. In his view the former is necessary to distinguish "my" movements as of a finger or holding my breath from such involuntary happenings as the growth of hair. Activity is added because it suggests the necessity for a feeling of efficaciousness requisite to agency. Richard Taylor, like Strawson, finds the notions of person and identity to be central to his case. "Hence, if it is really and unmetaphorically true, as I believe it to be, that I sometimes cause something to happen, this would seem to entail that it is *false* that any event, process, or state not identical with myself should be the real cause of it."[69]

Finally, mention should be made of Eugene Meehan's recent study, which seems to propose a functional account of explanation. He also finds the generalizing, deductive view of explanation inadequate and criticizes its overemphasis on logical elements or operations and an assertedly illegitimate fusion of the logical and the empirical. For this he would substitute a "system paradigm" of explanation. "The discussion that follows is therefore restricted to the kinds of organization of experience that enable man to anticipate and control events that take place in the physical and social environment—what would usually be called scientific knowledge."[70] In that the idea of system seems to stress coherence and possibly human purposes or needs, Meehan's substitute paradigm contains elements sympathetic to Wittgenstein and Richard Taylor, but also to Arthur Bentley. Bentley's unrelenting insistence on coherence,

[69] Richard Taylor, *Action and Purpose* (Englewood Cliffs, N.J.: Prentice-Hall, 1966), 111. Part One of this study is a critique of the symmetry thesis; for the several criteria of "action," see Chap. 8.

[70] Eugene J. Meehan, *Explanation in Social Science: A System Paradigm* (Homewood, Ill.: Dorsey, 1968), 16. Meehan is a political scientist, though he acknowledges his indebtedness to the historian and philosopher of science Stephen Toulmin. Toulmin's critique of the hypothetico-deductive account, insofar as it identifies prediction with explanation, can be found in his *Foresight and Understanding* (New York and Evanston, Ill.: Harper and Row, 1963).

244

organization, and function as criteria of description and analysis comes immediately to mind. Moreover, if it is not extending Meehan's notions of control to read them as calling for a philosophical anthropology to underlie explanatory theory, Bentley's interest in developing a behavioral theory to underpin logic may suggest another parallel.[71] I must leave these last considerations in this suggestive form and make a final attempt to evaluate the idea of process and the practice of political theory.

PROCESS AND POLITICAL THEORY

My earlier remarks about forms of equilibrium and process analysis apply to its use in social science generally, but there are respects in which the idea of process is uniquely related to the tradition of political science and political theory. Hannah Arendt has discussed the central importance of process to nineteenth- and twentieth-century political thought; her concern is more with the philosophy of history than with the process tradition itself, but many of her insights are directly relevant. She believes that the quarrel between the natural and historical sciences during the nineteenth century resulted in the twentieth-century belief in process as their "common denominator."[72] The modern age considered that both nature and history "imply that we think and consider everything in terms of processes and are not concerned with single entities or individual occurrences and their special separate courses."[73]

The notion of process deprives events of their individual importance, because they must all be related to the "meaningful" whole.

[71] Consideration of the control element in explanation suggests an extension to therapeutic success as theory validation. I have not been required to give specific attention to the case of psychoanalytic explanation, though it is surely a most interesting example to pursue. See Stephen Toulmin, "The Logical Status of Psycho-Analysis," *Analysis*, IX (1948), and the rejoinder by Anthony Flew, "Psycho-Analytic Explanation," in *Analysis*, X (1949).

[72] Hannah Arendt, "The Concept of History: Ancient and Modern," in Arendt, *Between Past and Future* (New York: Viking, 1961), 62. See also her extended argument in *The Human Condition* (Garden City, N.Y.: Doubleday, 1959).

[73] Arendt, *Between Past and Future*, 61.

"What the concept of process implies is that the concrete and the general, the single thing or event and the universal meaning, have parted company. The process, which alone makes meaningful whatever it happens to carry along, has thus acquired a monopoly of universality and significance."[74] Miss Arendt is especially concerned with the loss of meaning that deprives action of its aim, a deprivation that she characterizes as the replacement of antiquity's "immortality" by modernity's "history." I am less interested in her judgments about the treatment of time in political theory than in her perception that events are no longer considered meaningful in themselves. This is another way to describe the loss of faith in traditional units of investigation.

Political actors as well as political theorists have traditionally believed that they knew the important "segments" of political life; individuals, states, classes, and groups have had their vogues, but that there was, in politics, a unit of analysis was not doubted until our century. The choice of that unit not only determined the segmentations of experience but dictated the kinds of questions that could yield salient information about politics. Plato's famous remark that the state is man writ large enabled him to draw conclusions about the former by inquiring into the nature of man. When the state became the instrument of an oppressive class, the matter of individual virtue was irrelevant to political knowledge. Madison's political instrument was designed to control the effects of faction, and neither individual nor class units sufficed to contain its mischief. There was, in short, the conception of an acting unit confronting an environment, an *Umwelt,* from which it was actually, not simply analytically, set off.

The modern idea of history, in Miss Arendt's view, fails because we can make any number of constructions and theories about the process, and not only will we receive different answers to different questions, but there are no longer any unanswerable questions. Her remark that there is no longer a distinction between finding a "pattern" and locating a "meaning" in history is simply the corollary

[74] *Ibid.,* 64.

246

of Bentley's demand for the investigator's freedom of hypothesis. A striking example of this transformation is illustrated by Daniel Bell's comparison of two interpretations of America: Max Lerner's *America as a Civilization* and Harold Laski's *The American Democracy*.[75] Laski's interpretation is Marxian, employing socio-economic categories and the notions of ruling class and superstructure. Lerner, by contrast, explicitly rejects interpretative frameworks and declares that causation has given way to description of relation and interaction. Bell calls this the lack of a unifying vision.

> In the end there is no answer, but process. Lerner is forced to say that analysis consists only of "an interplay of the material world and the moral-psychological." And so while he has talked bravely of America as a "civilization"—and has defined the term as a "distinctly etched style of life, historically shaped and recognized by self and others as a new design for living"—in the end the "interplay" dissolves all coherence, and there is no unifying vision.[76]

Lerner certainly has a sense of a "whole," and Bell thinks his work exhibits a holistic bias. Lerner lacks, indeed explicitly rejects, "meaning" in the process. In specifically Bentleyan terms, it is the problem of segmentations, of discreteness. Abraham Edel has called this the "locus problem." "The question 'What is society?' raises what we may call the *locus problem*—the selection of basic unit or object in terms of which social and cultural traits or properties are to be analyzed, or subjects to which they are referred."[77] Edel has elsewhere shown how the choice of units provides a mode of entry for considerations of value; he speaks of a "value parameter."

What this kind of entry would be, if it actually exists, may be seen

---

[75] Daniel Bell, "The Refractions of the American Past: On the Question of National Character," in Bell, *End of Ideology*.

[76] *Ibid.*, 100.

[77] "The Concept of Levels in Social Theory," in *Symposium on Sociological Theory*, ed. Gross, 172. See also M. Brewster Smith's essay on the terms "culture" and "personality" in John Gillin (ed.), *For a Science of Social Man* (New York: Macmillan, 1954), and S. Stanfeld Sargent and Marian Smith (eds.), *Culture and Personality* (New York: Wenner-Gren Foundation, 1949), Part I.

by analogy. The sense intended is the same in which a theory of society is to involve a specific picture of the nature of man. We would then say that a social theory has a human-nature paramenter. The question would not be whether it can be eliminated, since some theory of human nature is unavoidable; rather it would be a choice of which picture to accept, or at least the realization that unsettled questions of social theory are in some definite part a function of unsettled questions in the theory of human nature.[78]

There must be some question about Edel's assertion that a view of human nature is necessary to the enterprise of social or political theory. What, we might ask, happens in the case of an account such as Lerner's, which at least attempts to dispense with interpretative frameworks, or Bentley's process statement, which seeks the elimination of entity language? It might, of course, be argued that neither attempt was successful, that entities or institutions or actors are implicit in the texts (as I have suggested above with respect to American group theory). This may well be the case, but I am here concerned to evaluate the announced goal, the recommendations rather than the accomplishments. It might also be said that Edel and I are guilty of implicitly legislating the boundaries or content of "political theorizing." What, it might be urged, prevents our defining "theory" in politics as the accumulation of behavioral uniformities and their statement in generalized, probabilistic form amenable to deductive operations? There is nothing to forbid a determination to define the enterprise in this fashion. We can, however, examine the possibilities and consequences of adopting this view (or others) and try to determine whether it is satisfactory—that is, can it provide a mode of inquiry and discourse appropriate to our sense of what political matters are all about? To do this is to give reasons for and against a particular viewpoint—to present, I take it, an argument.

It is difficult to avoid the feeling that the impact of the idea of process on the locus problem has raised more difficulties for political science and political theory than it has for others of the social

[78] Abraham Edel, "Social Science and Value," in *The New Sociology*, ed. Irving Louis Horowitz (New York: Oxford University Press, 1965), 220.

sciences, but it is also difficult to show persuasively why this should be the case. Historically, the study of politics has been particularly concerned with action and with such associations as agency and activity. Further, if social action itself takes place within a set of rules, conventions, or codes, then surely political practice is even more explicitly rule-observing. This is the case partly because of the public dimension of politics, its association with sacred or secular rituals of anointment, election, decision, and the like, but also because any leader or institution must face the problem of legitimation. A leader, that is, must secure the consent, the approval, certainly the attention of his constituency. This task of persuasion can be accomplished by appeal to a variety of sources—basic law, election, descent or lineage, special abilities, age, tradition, and many others which not only are ethical but must be understood as the ethico-political practices of the community. Political "games" are, consequently, more explicit and more visible than general social conventions. Bentley himself recognized this public dimension when, in *The Process of Government*, he suggested beginning group study with political interests because they were loci of ideas, articulators of demands, hence possessed of greater visibility.

This, then, would suggest that the science or theory game is a second-order activity, that is, it is an overlay played "upon" the game of political practice, itself a rather sophisticated and highly visible set of conventions.[79] Leo Strauss, in various works, has criticized contemporary political science for ignoring the "prescientific" understandings of politics.[80] His point can be given an historical interpretation and read as referring to understandings which existed prior to their articulation in theoretical abstractions, or it can be read as similar to the term "prereflexive" as used by phenomenologists like Alfred Schutz or existentialists like Maurice Merleau-Ponty.[81] In this latter sense prereflexive refers to the *Lebenswelt*, or

[79] I have previously raised some questions of this sort about contemporary political systems theory. See "Self, System and Significance."

[80] See, for example, his "An Epilogue," in Storing.

[81] Hwa Yol Jung has suggested this argument in "Communication to the Editor," *American Political Science Review*, LVIII (June, 1964).

the everyday world of lived meaning and experience.[82] When the theory game is severed from its anchorage and orientation in political practice, to what may it turn, or how does it generate direction from within itself? The comment by Almond and Verba might be recalled here: "The social scientist no longer assumes that the facts of social or political life are known . . . ," not even, we might add, through his own lived experience. This position seems to mark an advance from that of Lerner, for now not only are frameworks of interpretation suspect, but we are in doubt about the facts, even about the nature of the activity itself.

Of no less significance is Almond's and Verba's solution, which also merits repetition: "The ultimate criterion is the method by which they [facts] are gathered." This is the mistake Bentley made. Because experience resists formulation in what is conceived as the only acceptable scientific form, its categories and concepts cannot serve as the basis for an organization of knowledge. That Bentley arrived at this view through micro-analysis, while Almond and Verba discovered it at the macro level, is relatively unimportant, though it should not be forgotten that Bentley was much clearer about the theoretical demands of this fundamental reconstruction. Both recommendations sacrifice life, or the game of political practice, on the altar of a theory of explanation which is very likely mistaken, at least unnecessarily restrictive.[83]

It is not necessary here to confront the issue of whether the chronicle of Western political thought exhibits a pattern or tradition which could be held to constitute an identifiable enterprise within intellectual history. Leo Strauss and his students speak as if there were "political things" capable of cross-cultural specification, while Sheldon Wolin argues for the existence of a tradition conceived as diverse responses to recurring dilemmas of freedom, power, justice, etc. Lamenting the decline of the enterprise, Alfred

[82] A social science account bridging phenomenology and the sociology of knowledge is Peter Berger and Thomas Luckman, *The Social Construction of Reality* (Garden City, N.Y.: Doubleday, 1966).

[83] See my "Politics and Science: A Contemporary View of an Ancient Association," *Polity*, XI (Fall, 1969), for a historical sketch of the relation between the science and practice of politics.

Cobban attributes it to the theorist's isolation from the experience and responsibilities of policy-making authority. Whatever may be felt about these claims, my argument is satisfied by Oakshott's point that political order has a history and a set of conventions which yield "intimations" of proper action to those who know it well.[84] Whatever the content, mood, or style of political theory, it has assumed the existence of actors, whether persons or institutions (Strawson's particulars), to which the qualities of power, responsibility, and significance could be attributed and through which the activity of politics could be rendered intelligible. Moreover, the political practice or game of his culture has served as the theorist's point of departure, even though his purpose may have been to destroy that framework. The unique aspect of the idea of process is that it rejects the categories of practice and consequently finds its subject matter literally meaningless. Wolin has noted an interesting corollary of this posture: that theorists become preoccupied with the internal consistency of their descriptive propositions even while their subject game seems to disintegrate.[85] Whirl may reign in the outside world (or the "reference system"), but the house of theory remains calm.

If these contentions have merit, and political theory has been

---

[84] Leo Strauss, *What Is Political Philosophy?* (Glencoe, Ill.: Free Press, 1959); Sheldon Wolin, *Politics and Vision* (Boston: Little Brown, 1960); Alfred Cobban, "The Decline of Political Theory," *Political Science Quarterly*, LXVIII (September, 1953); and Michael Oakshott, *Rationalism in Politics* (New York: Basic Books, 1962). These efforts to elicit a definition of political theory from its historical practice should at least be distinguished formally from analytic definitions. These latter, stemming frequently from Max Weber, seek general, even universal, application through reliance on concepts such as the exercise of power or influence, the distribution of goods, and the allocation of values. Of these attempts Gunnell notes two difficulties: "First, there is little to support the contention that what is offered as a defining characteristic is anything more than an attribute of politics rather than the necessary or distinguishing feature. Second, such definitions are usually of equal or greater generality than that which is being defined, and thus rather than an explanation or meaningful distinction the result is conceptual reduplication." "Explanation," 162.

[85] Compare Strauss's remark that contemporary political science knows neither that it fiddles nor that Rome burns. "Epilogue," 327. Wolin's theme is brilliantly developed in his essay "Political Theory as a Vocation," *American Political Science Review*, LXIII (December, 1969).

concerned not simply with action, its meaning and consequences, but also with the role of "ordering" society in the sense of setting imperatives and assigning responsibilities, then my claim that it is more seriously threatened by the abolition of units, whether particulars, individuals, or persons, may have been vindicated. It is possible that there was a historical coincidence of the theory and practice of politics and Aristotelian logic, because the ontological implications of the latter reflected the distinctive political situation of men, set off and distinguished from a surrounding universe. In this respect, to substitute an ontology and methodology of process for a world of particulars would simply be to violate rules or conventions, to decline to play or play upon the game of politics.[86] If it is objected that my arguments might apply also to a process-oriented sociologist who studies the roles of father and teacher without much regard for the rules of family and school games, I would certainly concede the point, but I would reply that it is a matter of degree, and I believe that the nature of political games, the fact that their rules are more visible and explicit, renders them more vulnerable to process analysis.

"We seek a pattern, and we no longer ask what it is a pattern of or what it is a pattern in."[87] Burkhardt sounded the note of modern historiography when he said that history exhibits simply continuity. If it is true that events were engulfed by the total process of history in the nineteenth century, then history was itself swallowed by the process of society in the twentieth. This would suggest that, if there is a decline or some other malaise afflicting the political theory of our time, its roots lie far deeper than in disputes between behaviorists and traditionalists, normative and empirical orientations, tough- and tender-minded colleagues, Machiavellians and moralists, mainliners and marginals, or hipsters and squares. I have tried to illuminate some dimensions of the idea of process as it may contribute to a better understanding of our contemporary dis-

[86] I am indebted for this suggestion to my former colleague Matthew Stoltz.

[87] Jacob Burkhardt, quoted by Martin Johnson in "Science and Poetic Insight," in *Man in His Relationships*, ed. H. Westmann (London: Routledge and Kegan Paul, 1955), 31.

contents. Arthur Bentley's transactional analysis dissolved history, nature, and man in the universal process and posed a profound challenge to theoretical reconstruction. The conclusion of this analysis is that his own attempts failed, but political scientists as a whole have not yet confronted the demands of the process idea, and perhaps with good reason. It may well be that such demands, at least those of the maximum program of full transactional statement, are beyond human capability and, even if realizable, incur the prohibitive cost of impoverishing our experience. Bentley professed his willingness to suffer through the painful initial steps of reconstruction, confident, with the faith lent by a vision of despair, that social science could develop in no other direction. We surely cannot minimize the difficulties and ambiguities of his proposal, but neither may we profess ourselves his heirs or disciples if our work continues to ignore the critical basis from which process analysis emerged.

Bentley's great effort demands more from political scientists than a ritual footnote celebrating his "pioneering" role in the behavioral movement—more even than renewed attempts to refine and render in more acceptable fashion such transactional concepts as behavioral space-time. It demands that we critically examine and evaluate his revolution. Peter Strawson has written of our cognitive structures: "When we become sophisticated, we systematize the framework of calendars, maps, co-ordinate systems; but the use of such systems turns, fundamentally, on our knowing our place in them; though a man can lose his place, and have to be told it."[88] We owe no less to Bentley, and to ourselves.

[88] Strawson, 12.

Index

Abel, Theodore, 65, 108, 112–13

Activity: and becoming, 74; in Bentley, 129, 149, 156, 164, 206; and form, 128; as form of description, 78, 139; form and relation, 127; and group, 73, 76; group and interest, 67–68; group and interest in Bentley, 57, 61–62, 69–71, 172, 175, 221; and interest, 58; and interest in Bentley, 25; and interest in Small, 99; as process and relation, 121; and relation, 105, 112, 182; in Small, 96; and structure, 128; in Wiese, 106. *See also* Agency

Agency: and action, 244; and activity, 249

Allport, Gordon, 75

Almond, Gabriel, 185–86, 223–27, 250; on function and role, 189; on functionalism, 188; on process, 194; on system and process, 191–92

Anaximenes, 171

Angell, J. R., 17

Antoni, Carlo, 30

Archimedean point, 142, 202

Arendt, Hannah, 245–46

Aristotelian compromise, 171

Aristotelian tradition, 244

Aristotle, 3–4, 49, 171, 177; on becoming, 104; Bentley's critique, 143, 145, 151, 162; classification of governments, 71; on identity and ontology, 4, 143, 160, 211, 238, 252

Bailey, Stephen K., 231

Bain, Read, 117

Barnes, Harry Elmer, 82

Bauer, Raymond A., 228, 231

Beard, Charles A., 22, 25–26, 82

Becker, Howard, 105, 107, 112, 127, 142, 194; reply to Bentley, 114–15, 202

Becoming, 36, 122, 135–36; and analytic version of process, 116; in Aristotle, 4; and change, 128, 131; and process, 121; and relations, 123; in Small, 90, 101, 104. *See also* Activity; Process

"Behavioral": and behavior in Bentley, 158–59; in Bentley, 163

Bell, Daniel, 247

Bendix, Reinhard, 7

Bentham, Jeremy, 24

Bentley, Madison, 148

Berger, Bennett, 7

Bergson, Henri, 6, 9, 23, 31–32, 104, 122, 127, 131, 137

Bertalanffy, Ludwig von, 183

Boas, Franz, 17

Bogardus, Emory, 116

Bonner, Hubert, 209

Brandeis, Louis, 19

Braque, Georges, 6

255

A Note on the Author

Paul F. Kress is associate professor of political science at the University of North Carolina, Chapel Hill. He received his B.S. in 1956 and M.S. in 1958 from the University of Wisconsin, and his Ph.D. from the University of California, Berkeley, in 1964, where he was Social Science Research Council Fellow in Political Theory and Legal Philosophy, 1962–63. He has published several articles in political science journals and anthologies. *Social Science and the Idea of Process: The Ambiguous Legacy of Arthur F. Bentley* is his first book.

UNIVERSITY OF ILLINOIS PRESS